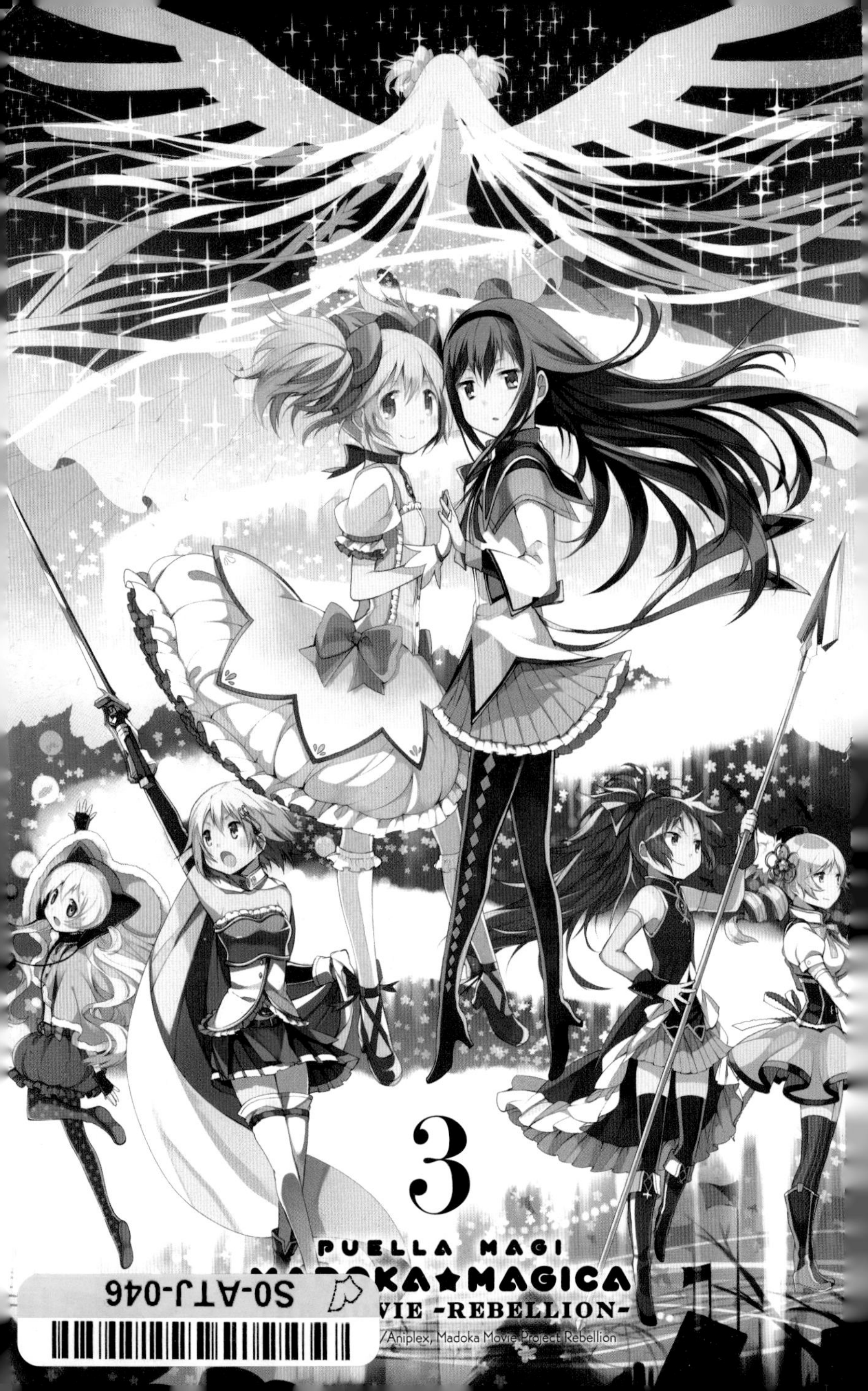
3
PUELLA MAGI
MAGICA
-REBELLION-
/Aniplex, Madoka Movie Project Rebellion

CONTENTS

PUELLA MAGI MADOKA MAGICA
THE MOVIE -REBELLION-
VOLUME THREE

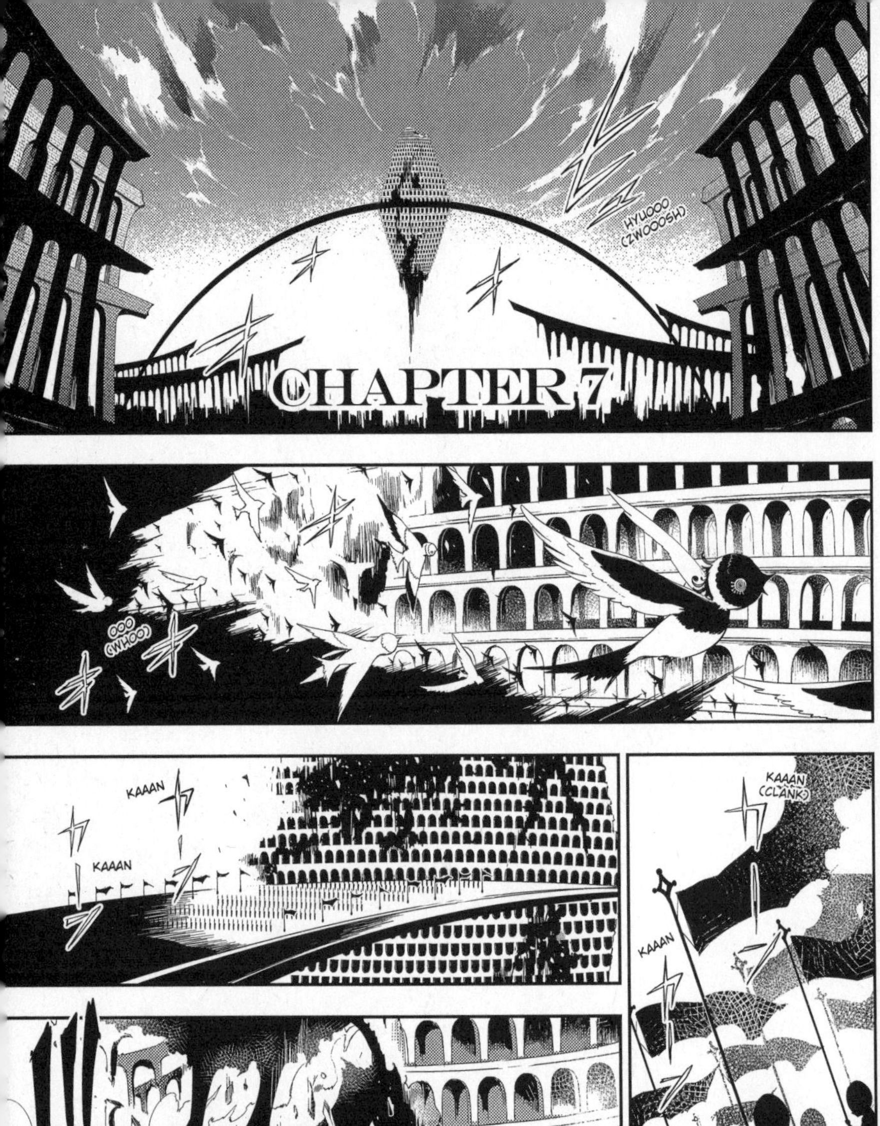
HYUOOO (ZWOOOSH)
CHAPTER 7
OOO (WHOO)
KAAAN (CLANK)
KAAAN
KAAAN
KAAAN
DOOO (THOOM)

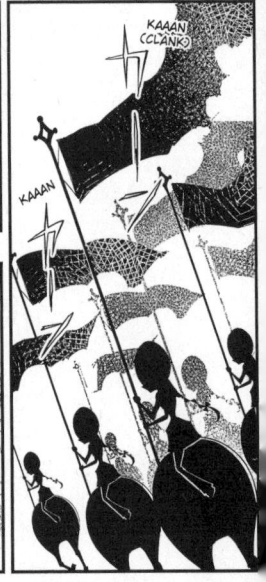

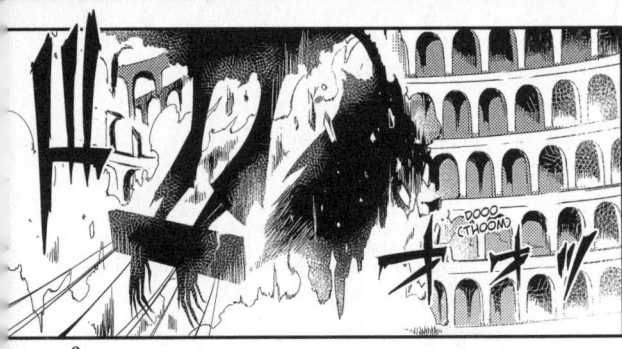

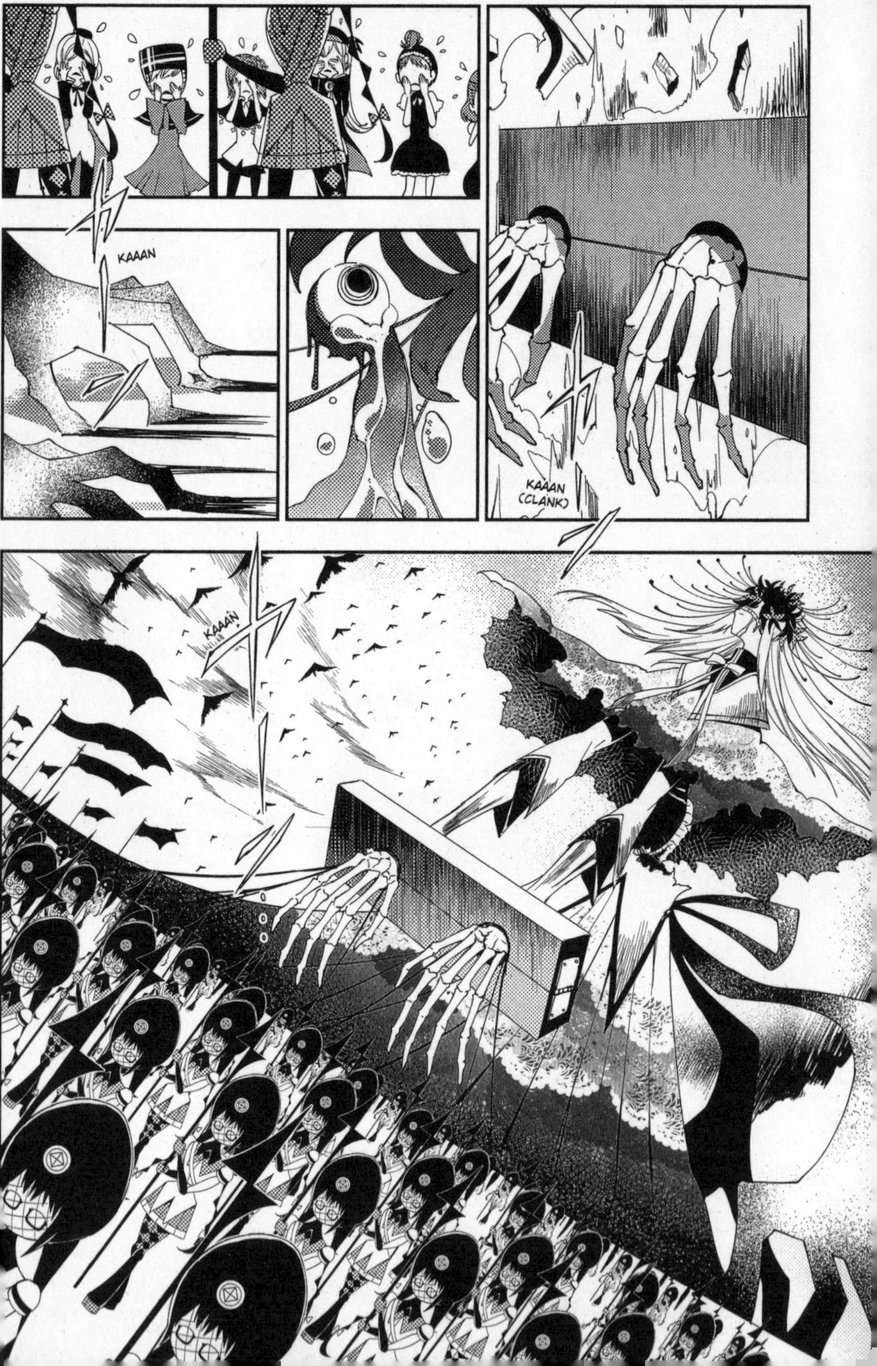
KAAAN (CLANK)
KAAAN
KAAAN

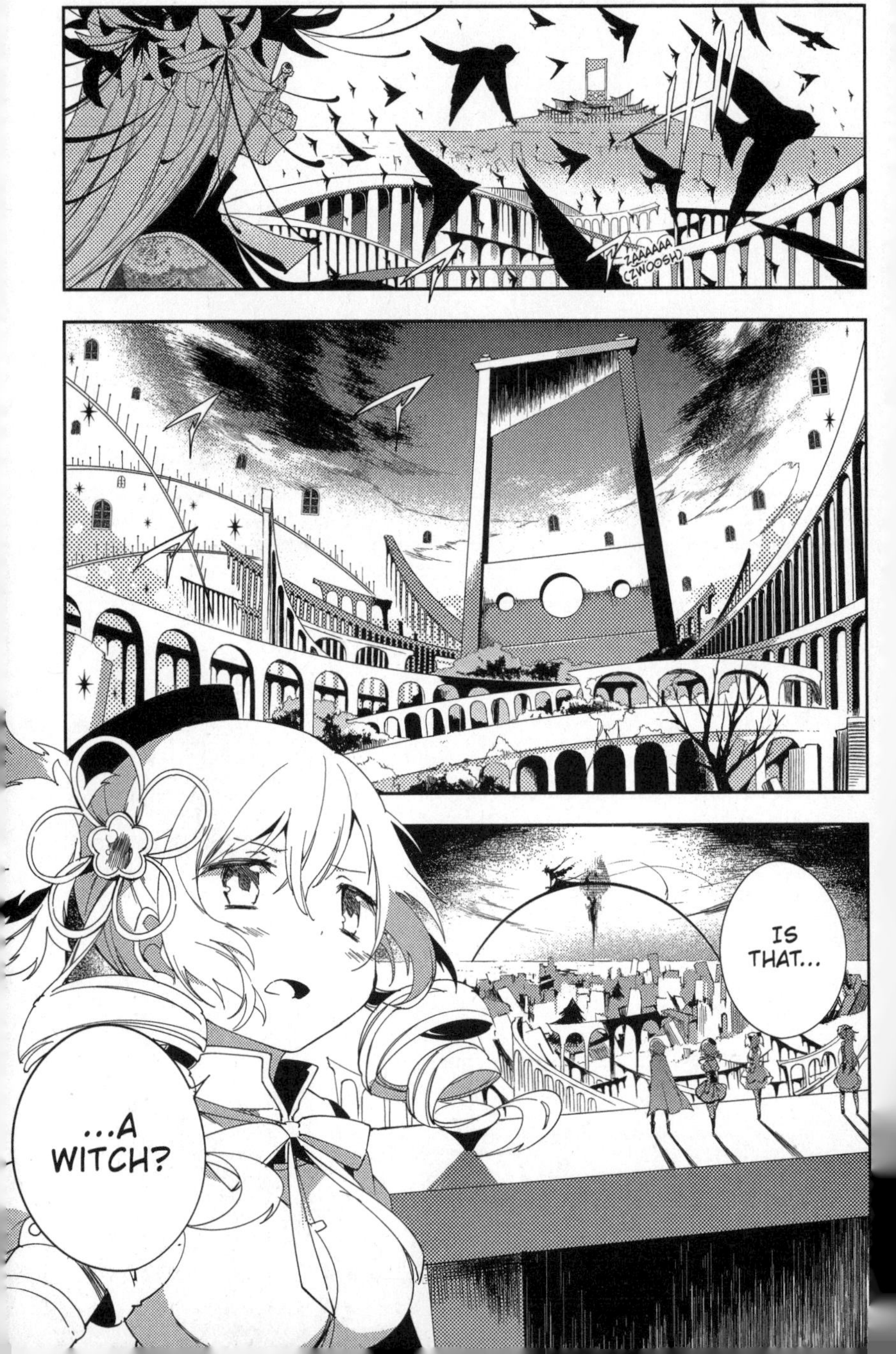
ZAAAAAA (ZWOOSH)
IS THAT...
...A WITCH?

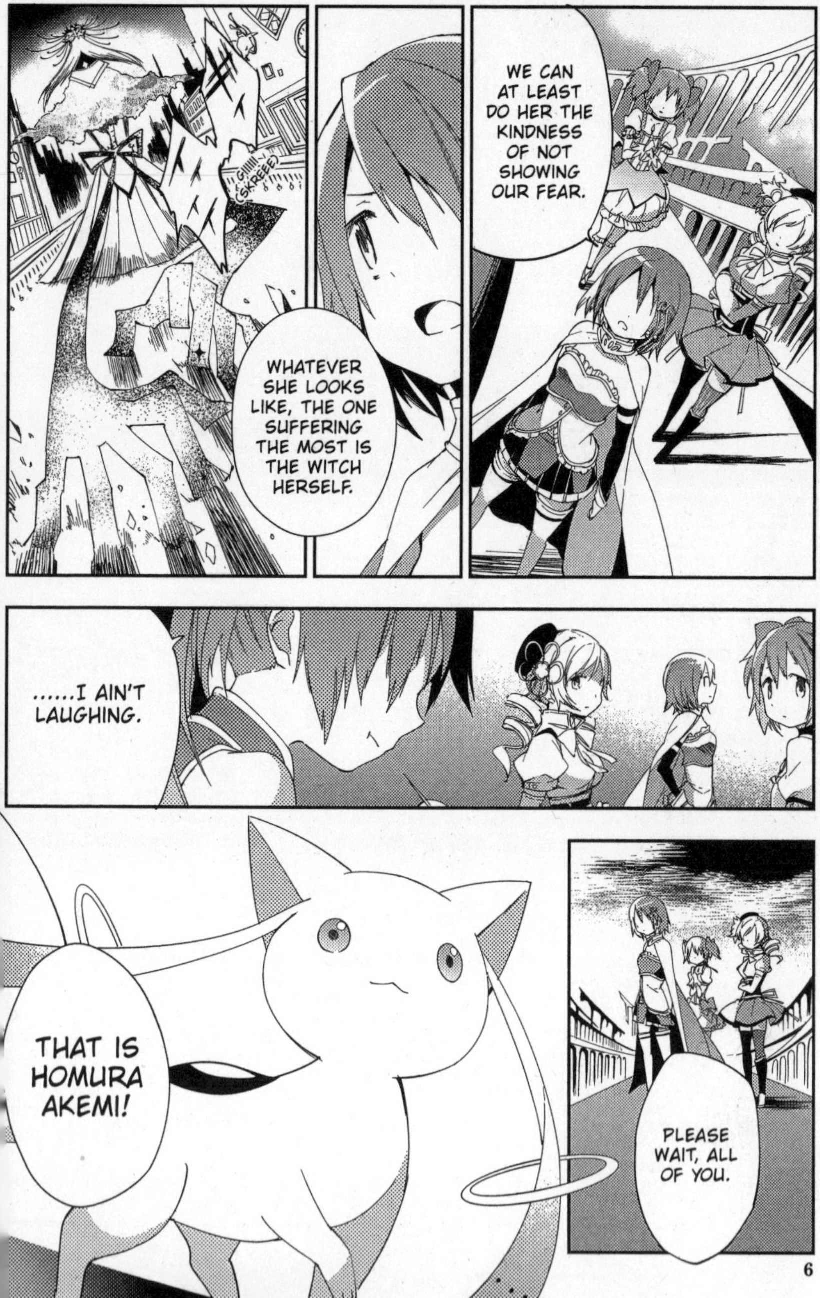
WE CAN AT LEAST DO HER THE KINDNESS OF NOT SHOWING OUR FEAR.
WHATEVER SHE LOOKS LIKE, THE ONE SUFFERING THE MOST IS THE WITCH HERSELF.
GIIII!!-! (SKREEE)
......I AIN'T LAUGHING.
PLEASE WAIT, ALL OF YOU.
THAT IS HOMURA AKEMI!

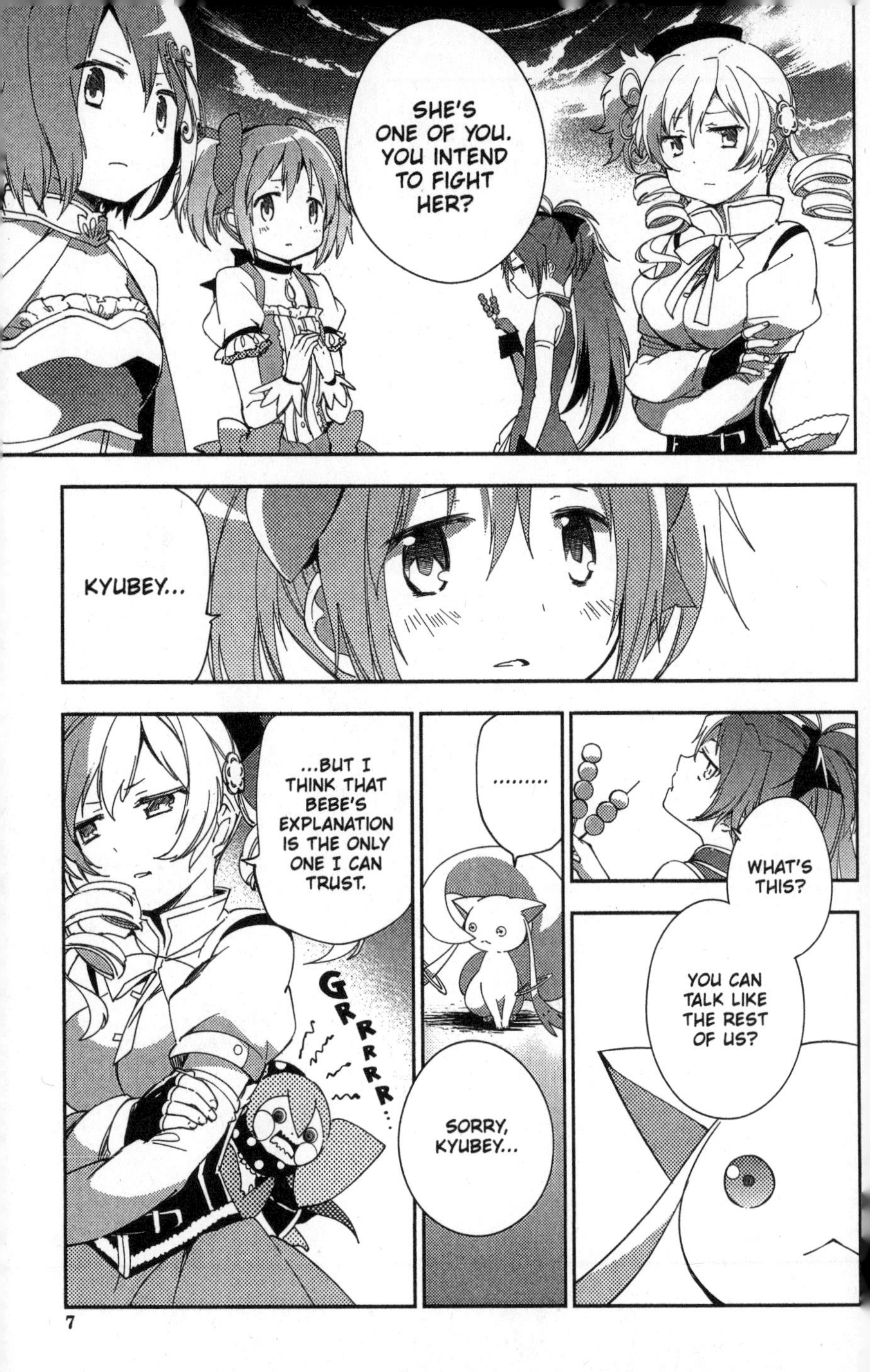
SHE'S ONE OF YOU. YOU INTEND TO FIGHT HER?
KYUBEY...
WHAT'S THIS?
YOU CAN TALK LIKE THE REST OF US?
....
SORRY, KYUBEY...
...BUT I THINK THAT BEBE'S EXPLANATION IS THE ONLY ONE I CAN TRUST.
GRRRR...

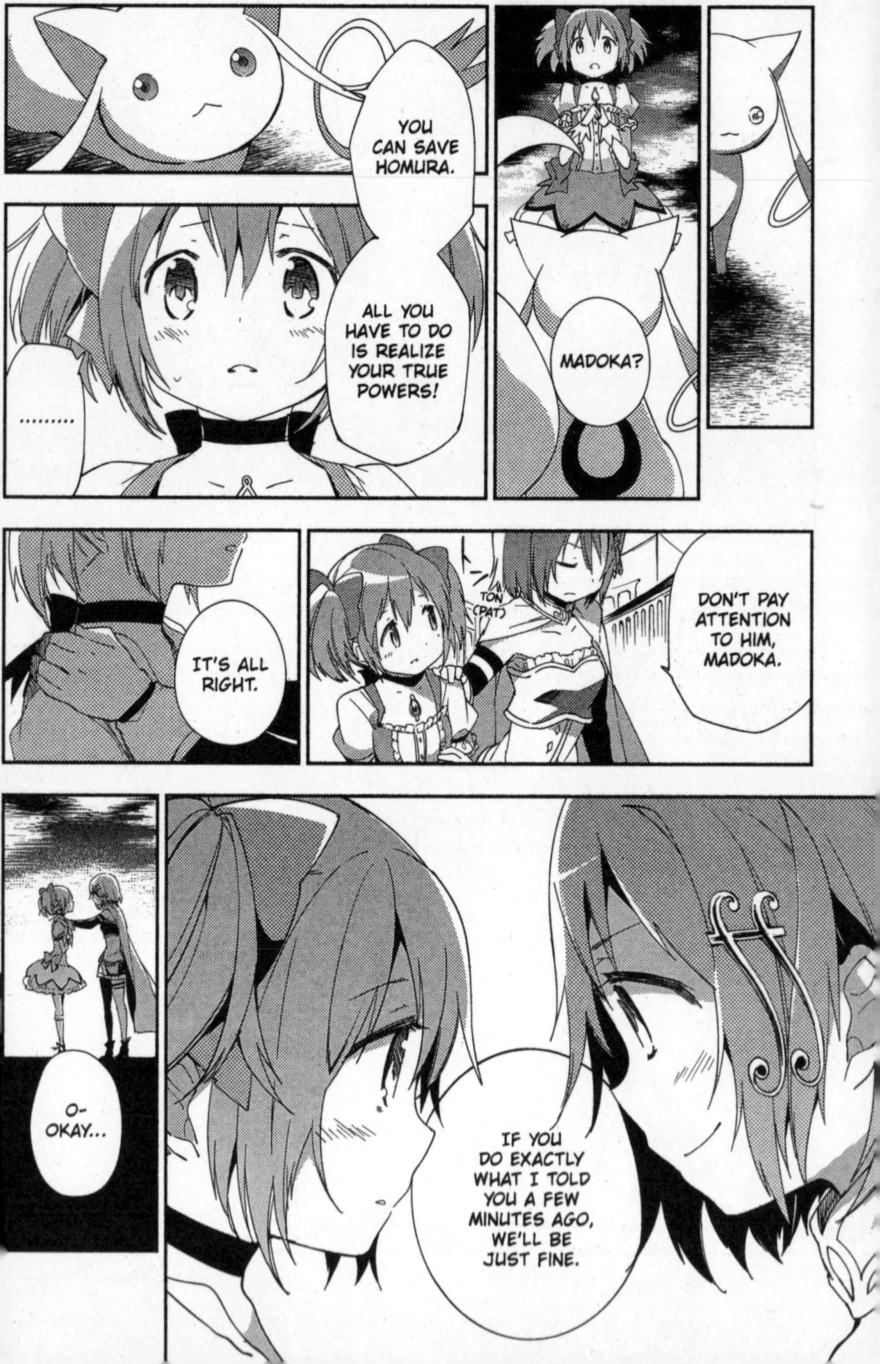
MADOKA?
YOU CAN SAVE HOMURA.
ALL YOU HAVE TO DO IS REALIZE YOUR TRUE POWERS!
....
DON'T PAY ATTENTION TO HIM, MADOKA.
TON (PAT)
IT'S ALL RIGHT.
IF YOU DO EXACTLY WHAT I TOLD YOU A FEW MINUTES AGO, WE'LL BE JUST FINE.
O-OKAY...

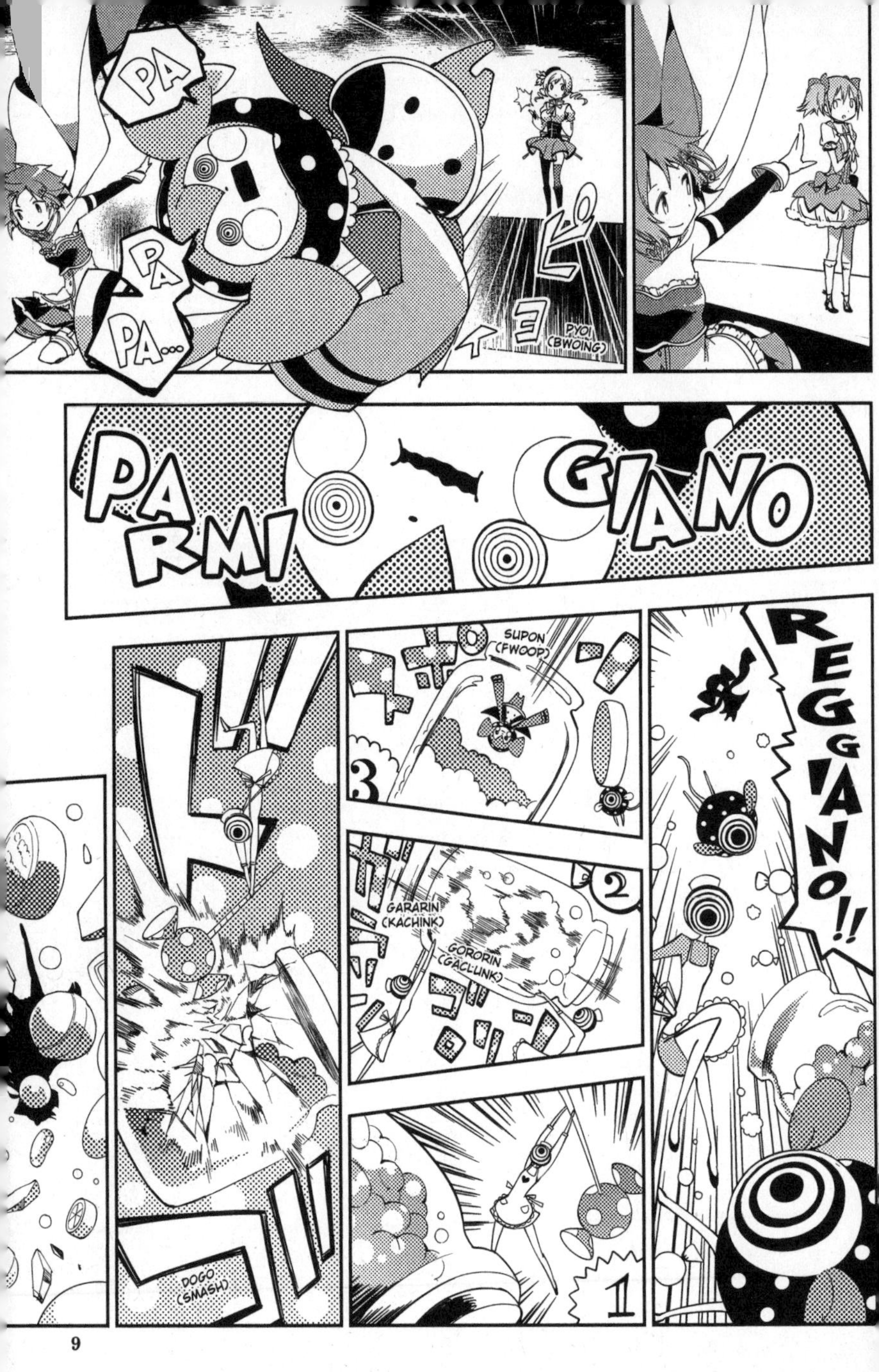
PYOI (BWOING)
PA
PA
PA...
PARMIGIANO
REGGIANO!!
1
2
GARARIN (KACHINK)
GORORIN (GACLUNK)
3
SUPON (FWOOP)
DOGO (SMASH)

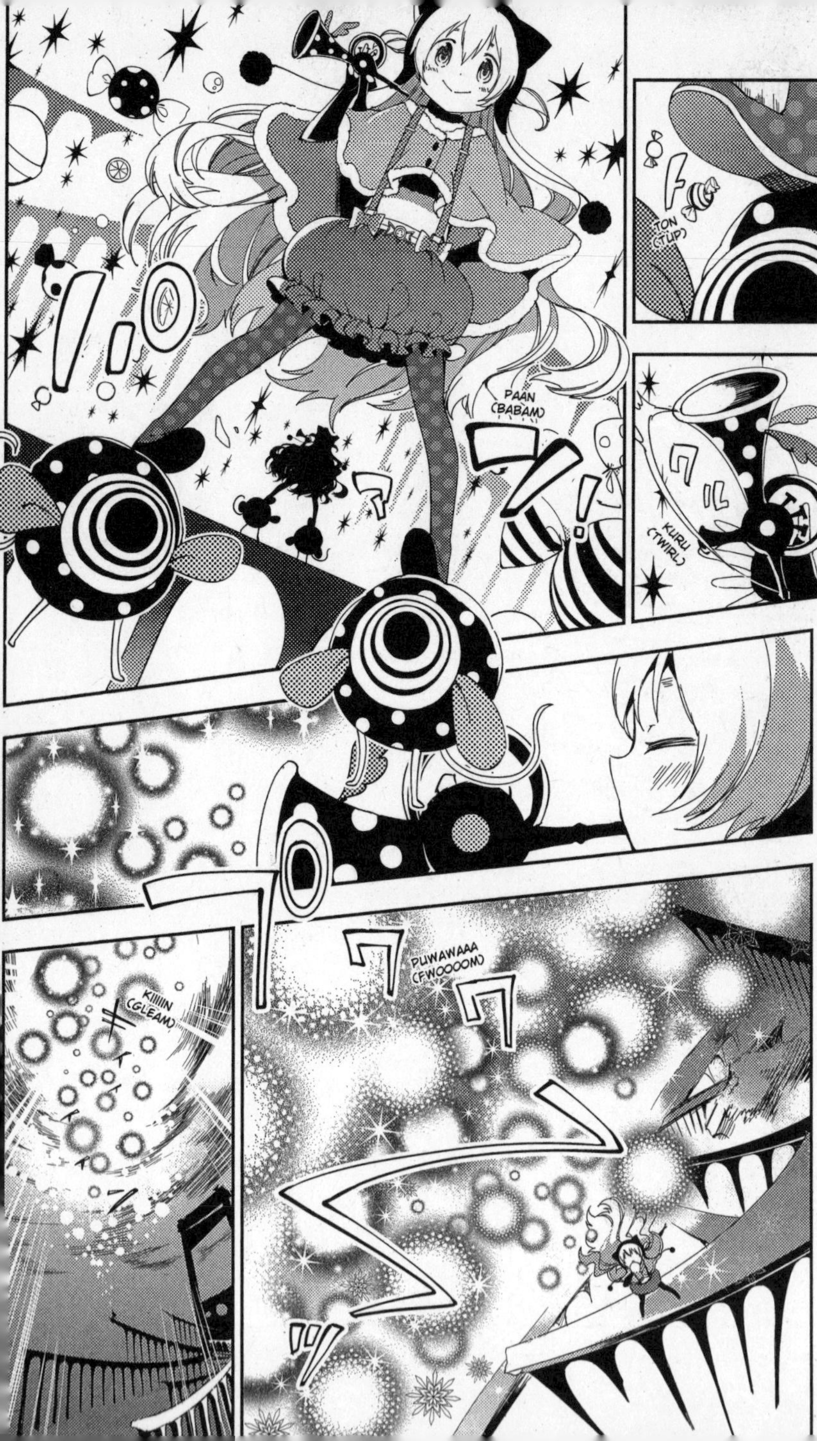
TON (TUP)
KURU (TWIRL)
PAAN (BABAM)
PUWAWAAA (FWOOOOM)
KIIIIN (GLEAM)

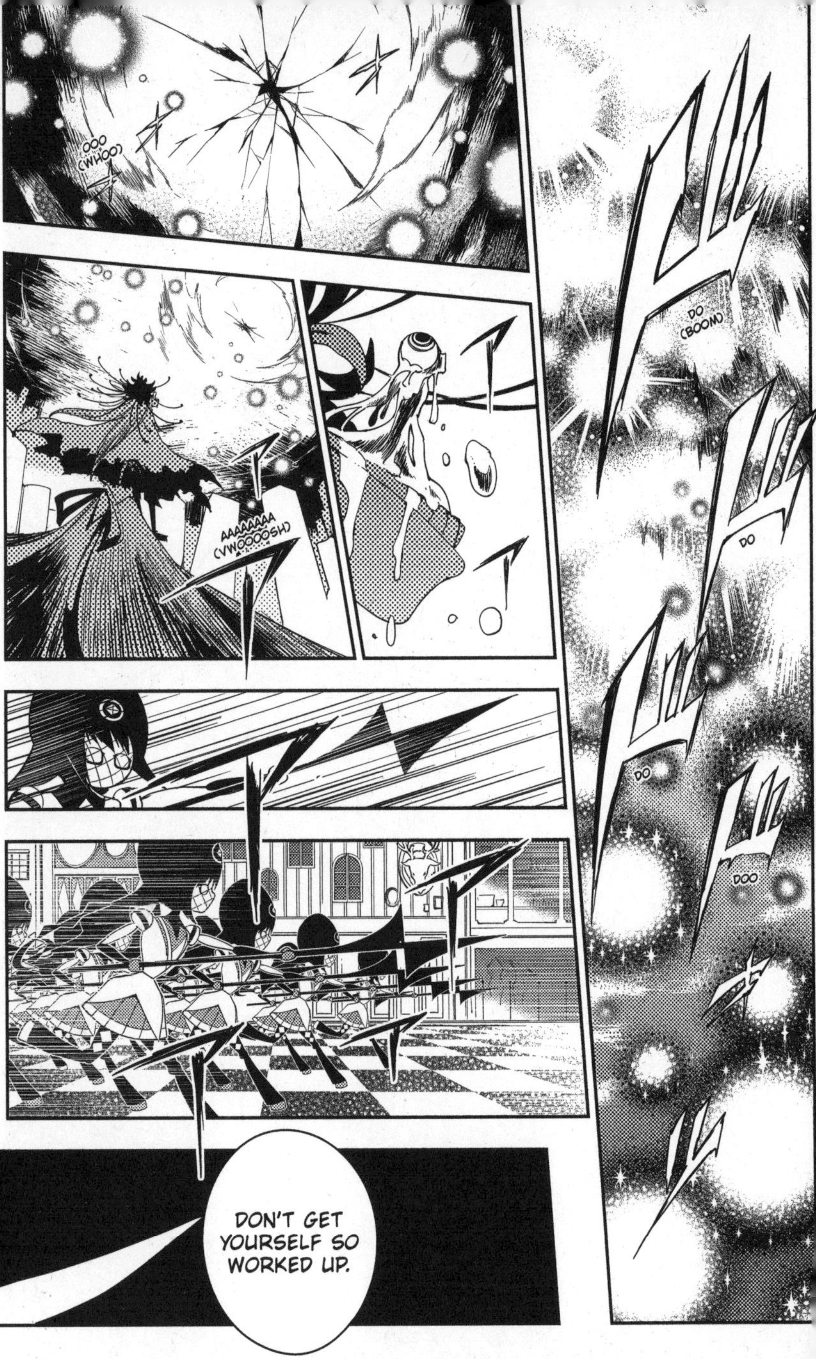
DO
(BOOM)
DO
DO
DOO
OOO
(WHOO)
AAAAAAAA
(VWOOOOSH)
DON'T GET YOURSELF SO WORKED UP.

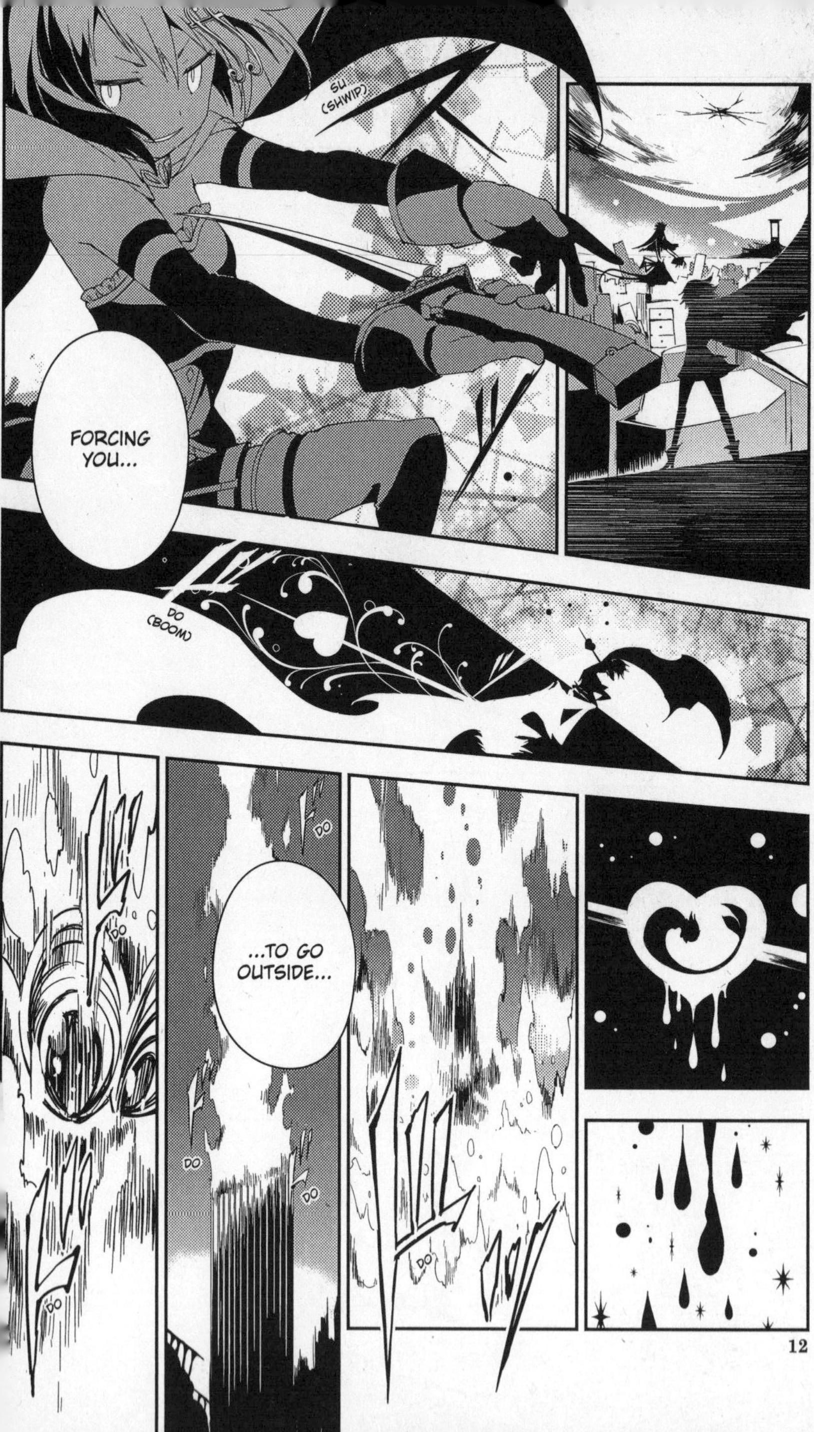
SU (SHWIP)
FORCING YOU...
DO (BOOM)
DO
DO
...TO GO OUTSIDE...
DO
DO
DO
DO

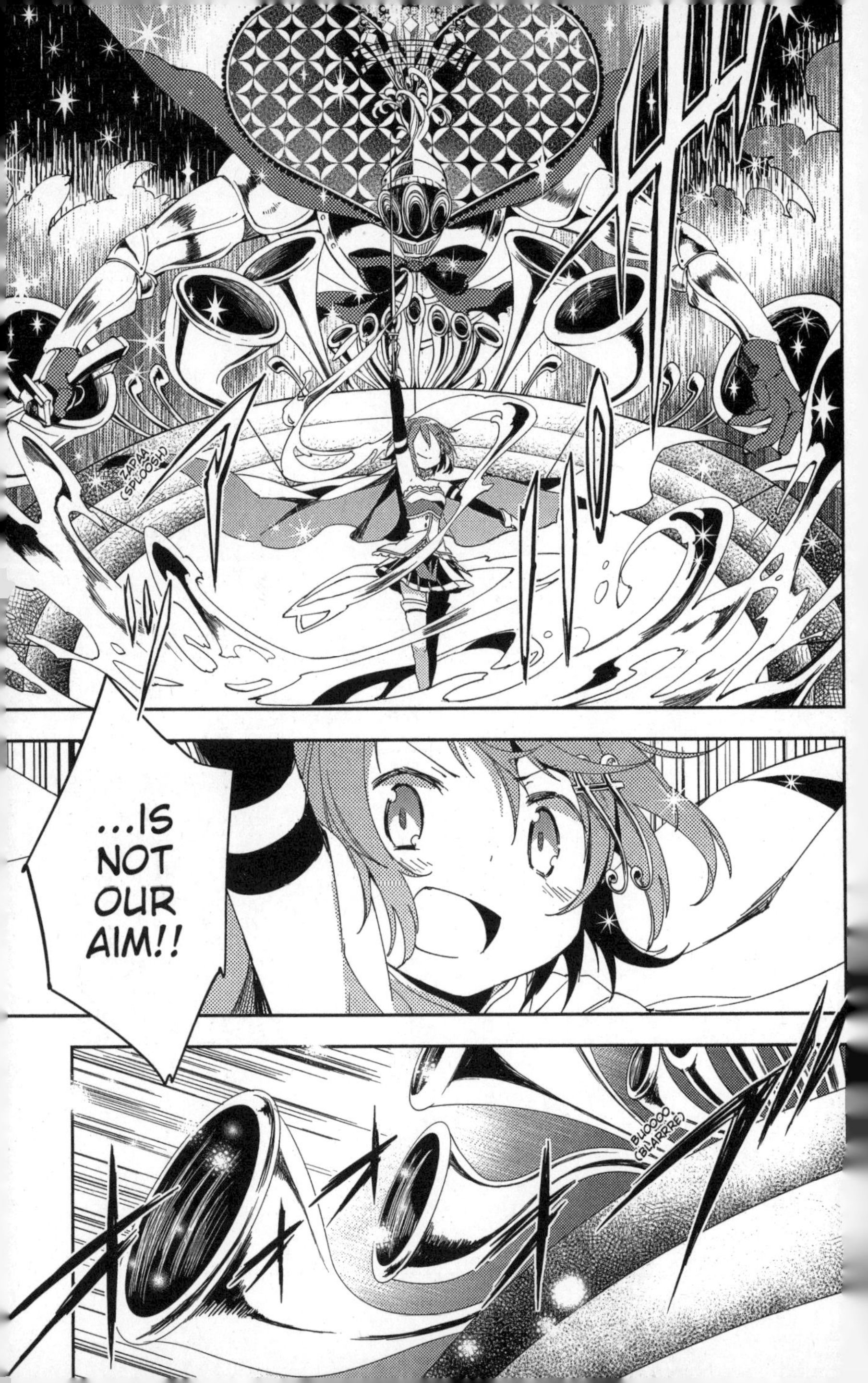
ZAPAA (SPLOOSH)
...IS NOT OUR AIM!!
BUOOOO. (BLARRE)

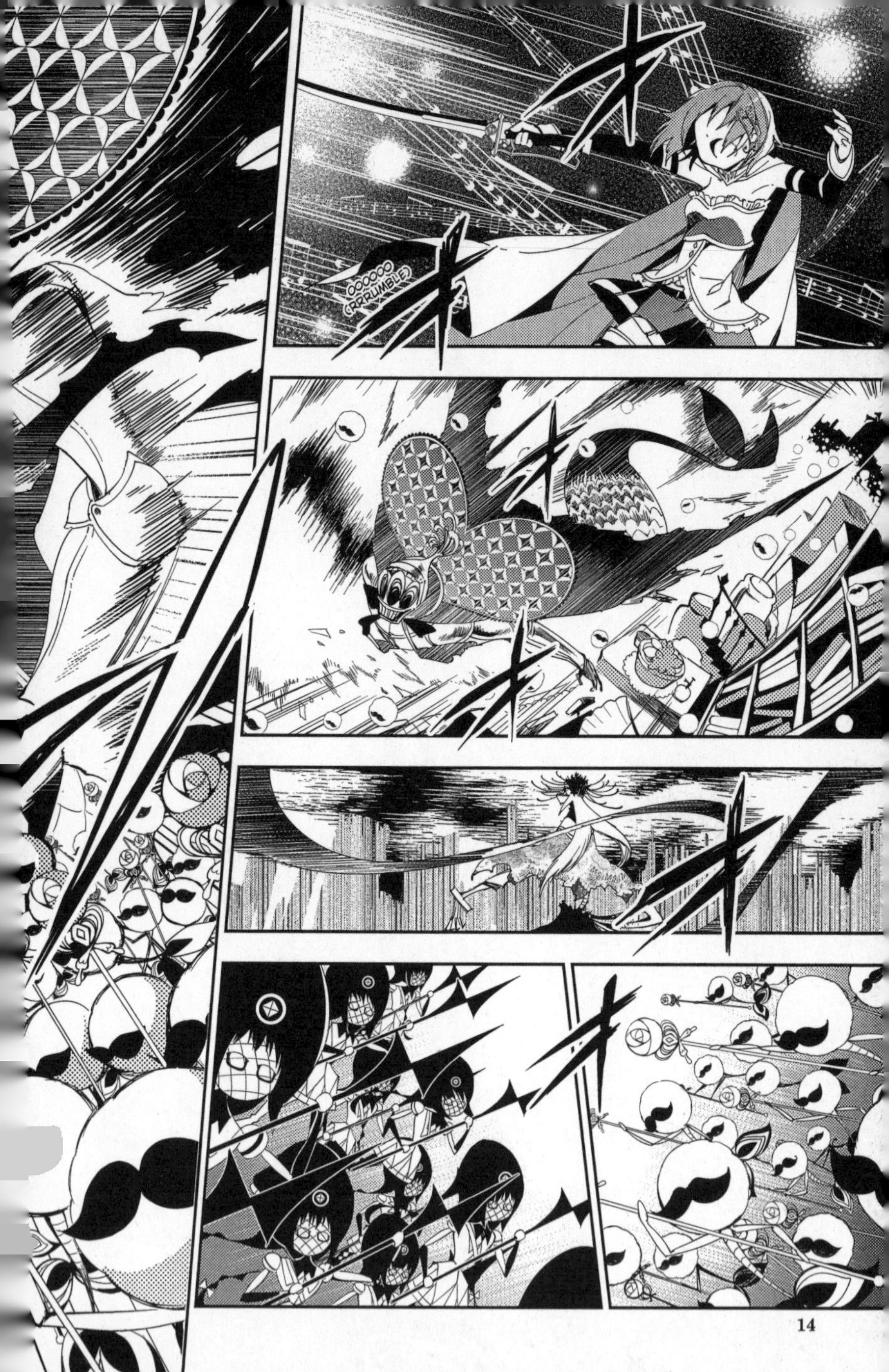
OOOOOO
(RRRUMBLE)

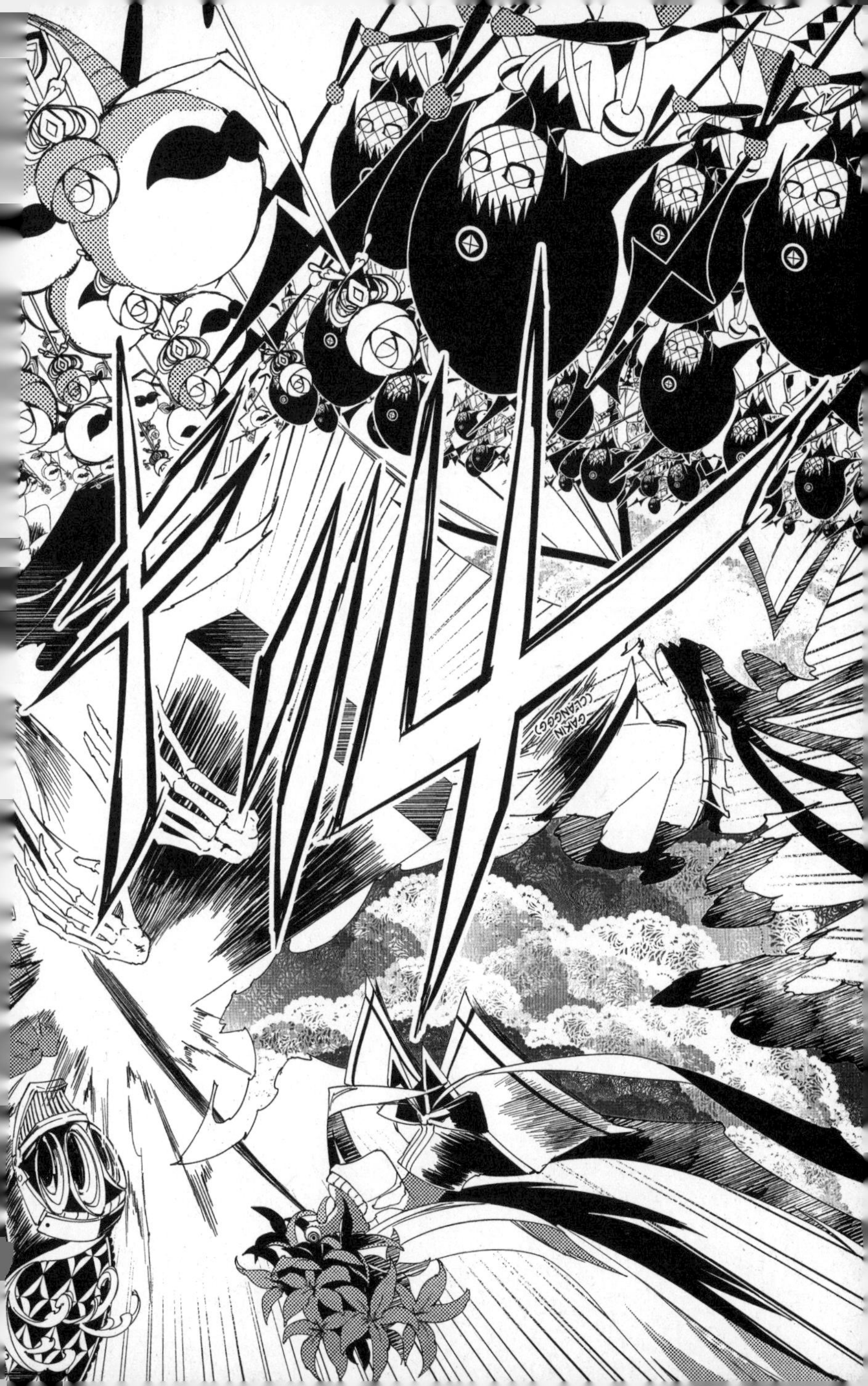
GAKIN
(CLANGGG)

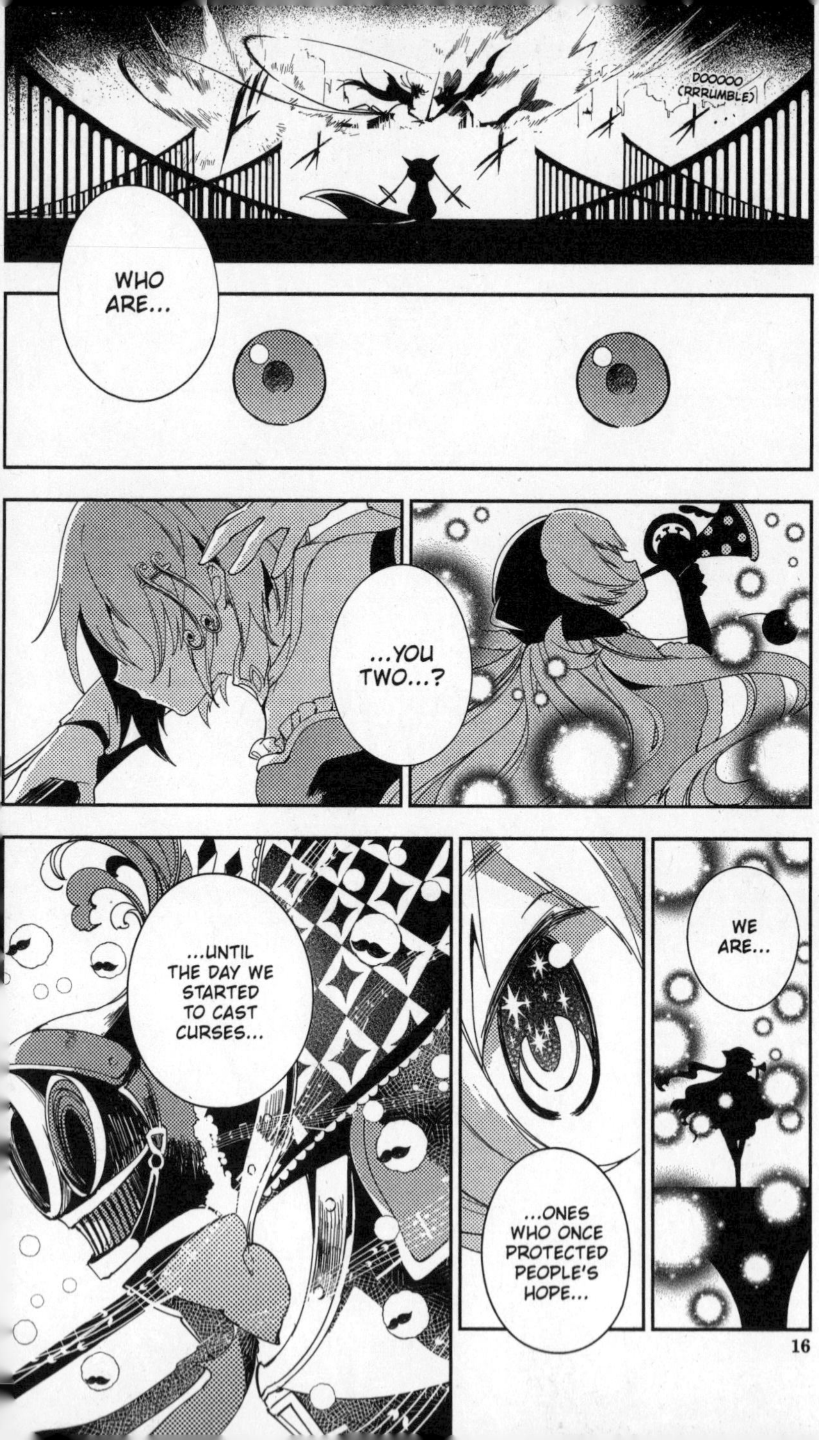
DOOOOO (RRRUMBLE) ...
WHO ARE...
...YOU TWO...?
WE ARE...
...ONES WHO ONCE PROTECTED PEOPLE'S HOPE...
...UNTIL THE DAY WE STARTED TO CAST CURSES...

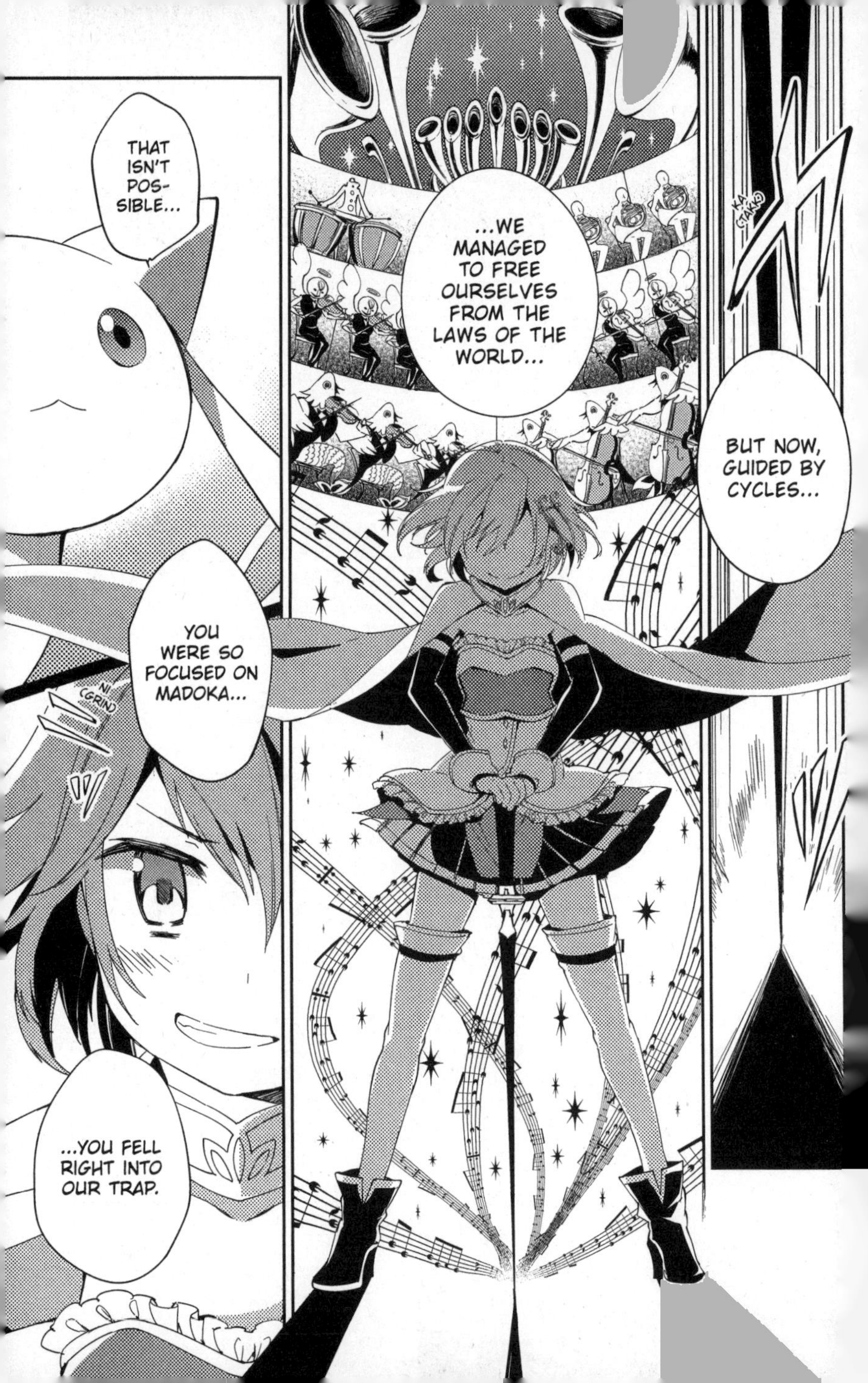
KA (TAKK)
BUT NOW, GUIDED BY CYCLES...
...WE MANAGED TO FREE OURSELVES FROM THE LAWS OF THE WORLD...
THAT ISN'T POS-SIBLE...
YOU WERE SO FOCUSED ON MADOKA...
NI (GRIN)
...YOU FELL RIGHT INTO OUR TRAP.

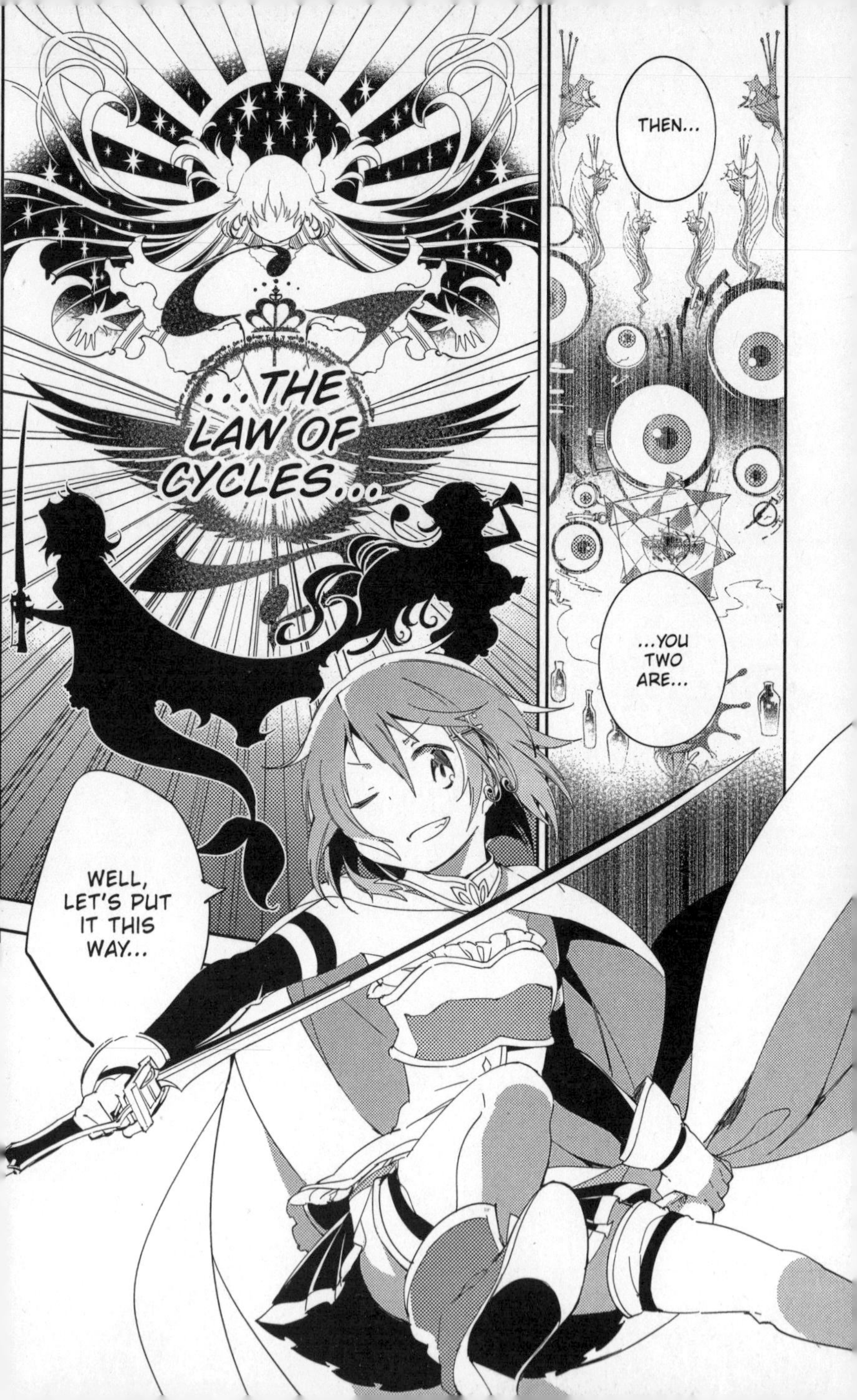
THEN...
...YOU TWO ARE...
...THE LAW OF CYCLES...
WELL, LET'S PUT IT THIS WAY...

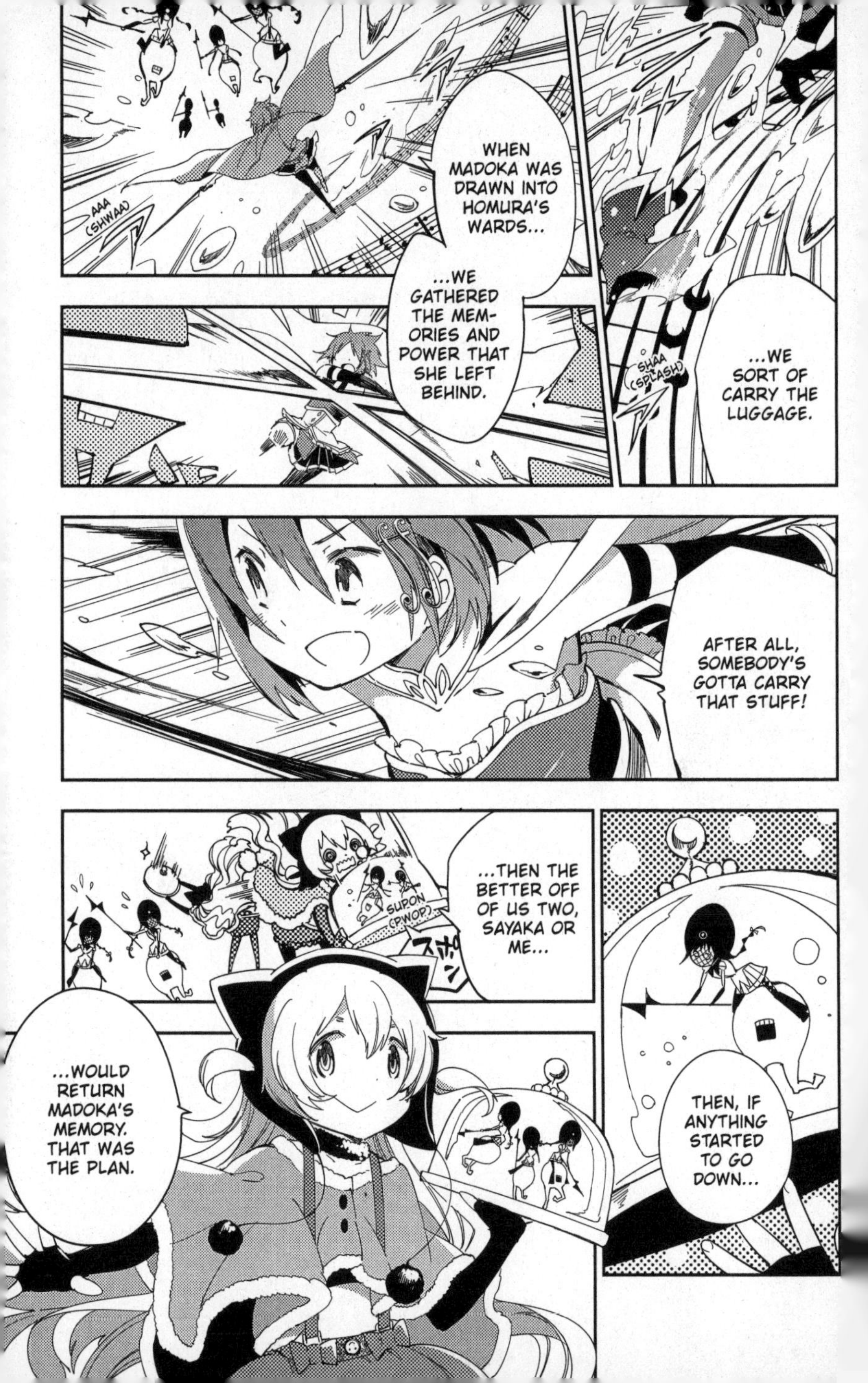
SHAA (SPLASH)
...WE SORT OF CARRY THE LUGGAGE.
WHEN MADOKA WAS DRAWN INTO HOMURA'S WARDS...
...WE GATHERED THE MEMORIES AND POWER THAT SHE LEFT BEHIND.
AAA (SHWAA)
AFTER ALL, SOMEBODY'S GOTTA CARRY THAT STUFF!
THEN, IF ANYTHING STARTED TO GO DOWN...
...THEN THE BETTER OFF OF US TWO, SAYAKA OR ME...
SUPON (PWOP)
...WOULD RETURN MADOKA'S MEMORY. THAT WAS THE PLAN.

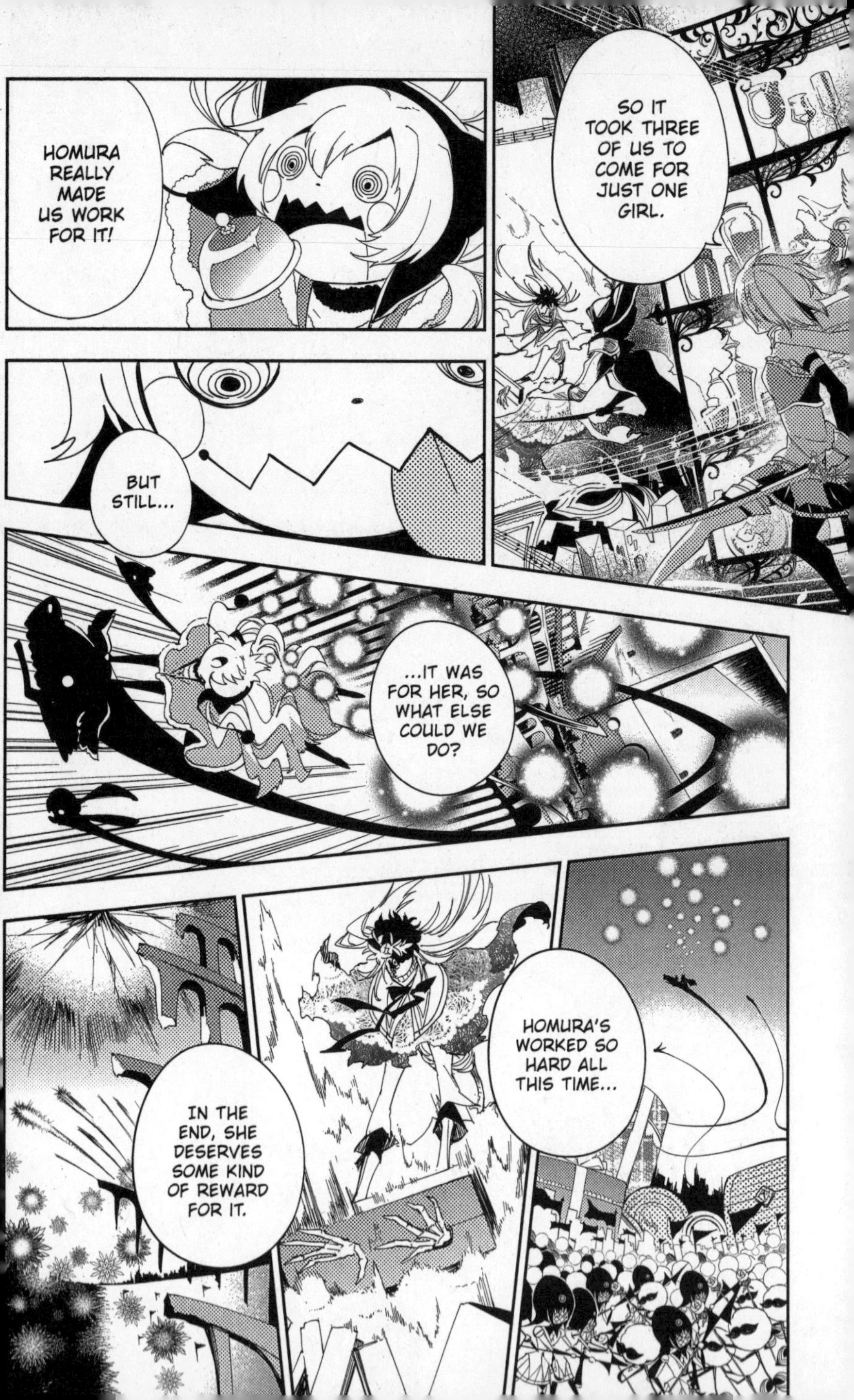
SO IT TOOK THREE OF US TO COME FOR JUST ONE GIRL.
HOMURA REALLY MADE US WORK FOR IT!
BUT STILL...
...IT WAS FOR HER, SO WHAT ELSE COULD WE DO?
HOMURA'S WORKED SO HARD ALL THIS TIME...
IN THE END, SHE DESERVES SOME KIND OF REWARD FOR IT.

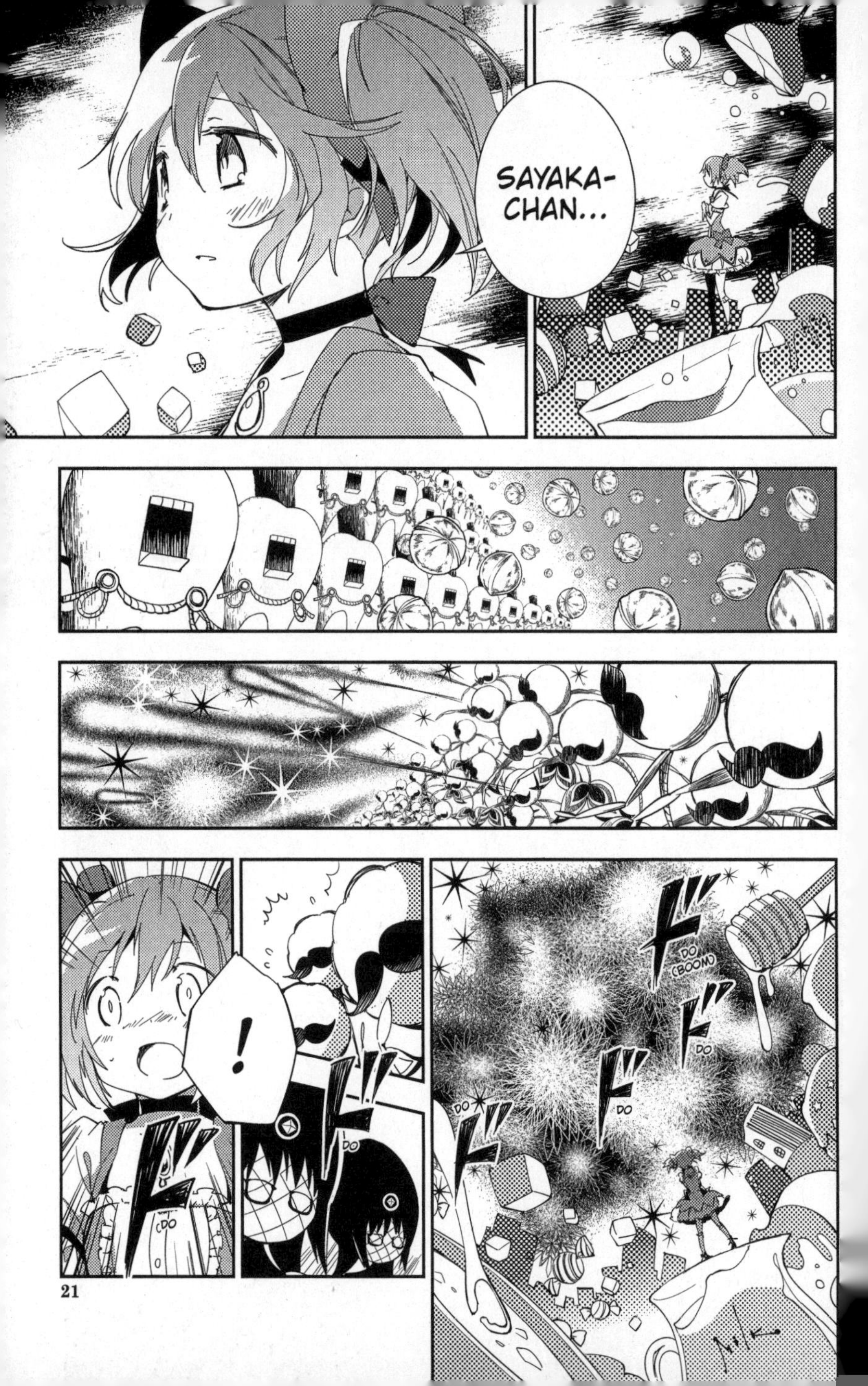
SAYAKA-CHAN...
DO (BOOM)
DO
DO
DO
!
DO
DO

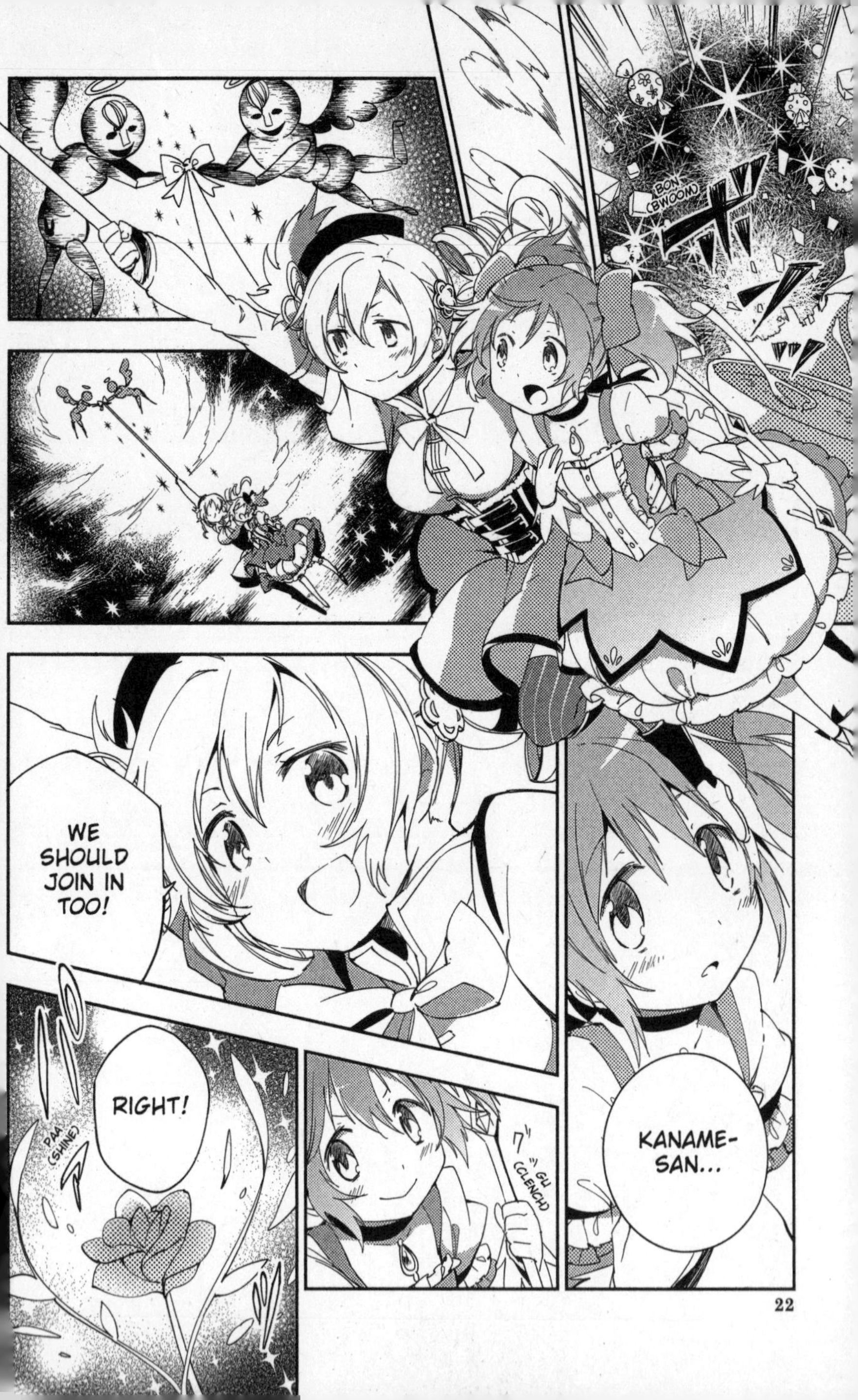
BON
(BWOOM)
KANAME-SAN...
WE SHOULD JOIN IN TOO!
GU
(CLENCH)
RIGHT!
PAA
(SHINE)

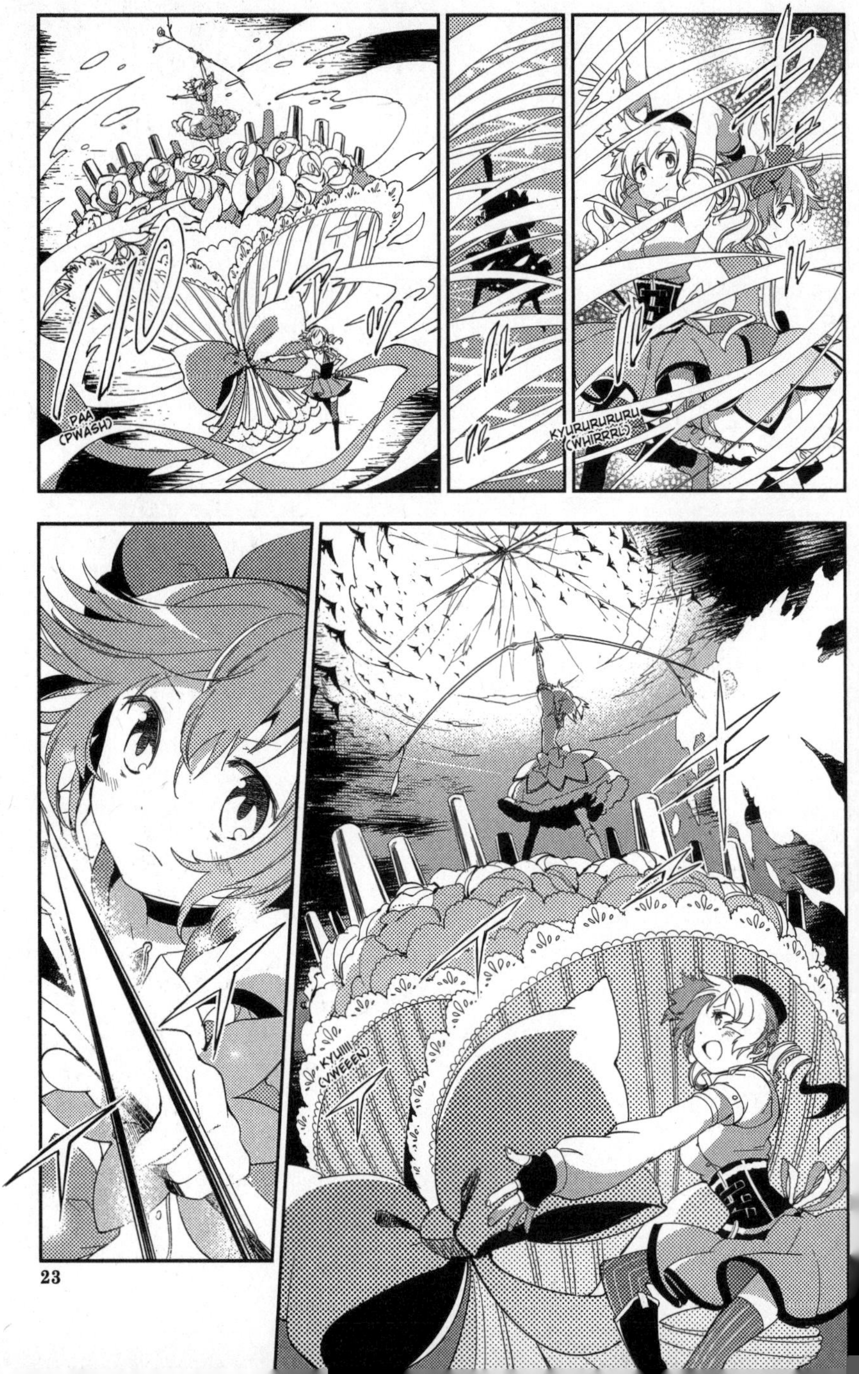
KYURURURURU
(WHIRRRL)
PAA
(PWASH)
KYUIIII
(CWEEEN)

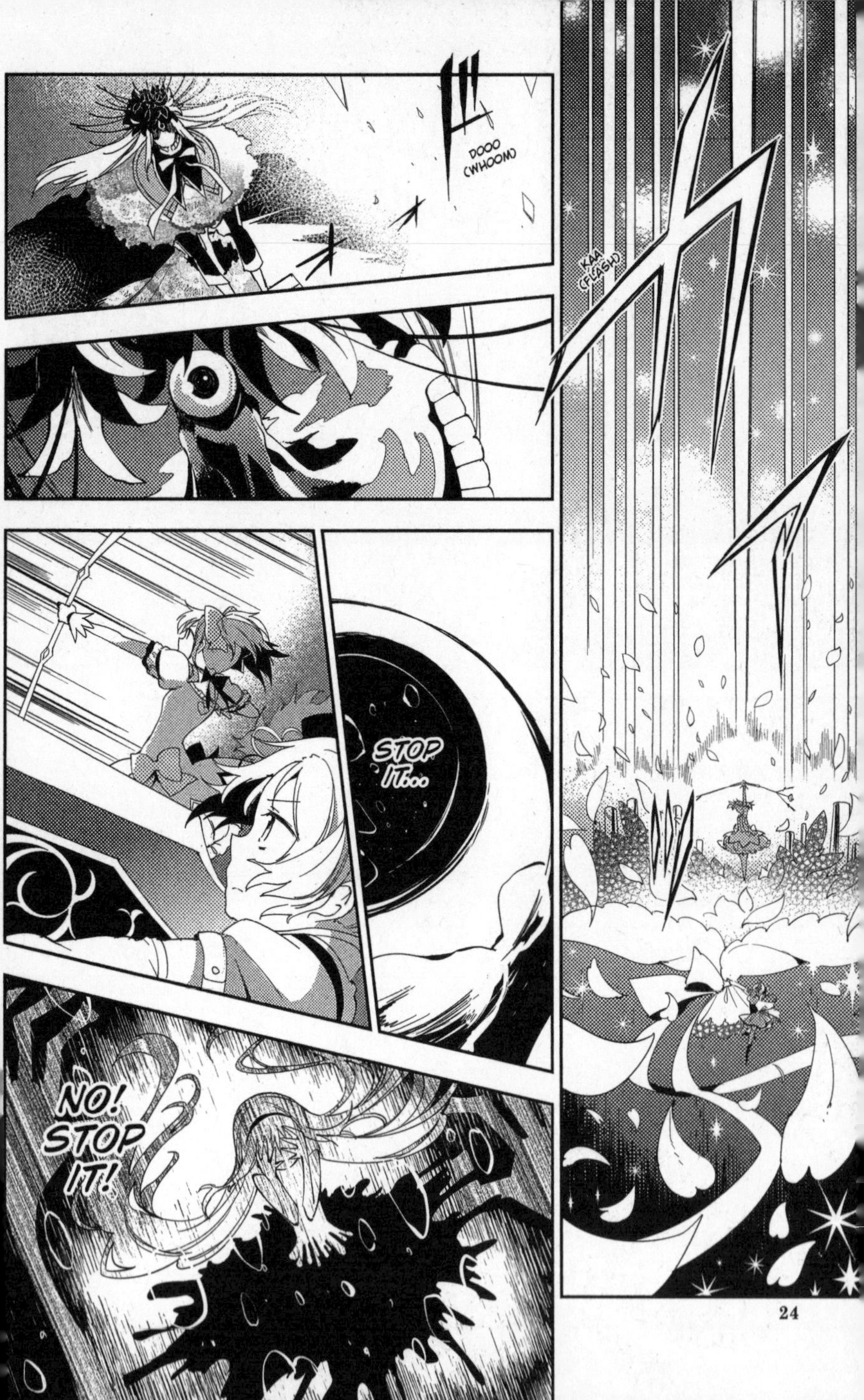
KAA (FLASH)
DOOO (WHOOM)
STOP IT...
NO! STOP IT!

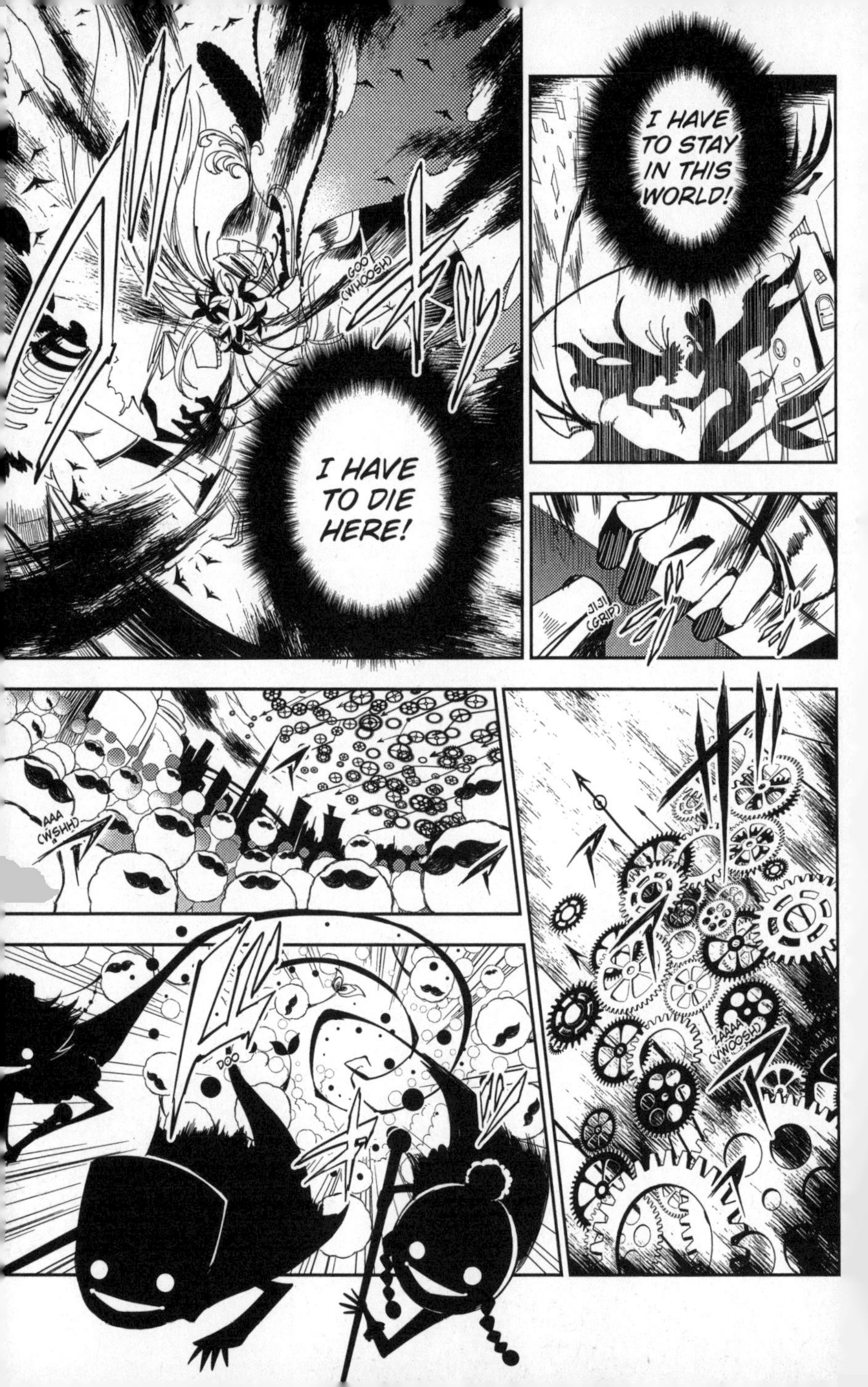
I HAVE TO STAY IN THIS WORLD!
JIJI (GRIP)
GOO (WHOOSH)
I HAVE TO DIE HERE!
ZAAAA (WOOSH)
AAA (WSHH)
DOO

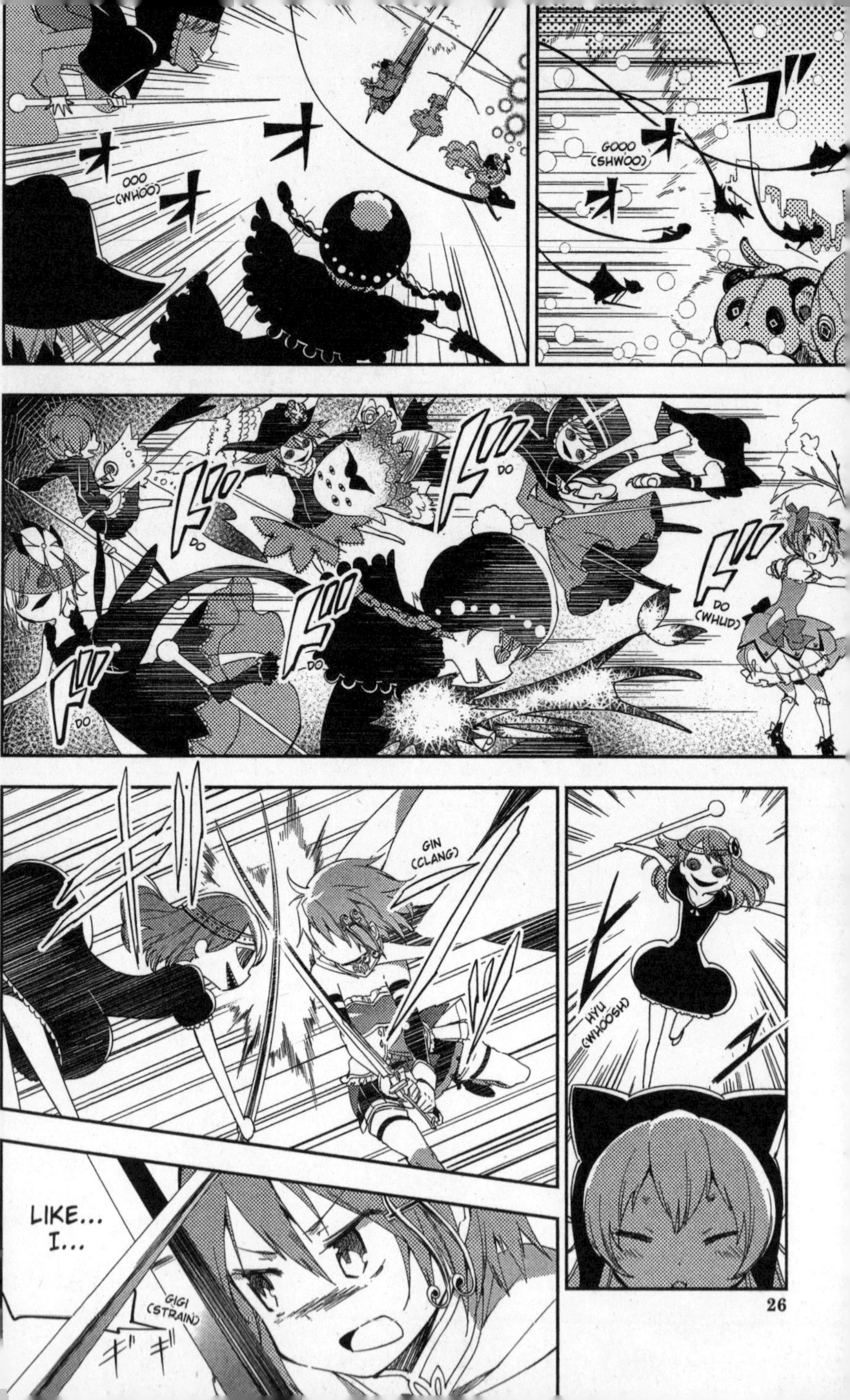
GOOO (SHWOO)
OOO (WHOO)
DO (WHUD)
DO
DO
DO
DO
HYU (WHOOSH)
GIN (CLANG)
LIKE... I...
GIGI (STRAIN)

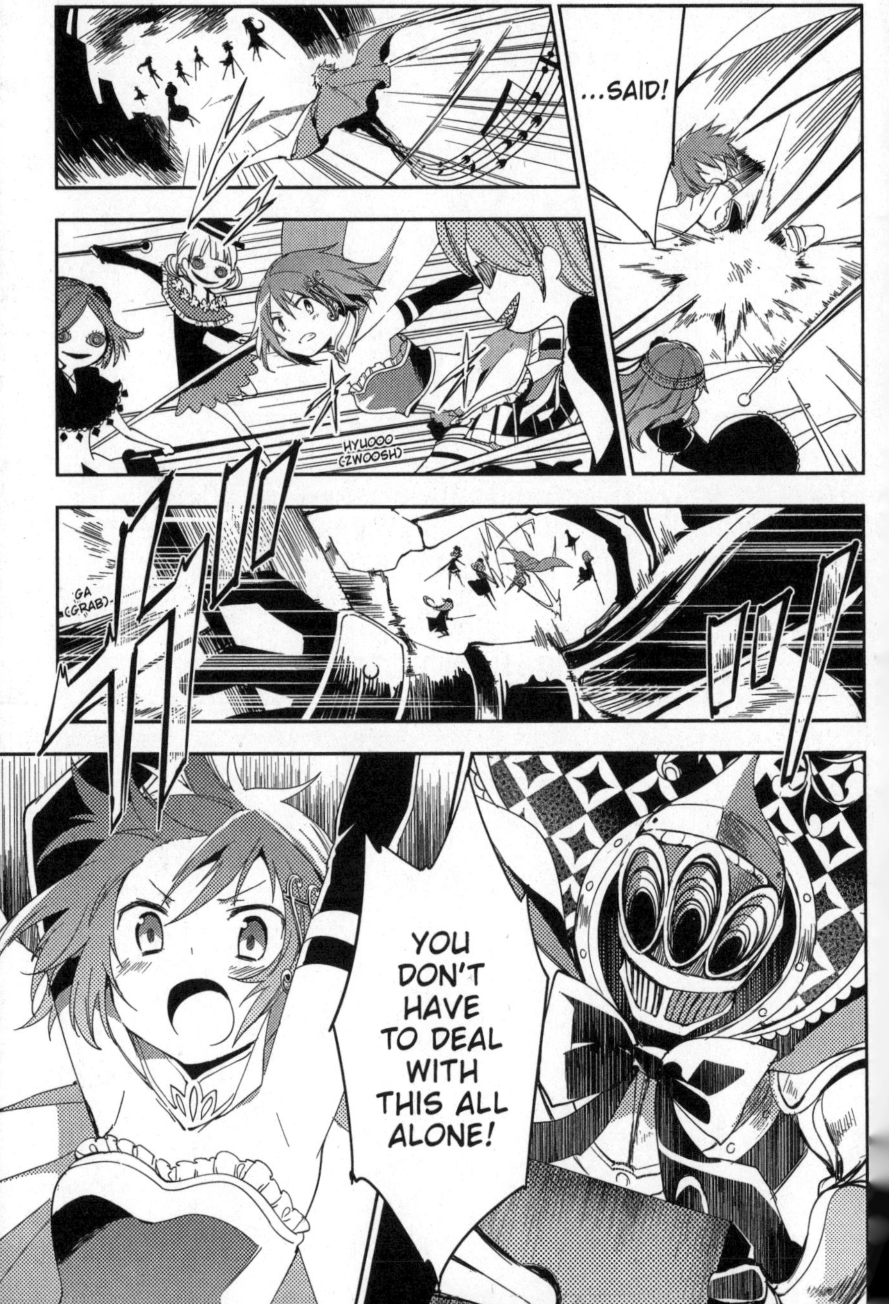
...SAID!
HYUOOO (ZWOOSH)
GA (GRAB)
YOU DON'T HAVE TO DEAL WITH THIS ALL ALONE!

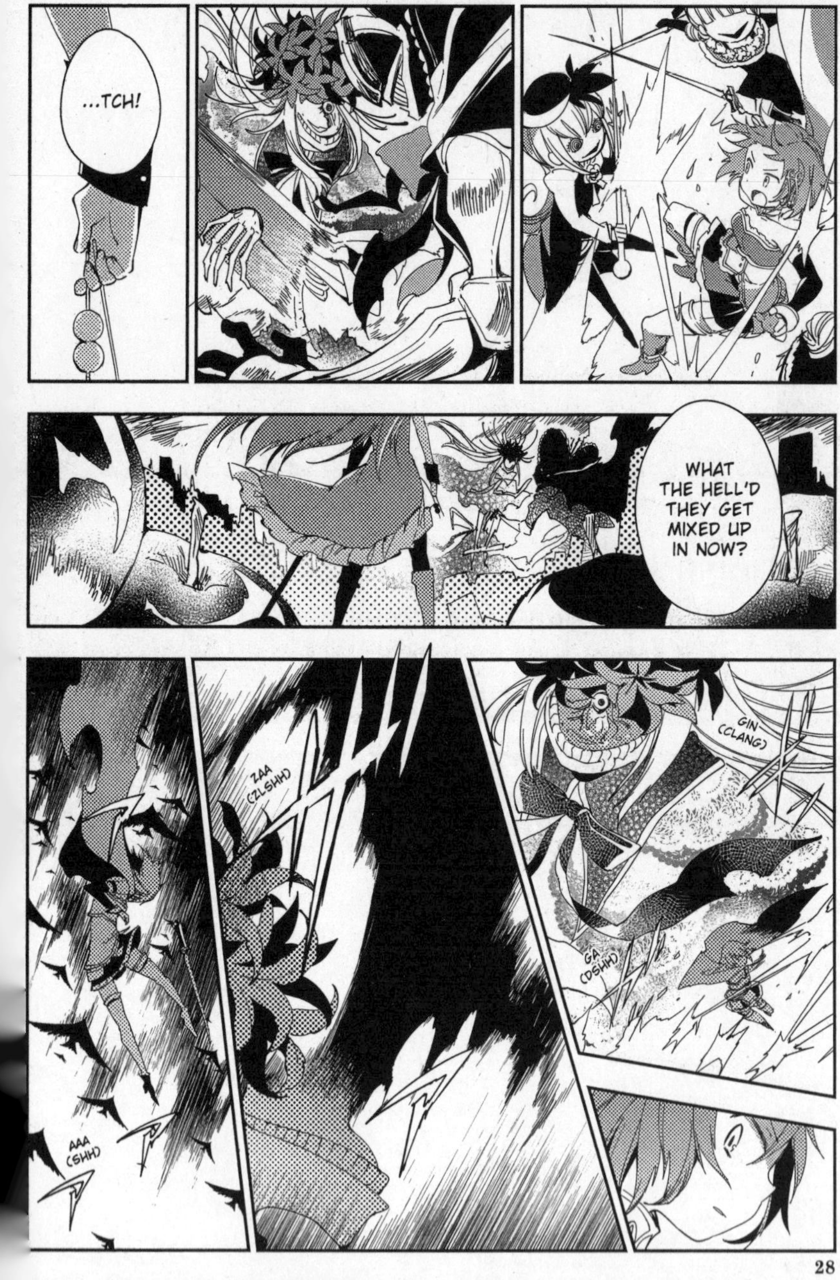
...TCH!
WHAT THE HELL'D THEY GET MIXED UP IN NOW?
GIN (CLANG)
GA (DSHH)
ZAA (ZLSHH)
AAA (SHH)

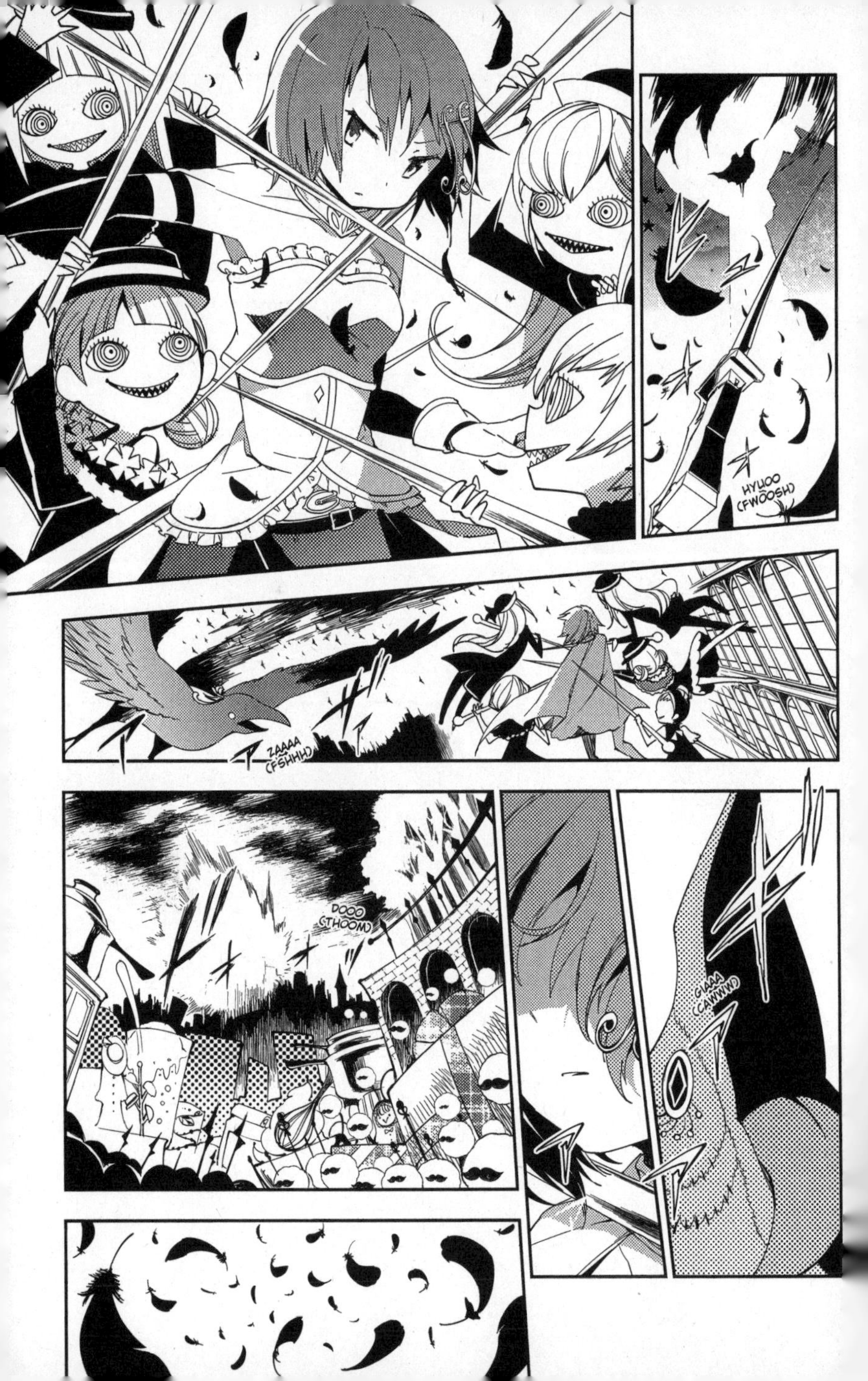
HYUOO (FWOOSH)
ZAAAA (FSHHH)
GIAAA (CAWWW)
DOOO (THOOM)

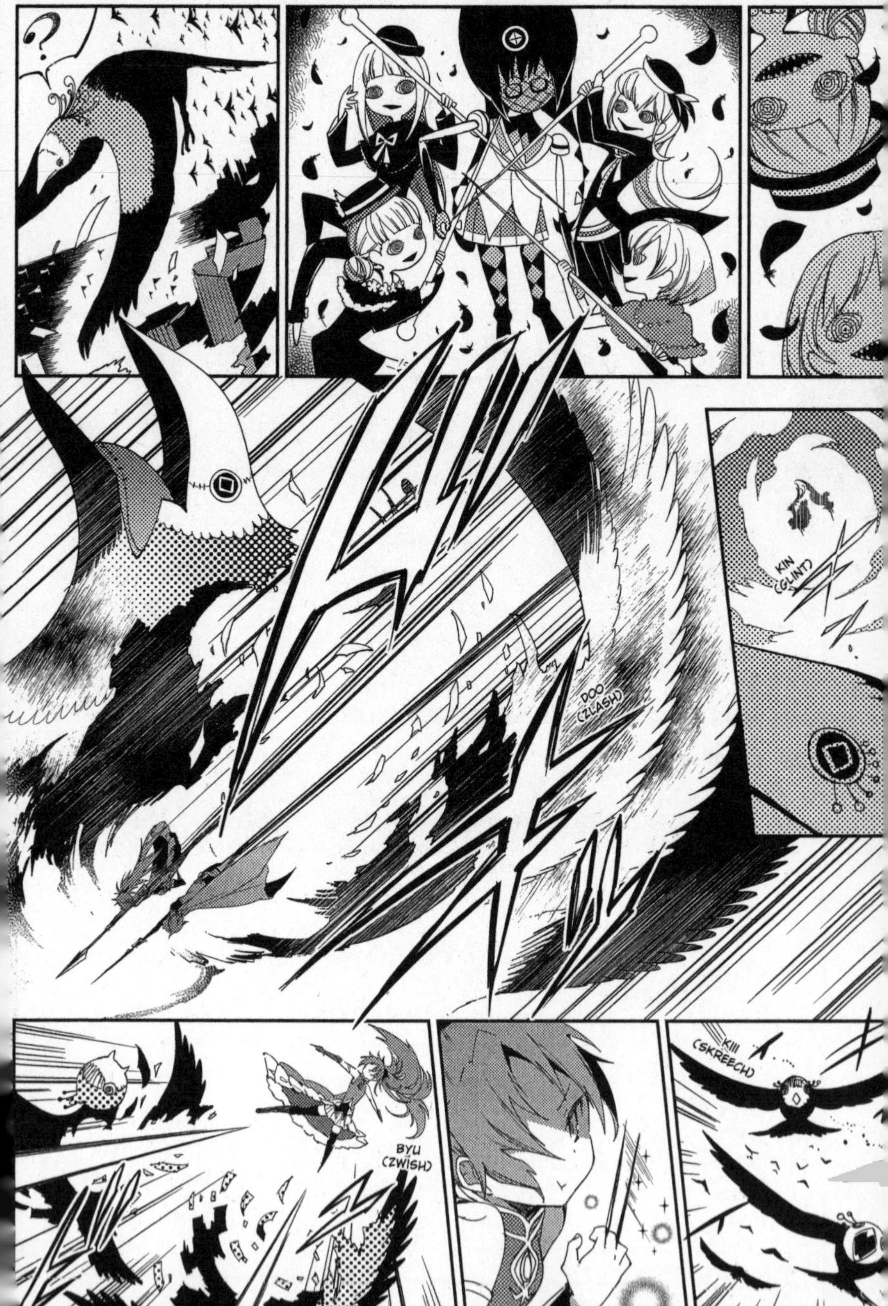
?
KIN
(GLINT)
DOO
(ZLASH)
KIII
(SKREECH)
BYU
(ZWISH)

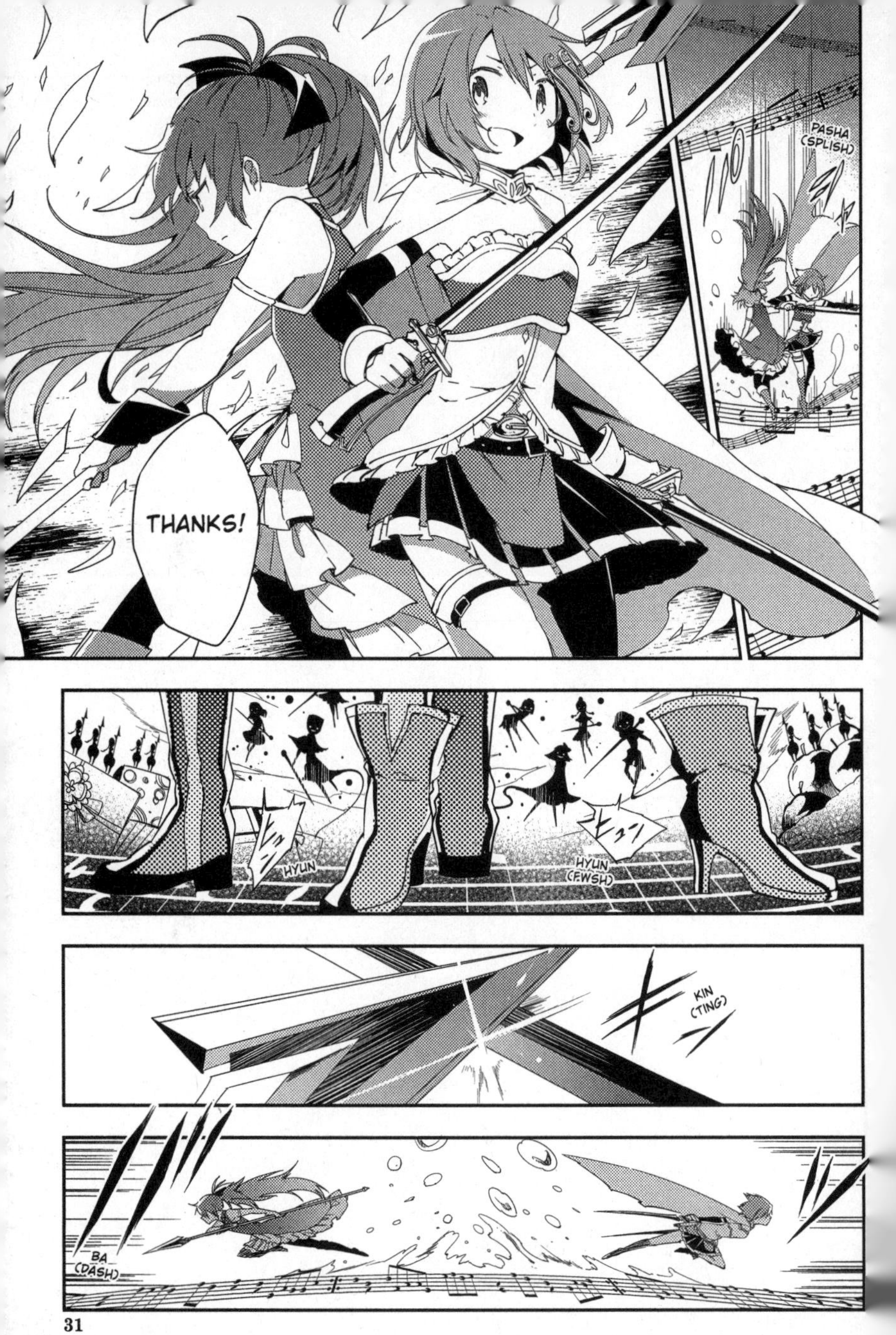
PASHA (SPLISH)
THANKS!
HYUN (FWSH)
HYUN
KIN (TING)
BA (DASH)

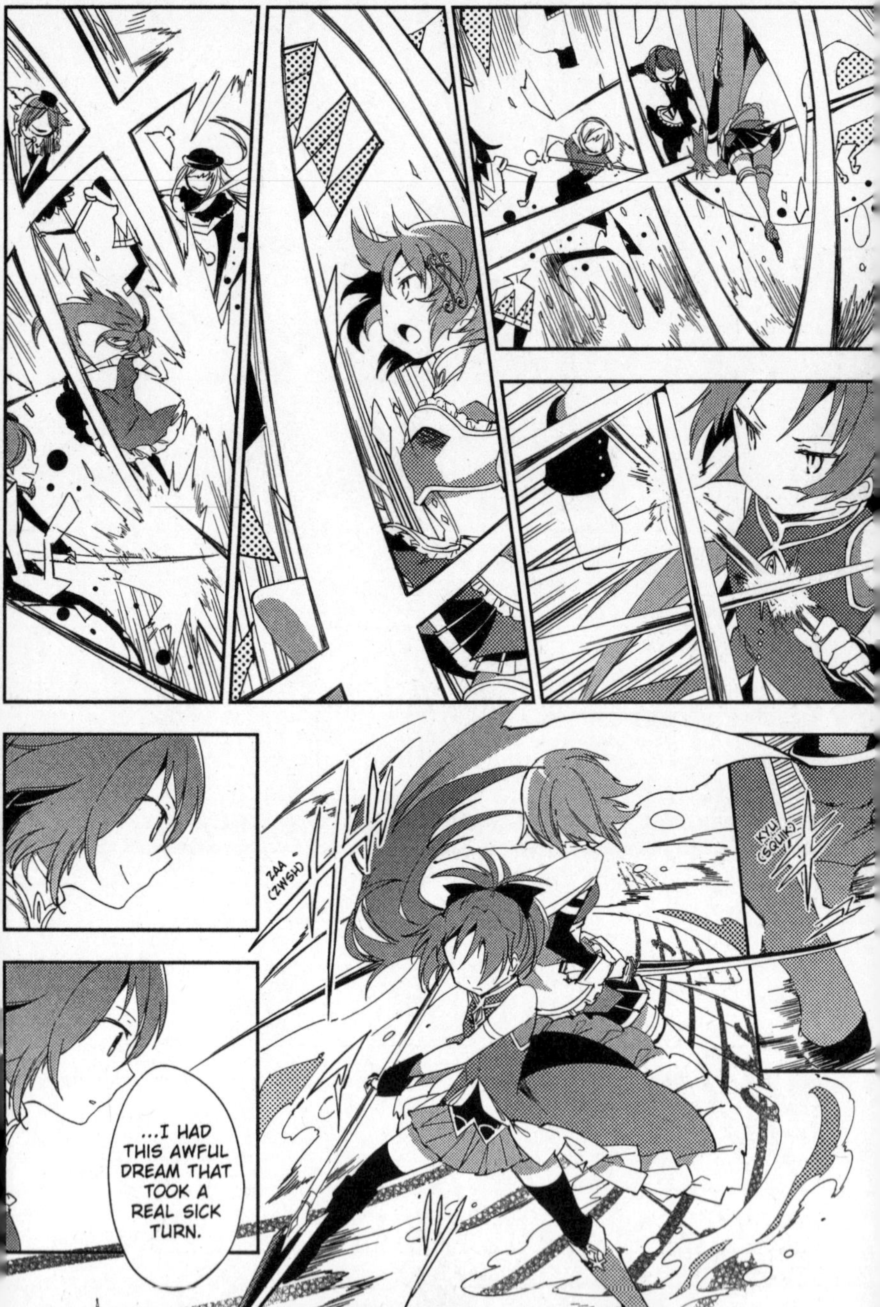
KYU (SQUIK)
ZAA (ZWSH)
...I HAD THIS AWFUL DREAM THAT TOOK A REAL SICK TURN.

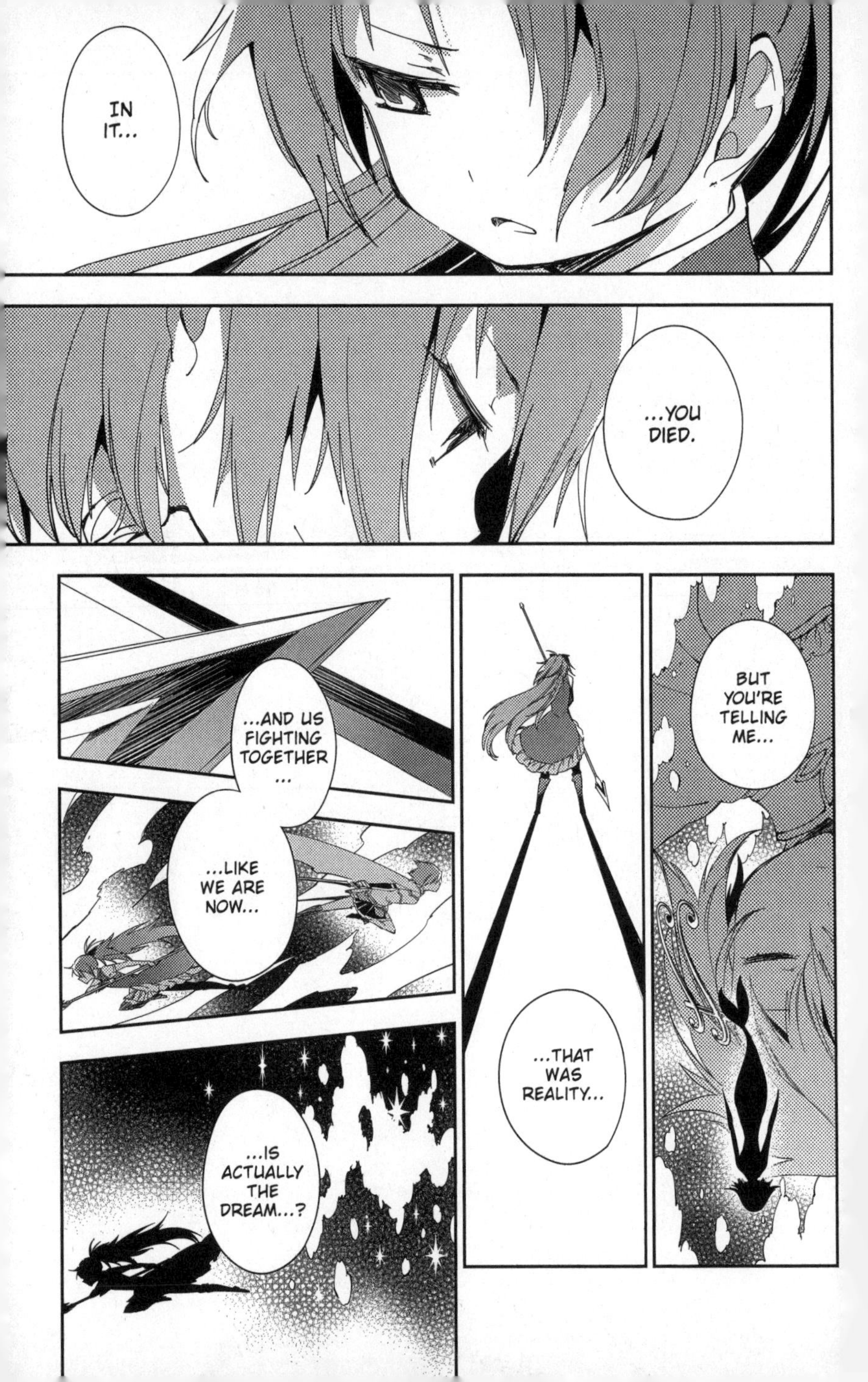
IN IT...
...YOU DIED.
BUT YOU'RE TELLING ME...
...THAT WAS REALITY...
...AND US FIGHTING TOGETHER ...
...LIKE WE ARE NOW...
...IS ACTUALLY THE DREAM...?

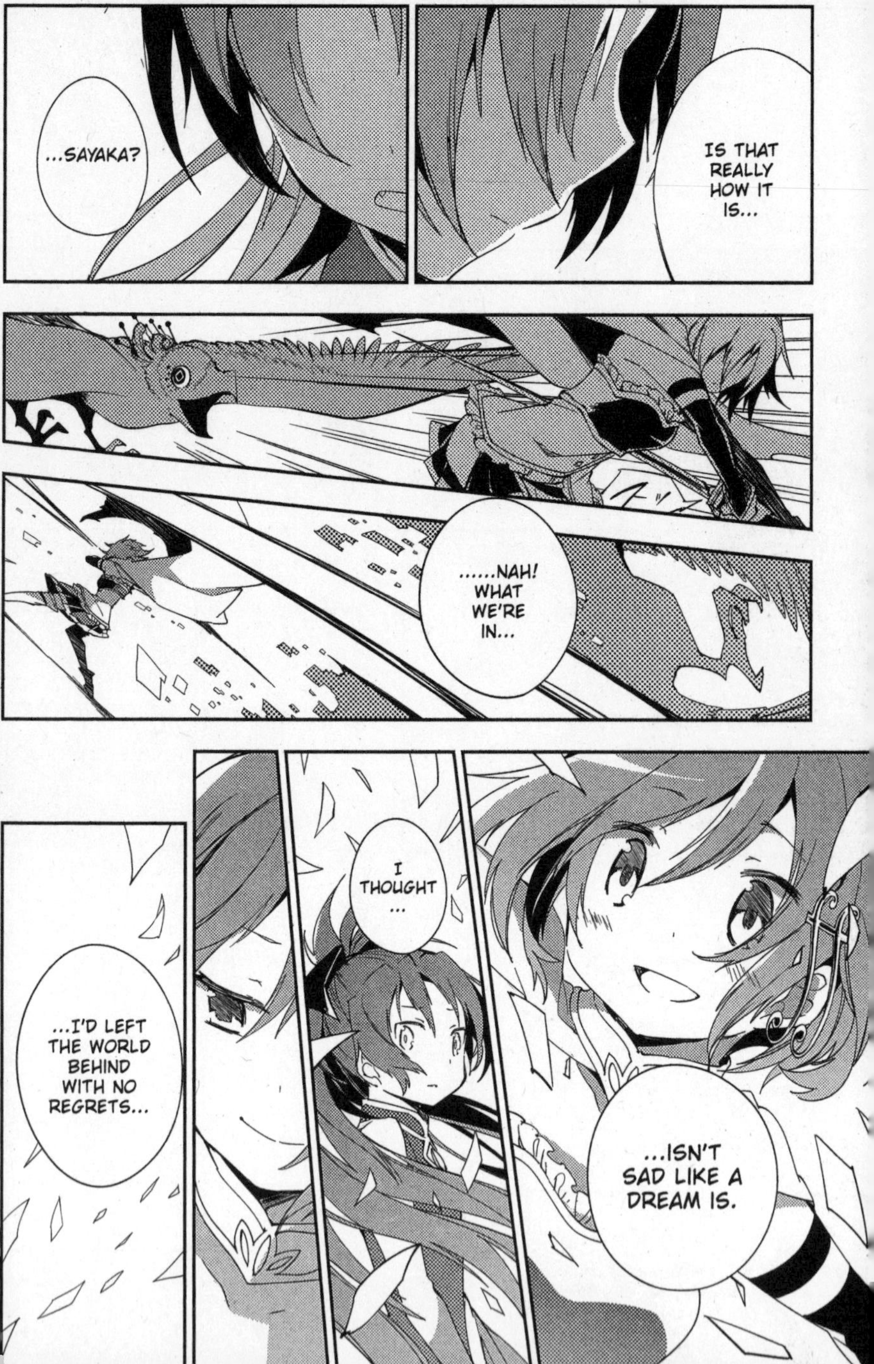
IS THAT REALLY HOW IT IS...
...SAYAKA?
......NAH! WHAT WE'RE IN...
...ISN'T SAD LIKE A DREAM IS.
I THOUGHT ...
...I'D LEFT THE WORLD BEHIND WITH NO REGRETS...

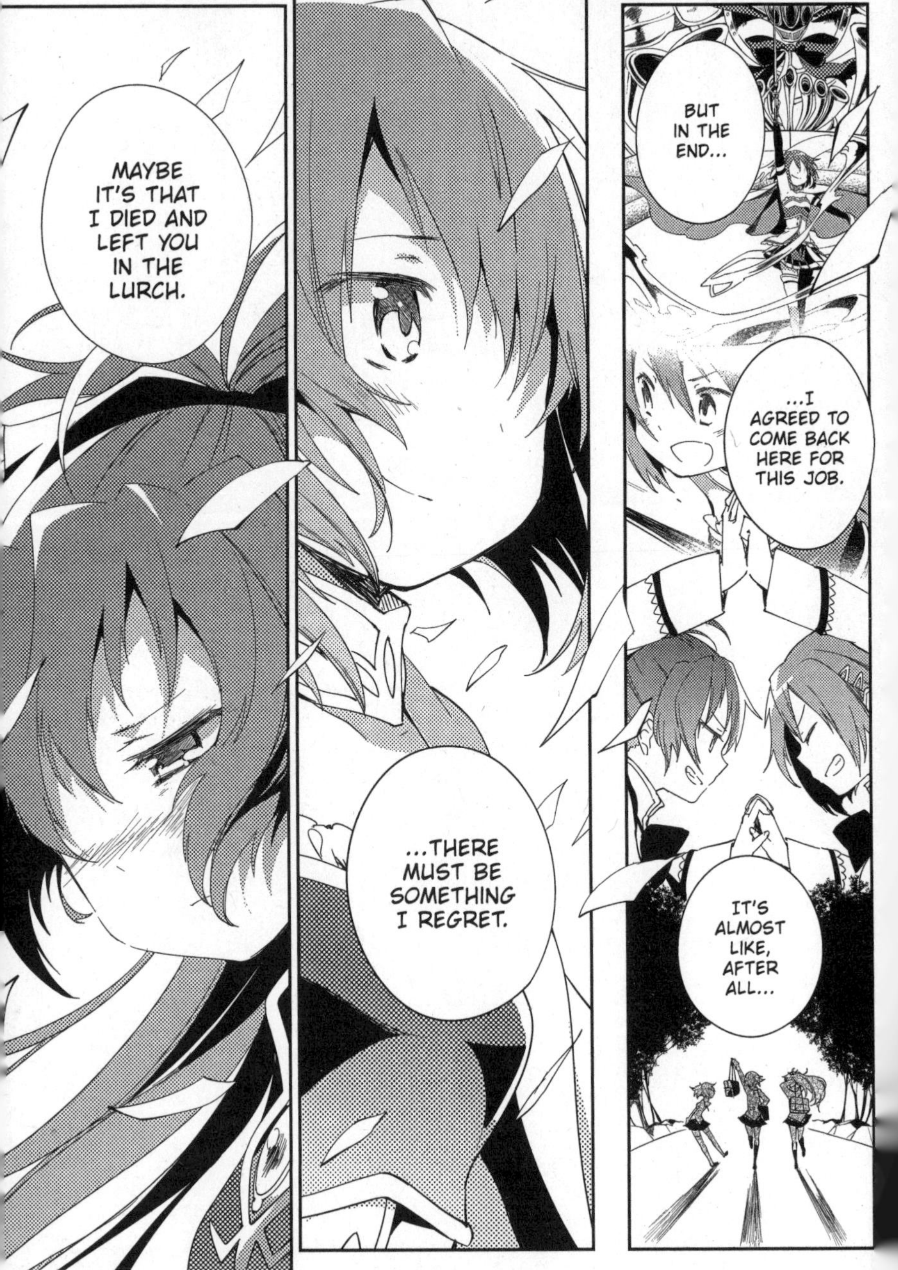
BUT IN THE END...
...I AGREED TO COME BACK HERE FOR THIS JOB.
IT'S ALMOST LIKE, AFTER ALL...
...THERE MUST BE SOMETHING I REGRET.
MAYBE IT'S THAT I DIED AND LEFT YOU IN THE LURCH.

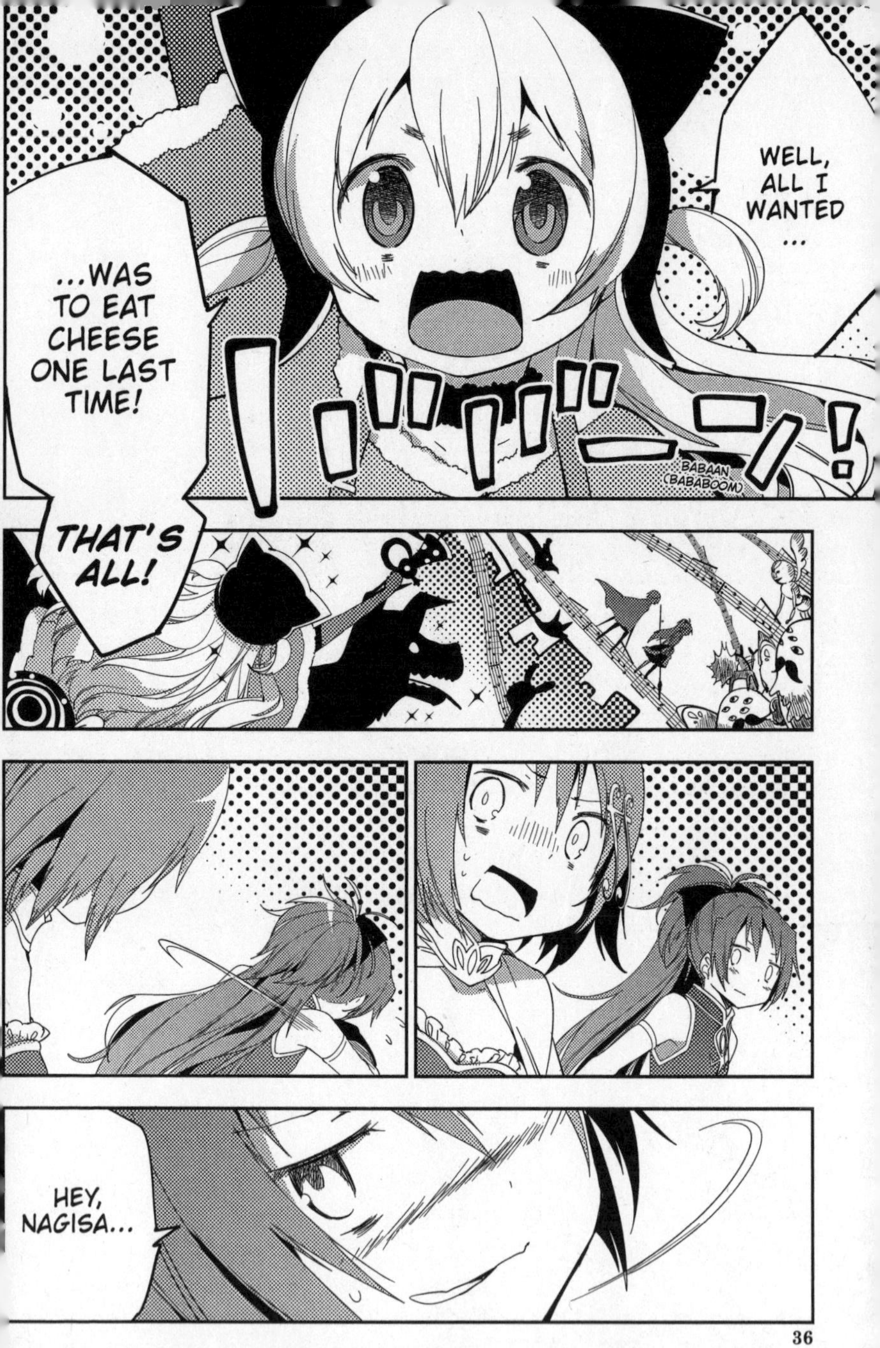
WELL, ALL I WANTED ...
...WAS TO EAT CHEESE ONE LAST TIME!
BABAAN (BABABOOM)
THAT'S ALL!
HEY, NAGISA...

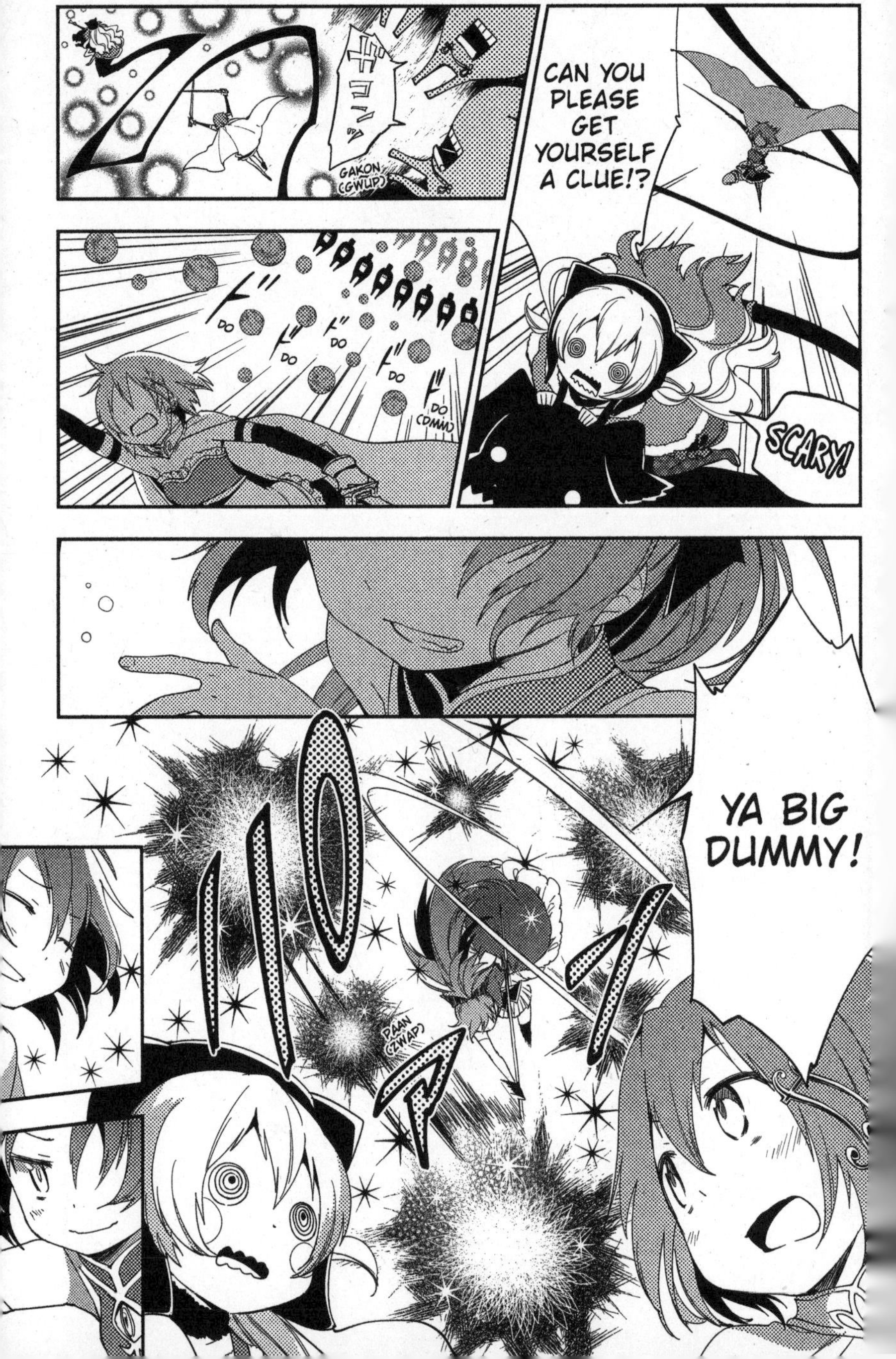
CAN YOU PLEASE GET YOURSELF A CLUE!?
SCARY!
GAKON (GWUP)
DO
DO
DO
DO
DO (DMM)
YA BIG DUMMY!
PAAN (ZWAP)

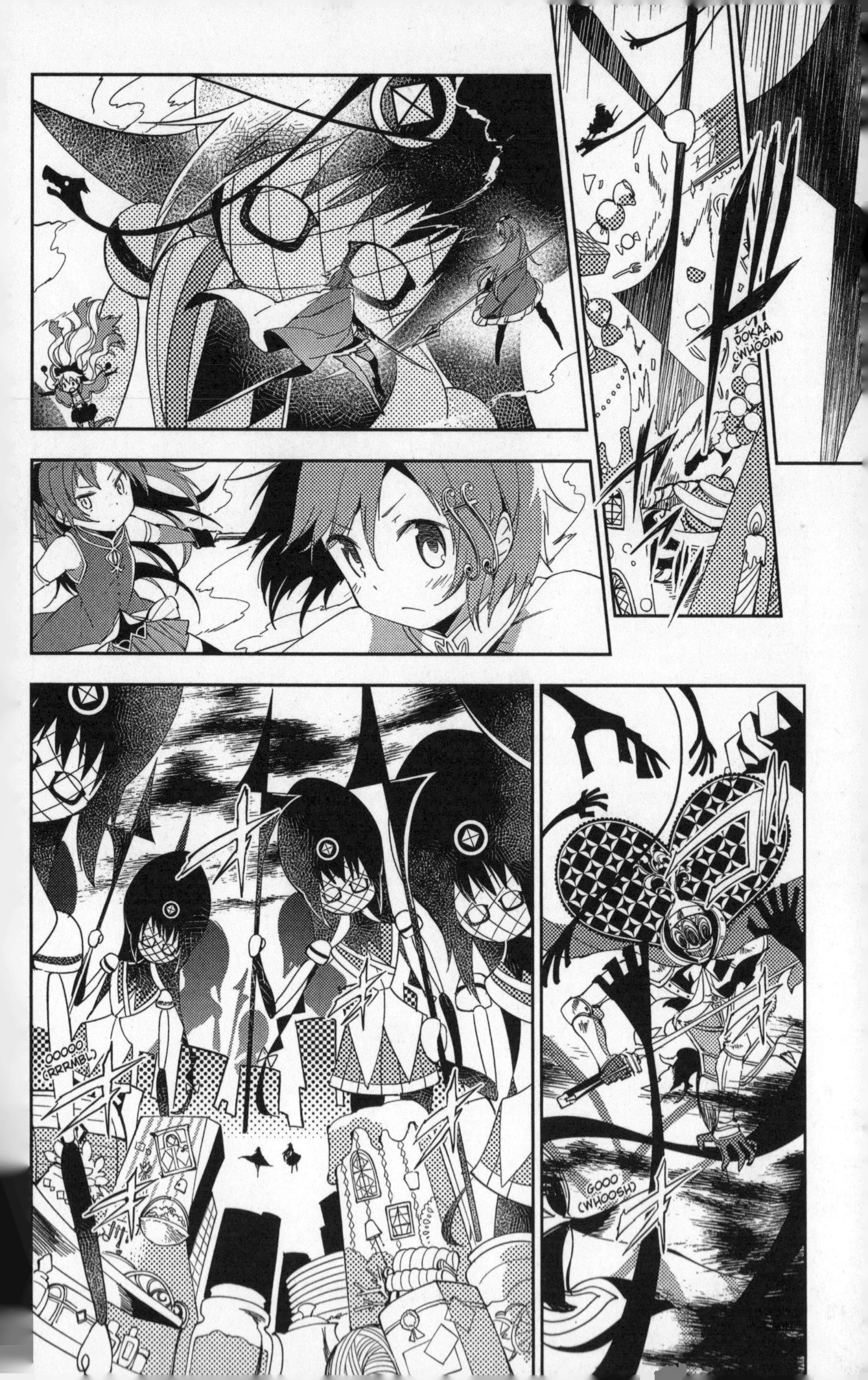
DOKAA (WHOOM)
GOOO (WHOOSH)
OOOOO (RRRMBL)

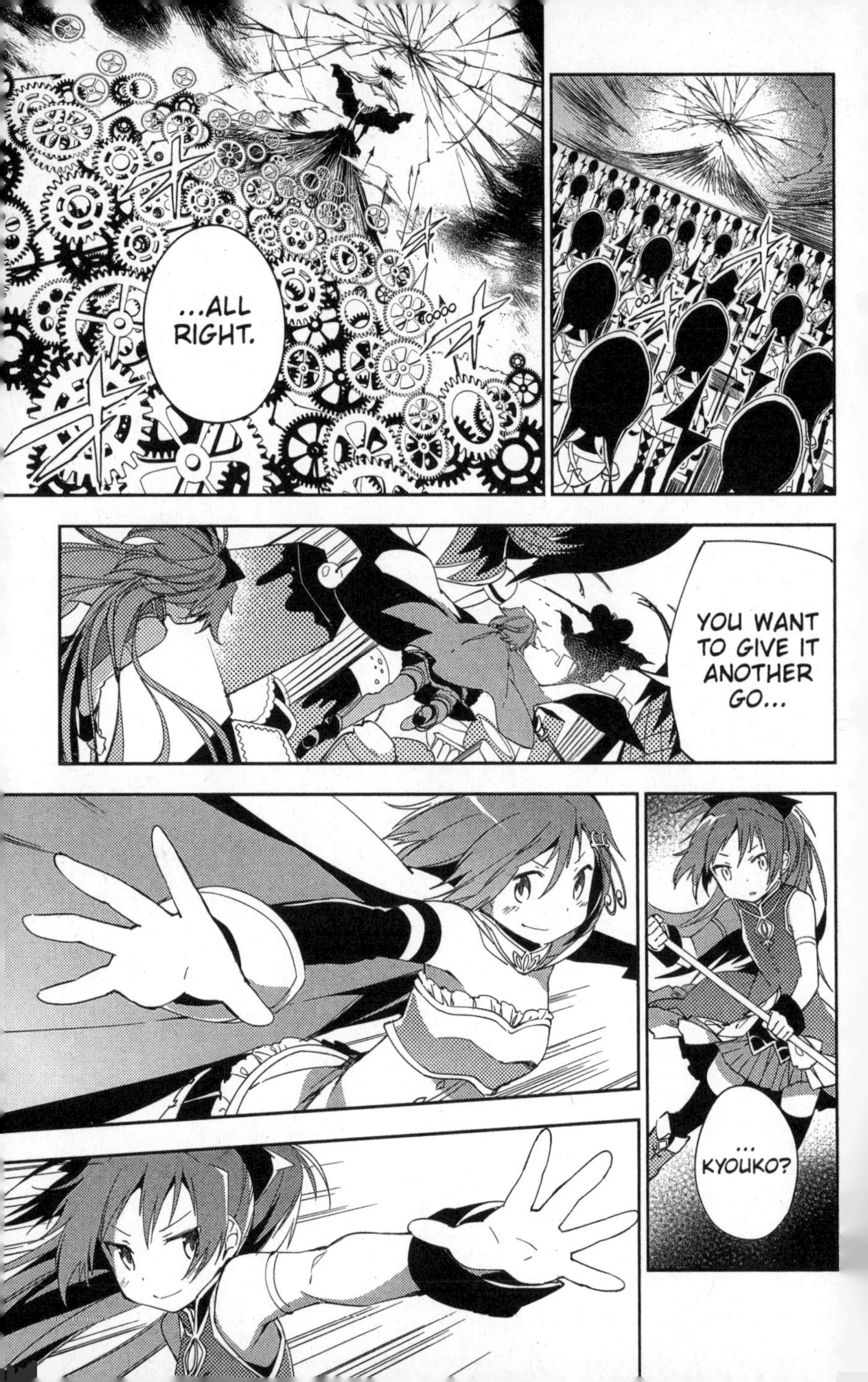
...ALL RIGHT.
YOU WANT TO GIVE IT ANOTHER GO...
...KYOUKO?

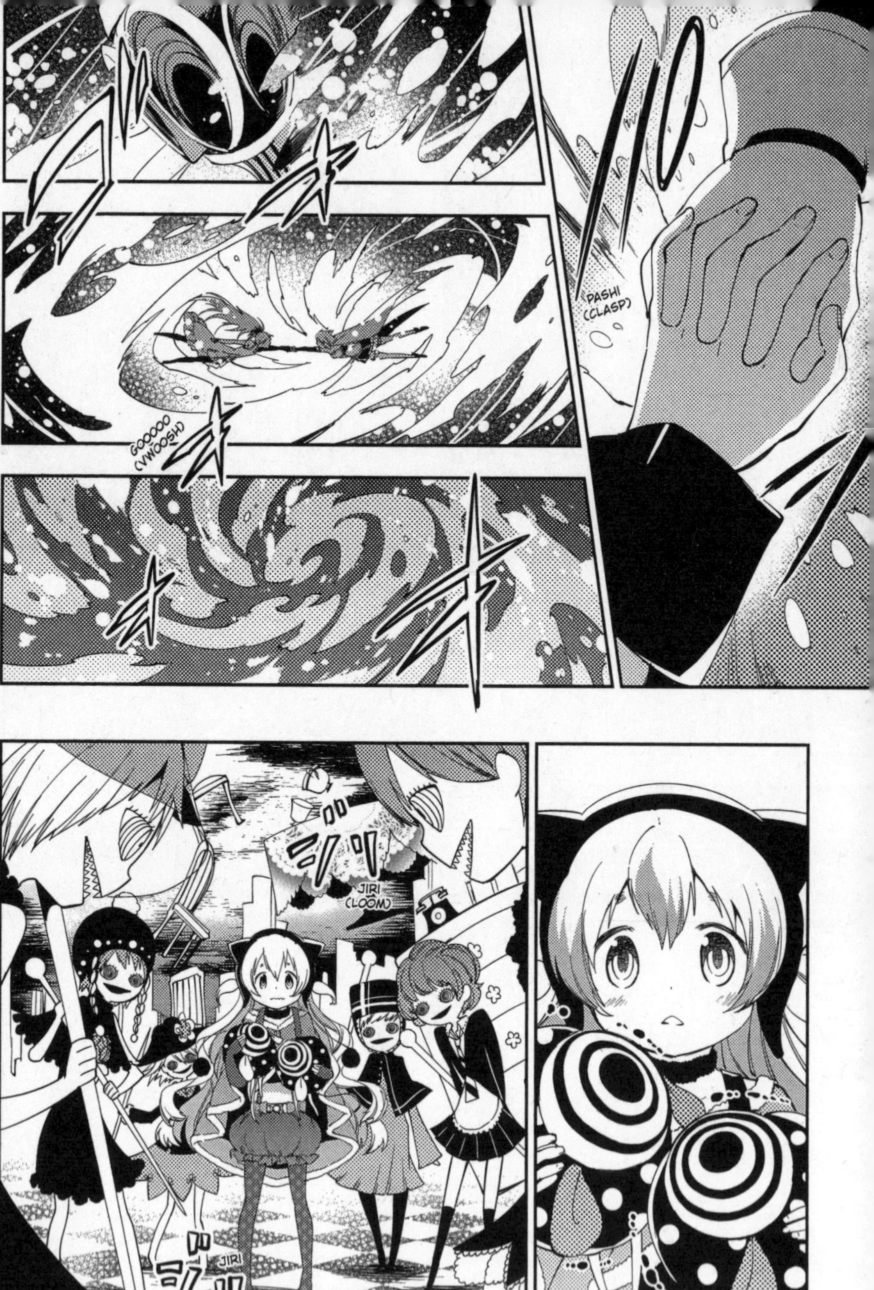
PASHI (CLASP)
GOOOOO (VWOOSH)
JIRI (LOOM)
JIRI

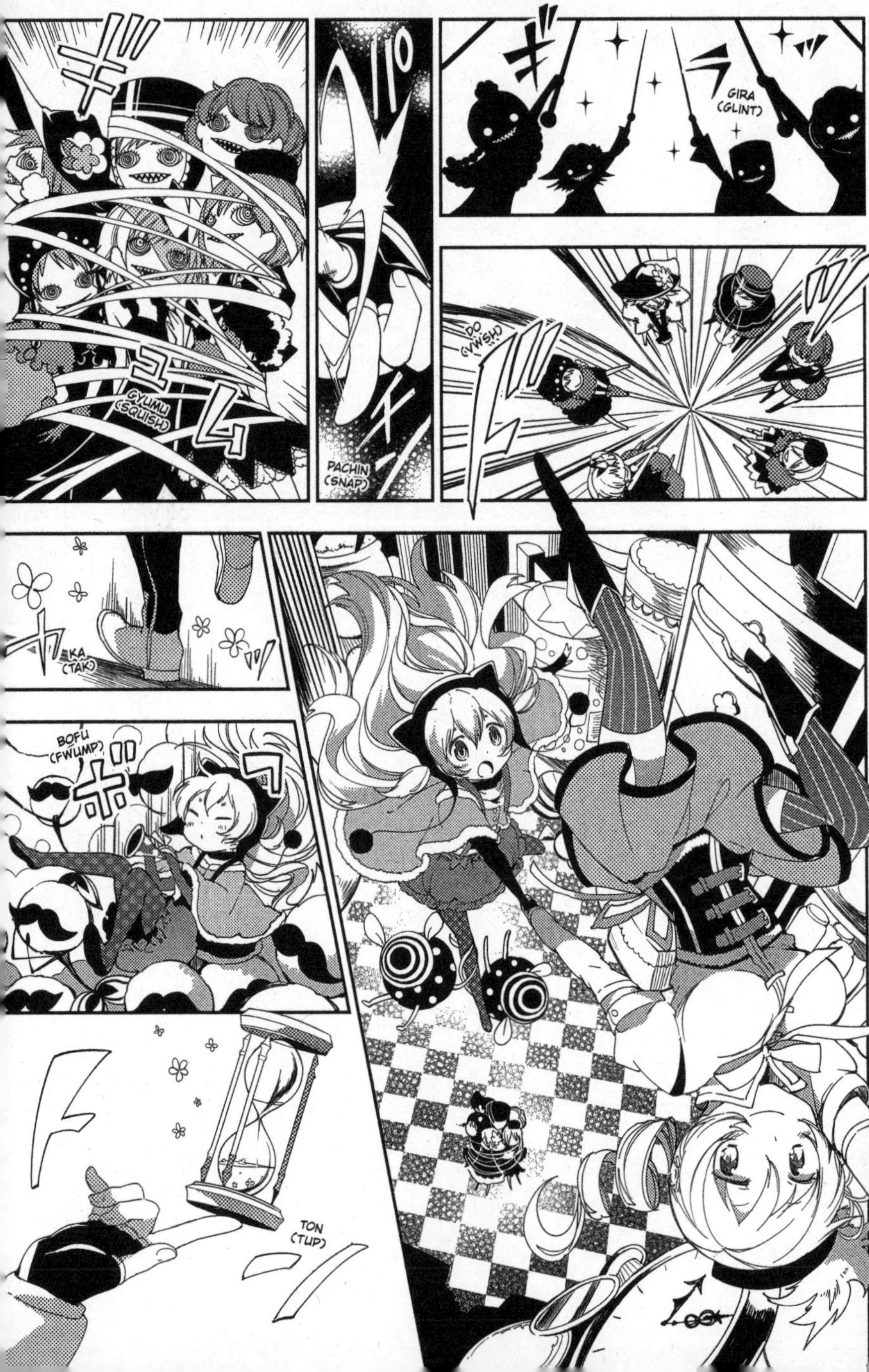
GIRA (GLINT)
DO (VWSH)
PACHIN (SNAP)
GYUMU (SQUISH)
KA (TAK)
BOFU (FWUMP)
TON (TUP)

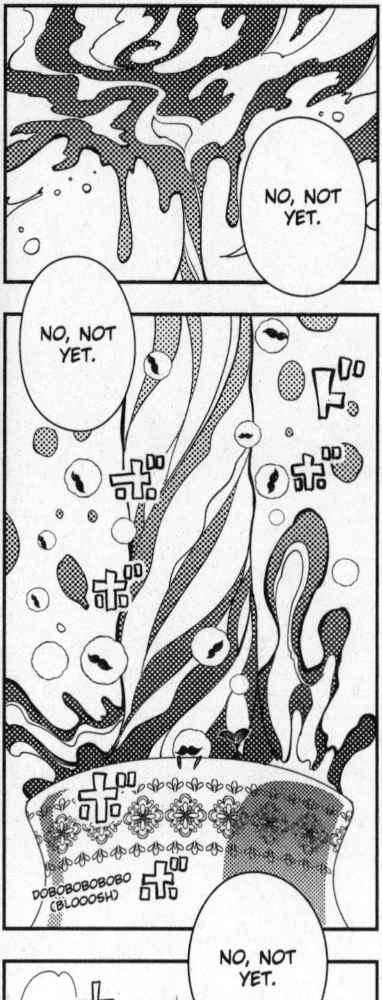
NO, NOT YET.
NO, NOT YET.
DOBOBOBOBOBO (BLOOOSH)
NO, NOT YET.
KAPON (CLUNK)
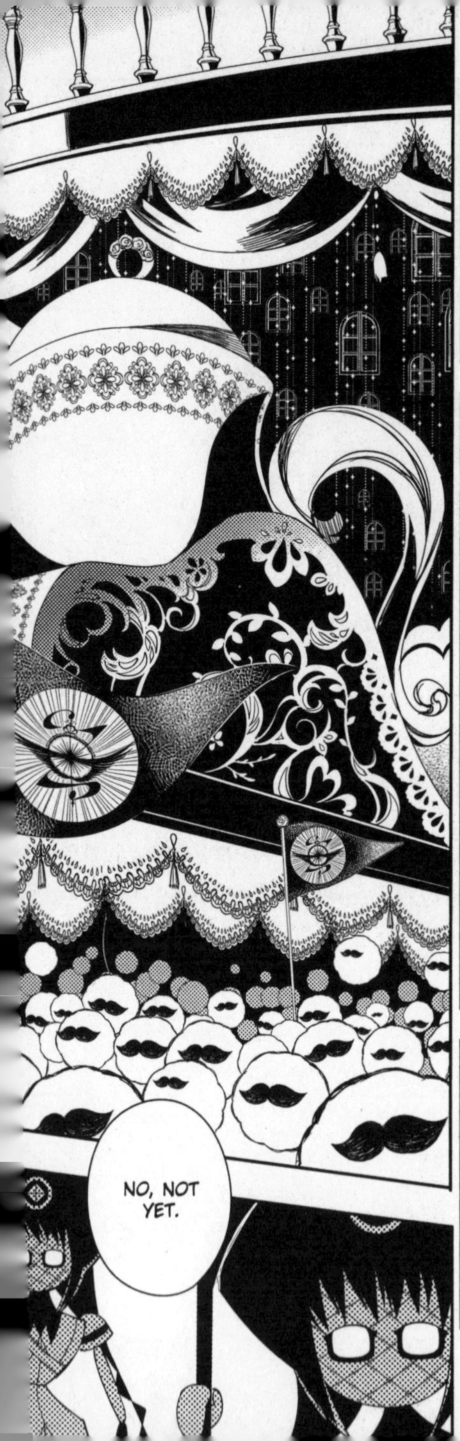
NO, NOT YET.

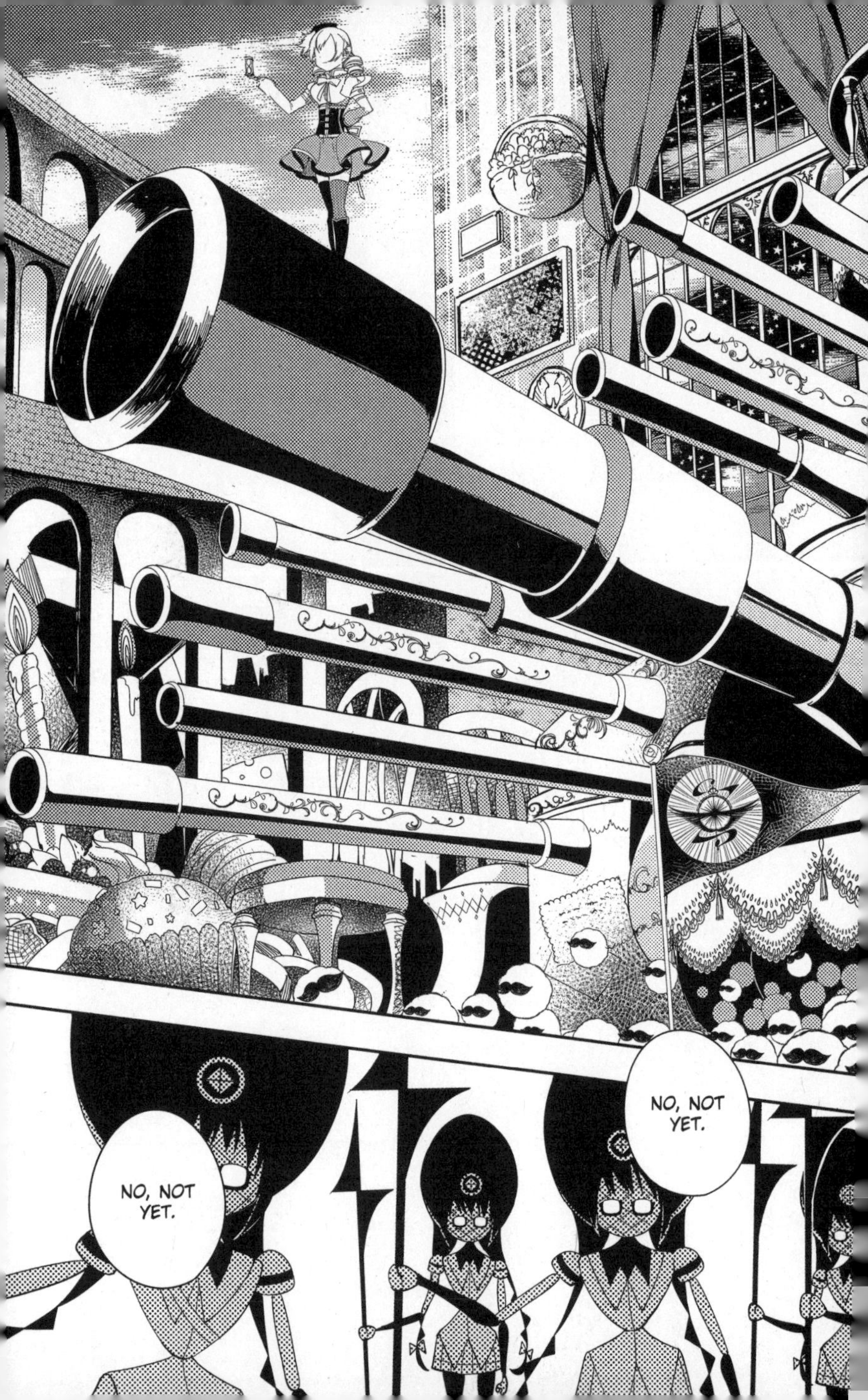
NO, NOT YET.
NO, NOT YET.

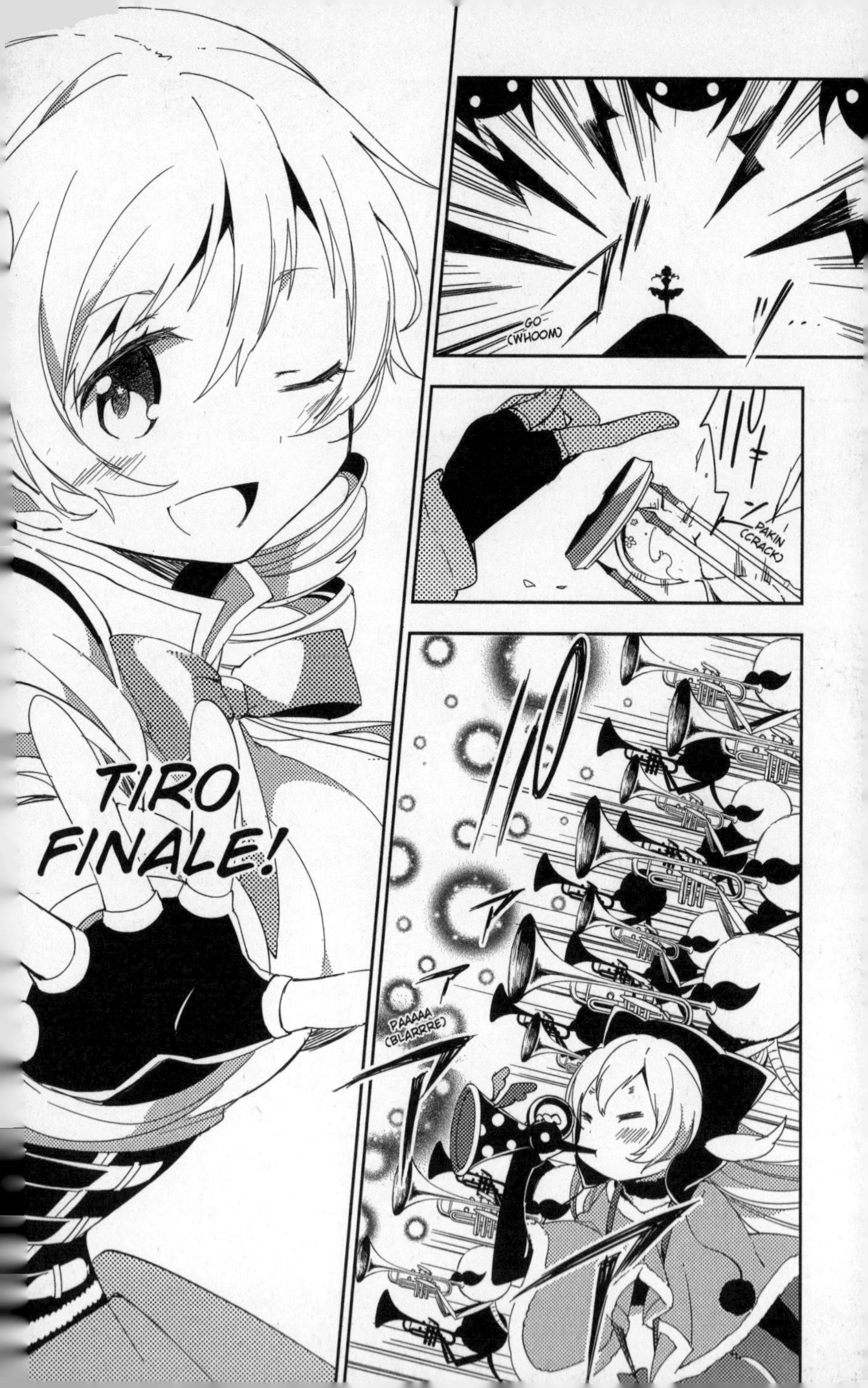
GO (WHOOM)
PAKIN (CRACK)
PAAAAA (BLARRRE)
TIRO FINALE!

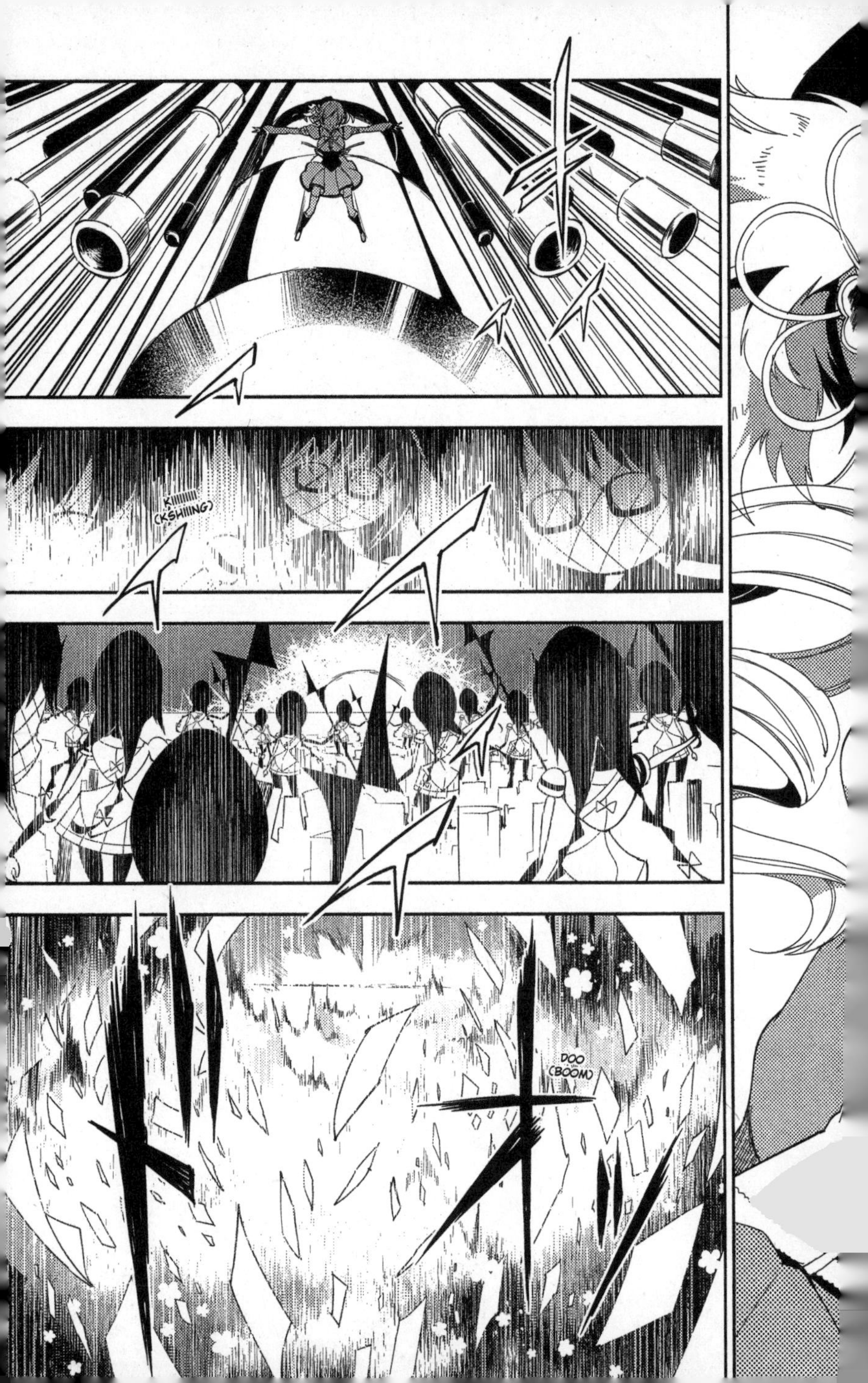
KIIIIIIII
(KSHIIING)
DOO
(BOOM)

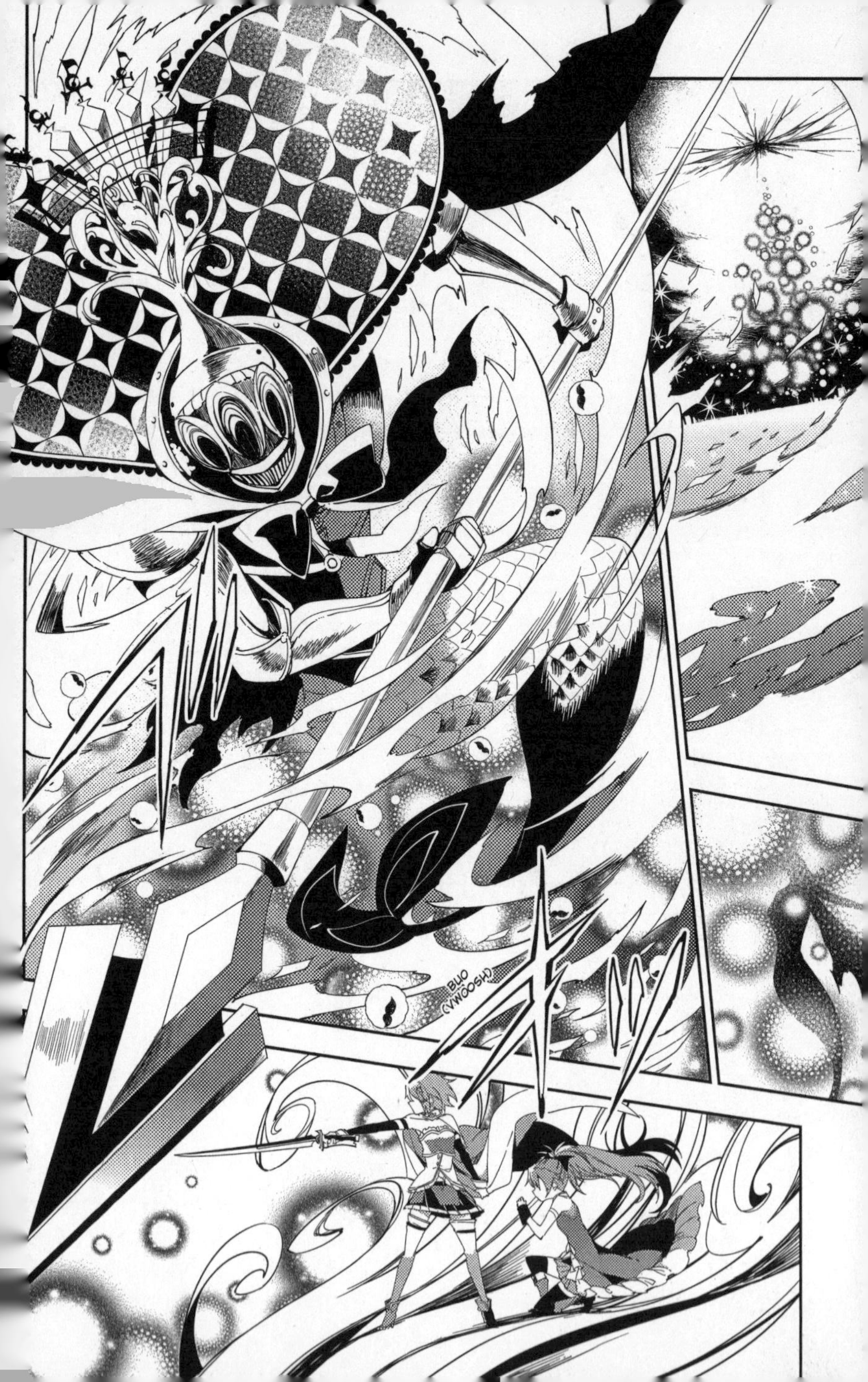
BUO
(VWOOSH)

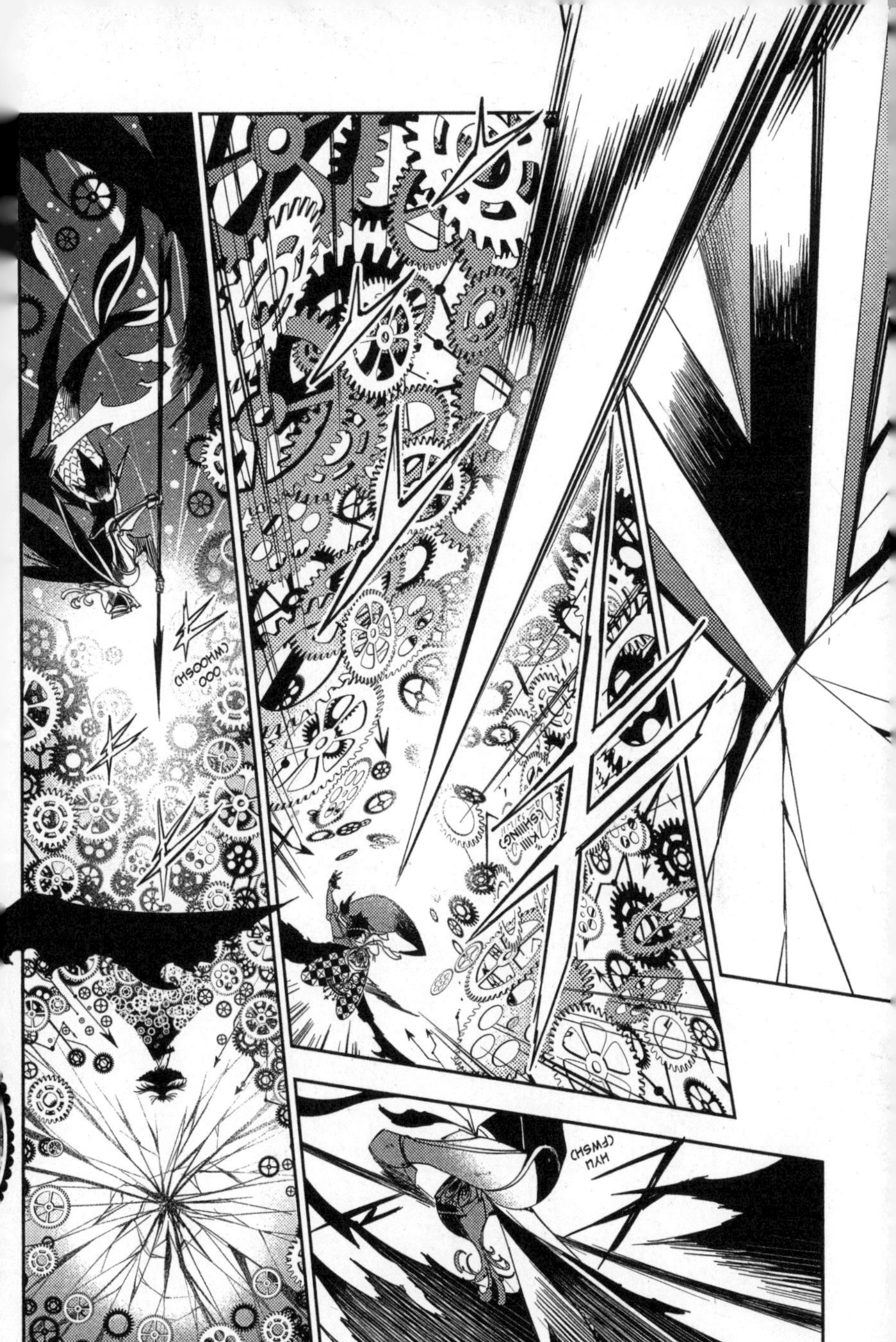
KIIII (SHIIING)
HYU (FWSH)
OOO (WHOOSH)

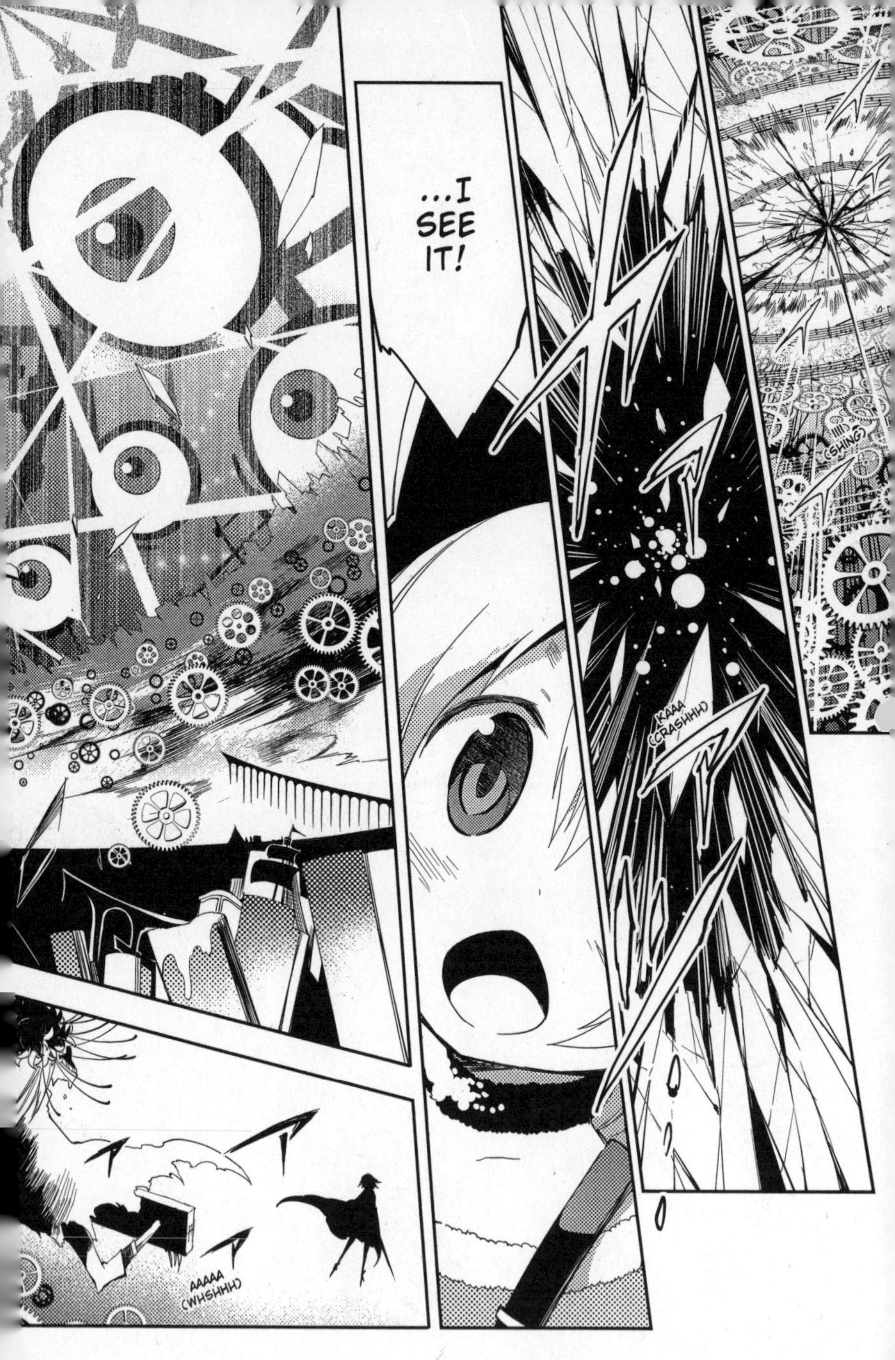
(SHING)
KAAA (CRASHHH)
...I SEE IT!
AAAAA (WHSHHH)

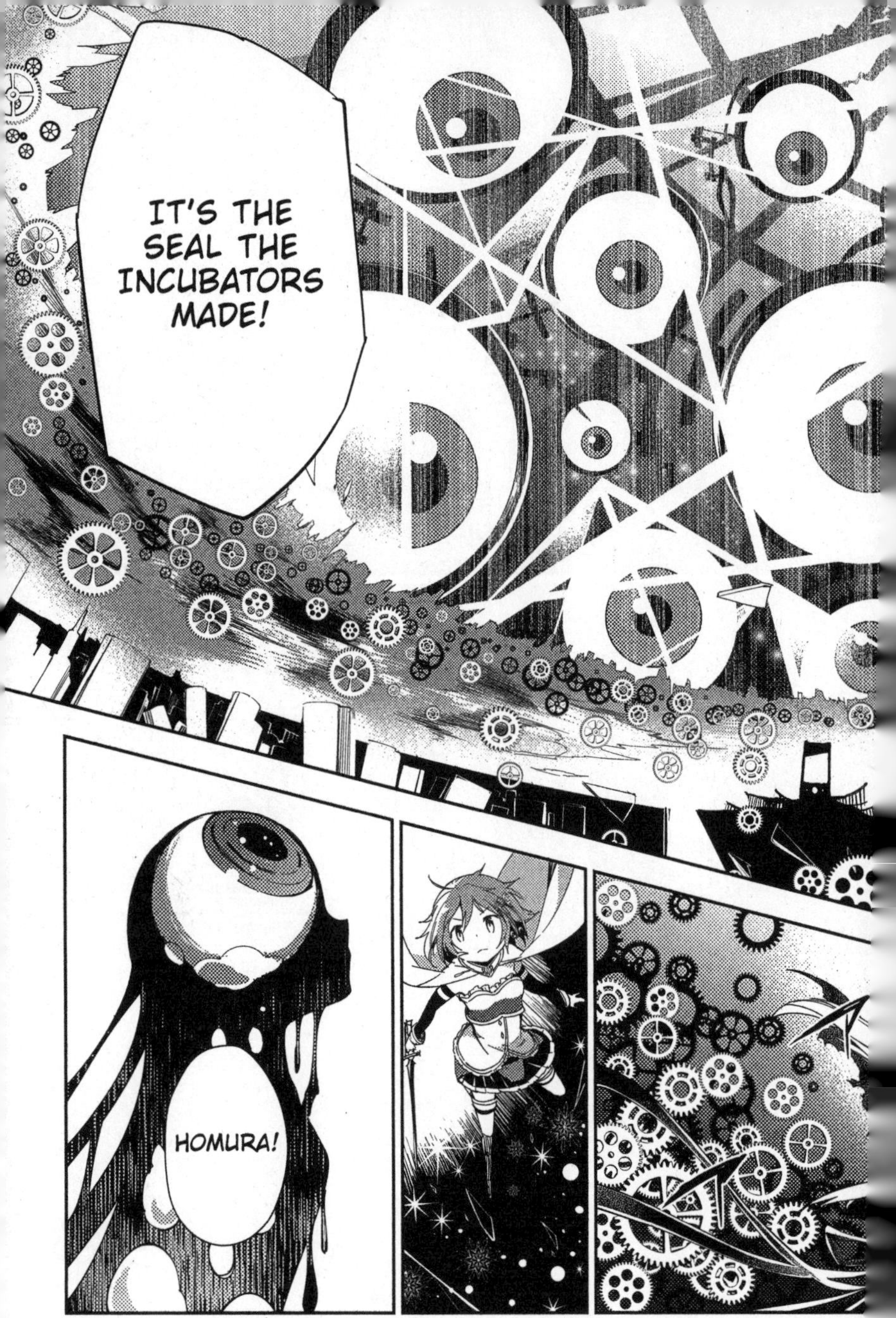
IT'S THE SEAL THE INCUBATORS MADE!
HOMURA!

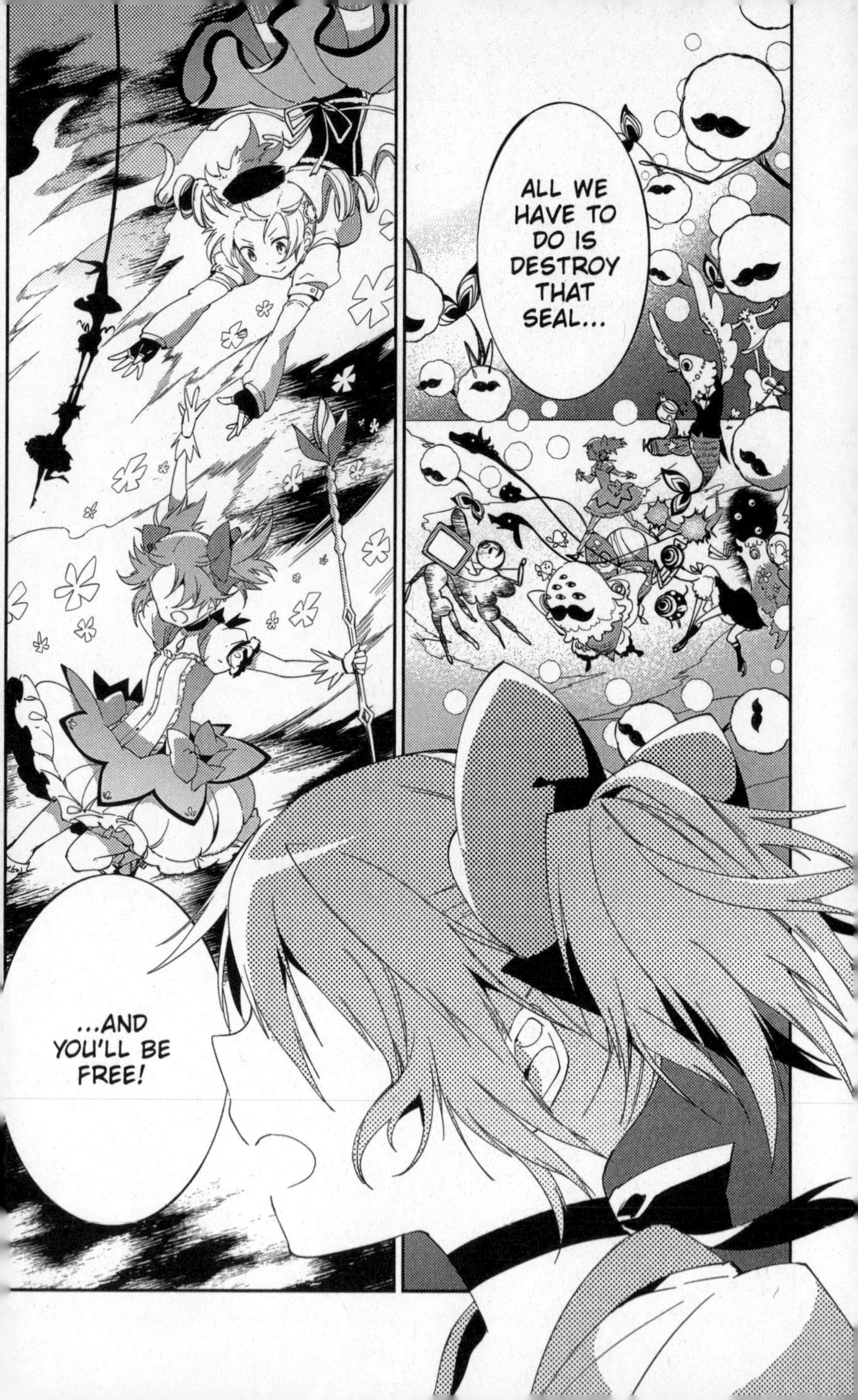
ALL WE HAVE TO DO IS DESTROY THAT SEAL...
...AND YOU'LL BE FREE!

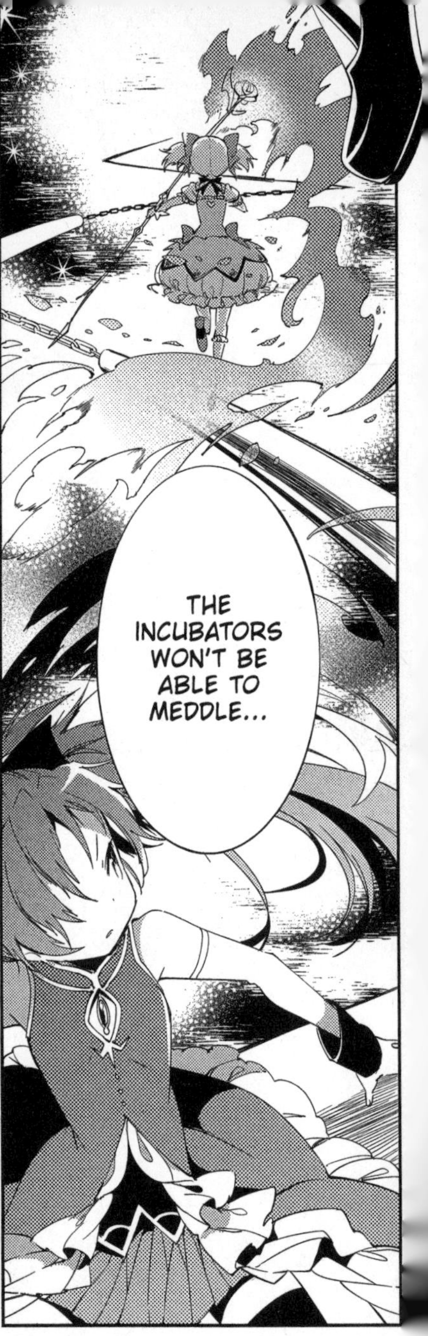
THE INCUBATORS WON'T BE ABLE TO MEDDLE...

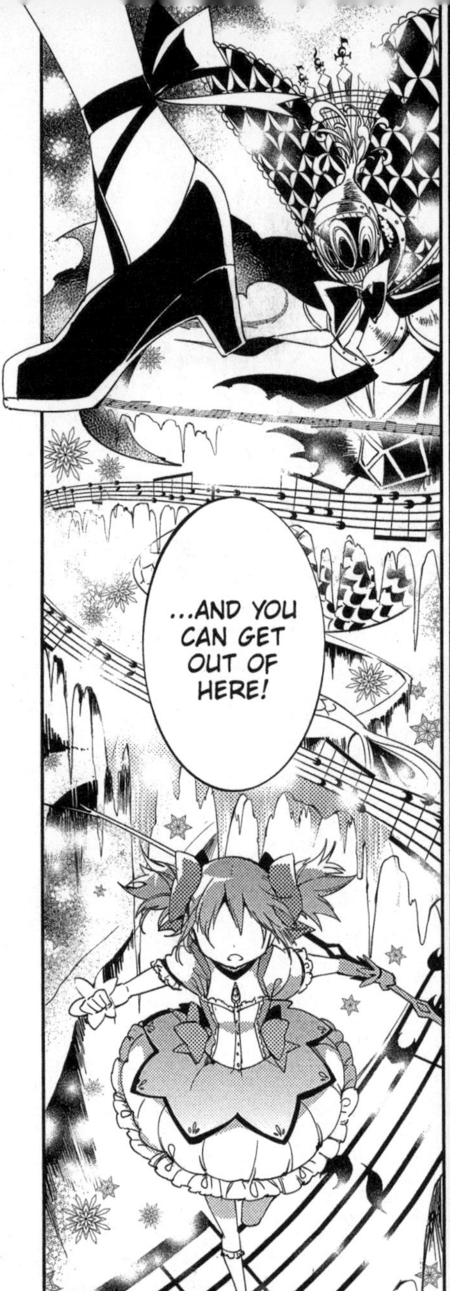
...AND YOU CAN GET OUT OF HERE!

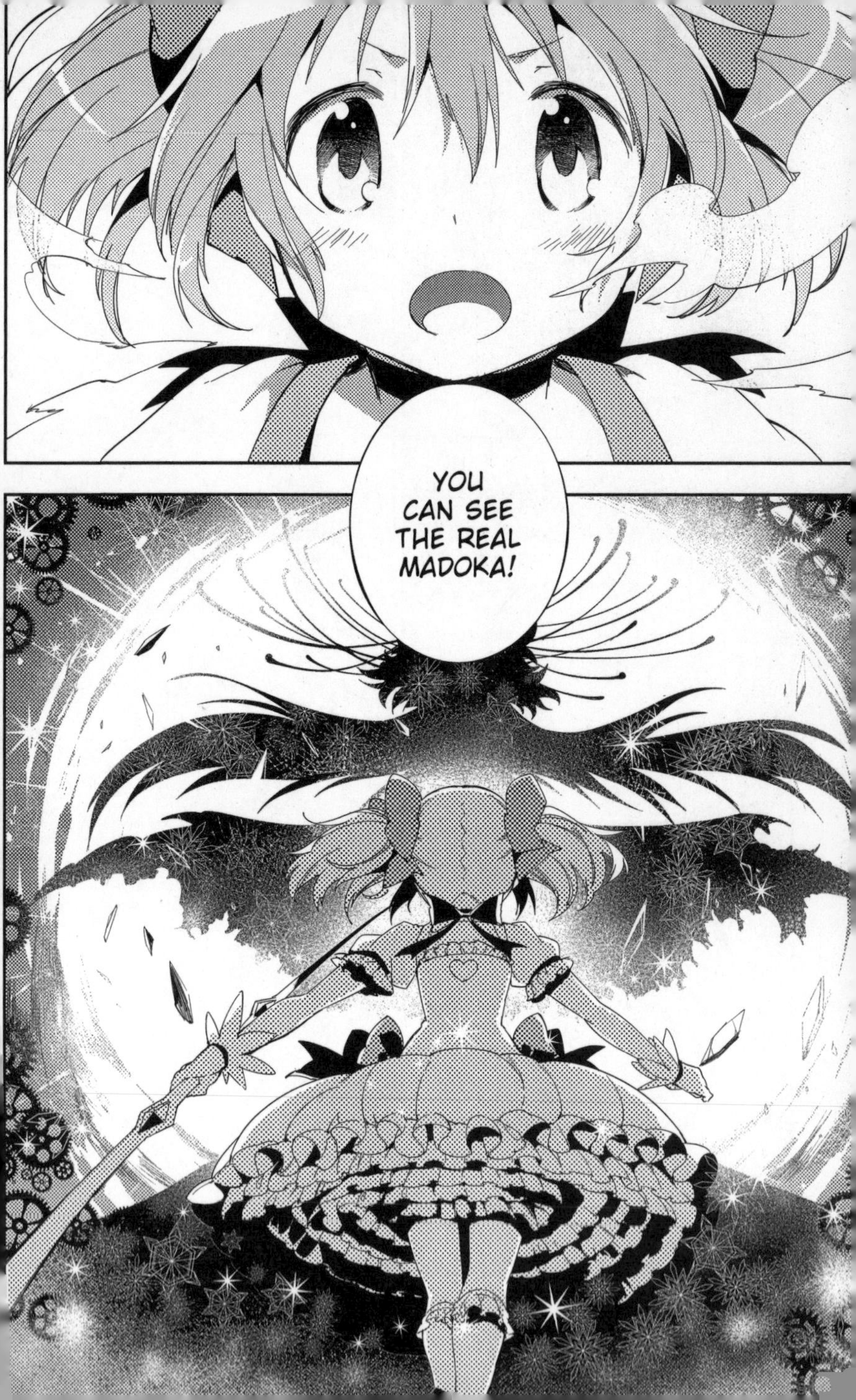
YOU CAN SEE THE REAL MADOKA!

PUELLA MAGI
MADOKA★MAGICA
THE MOVIE -REBELLION-

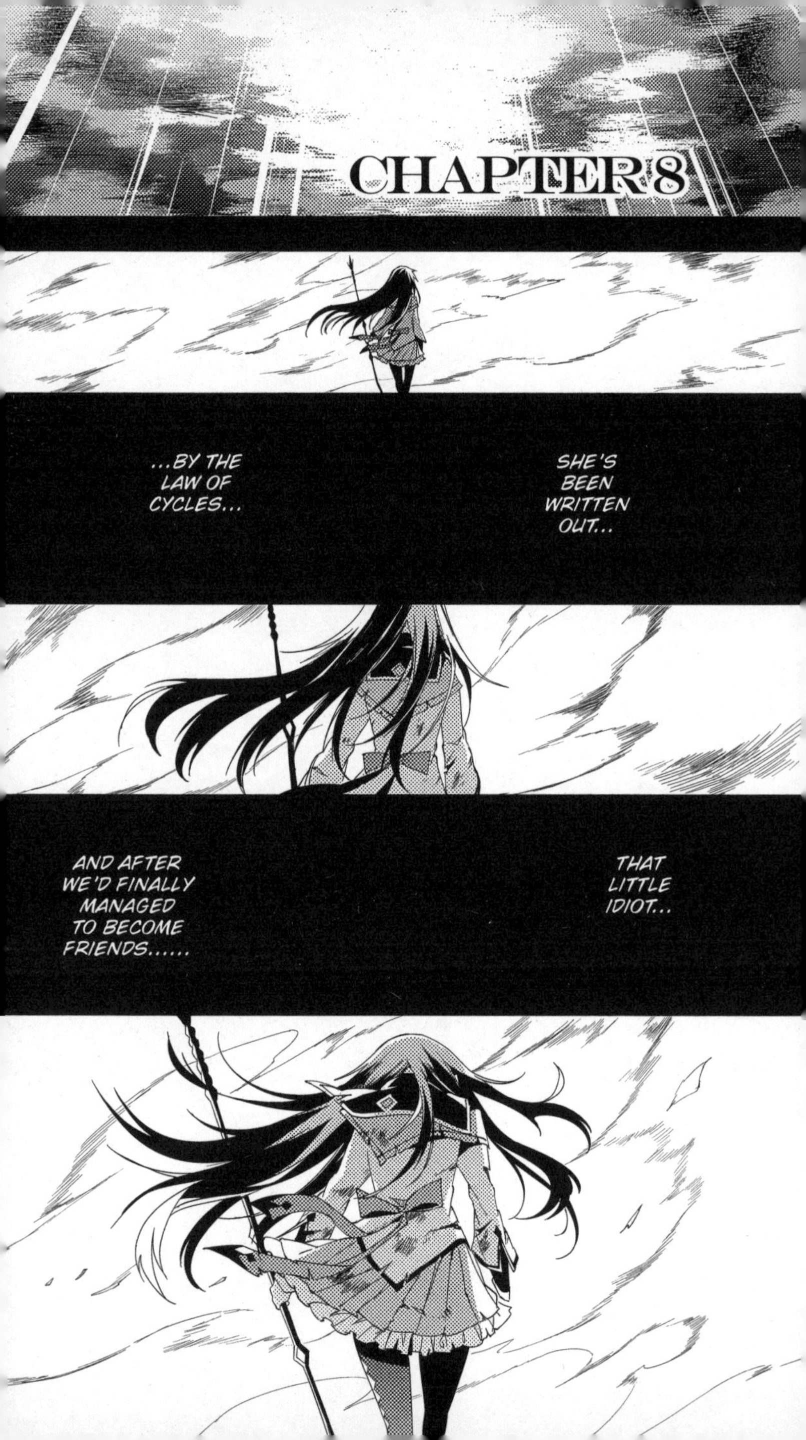
CHAPTER 8
SHE'S BEEN WRITTEN OUT...
...BY THE LAW OF CYCLES...
THAT LITTLE IDIOT...
AND AFTER WE'D FINALLY MANAGED TO BECOME FRIENDS......

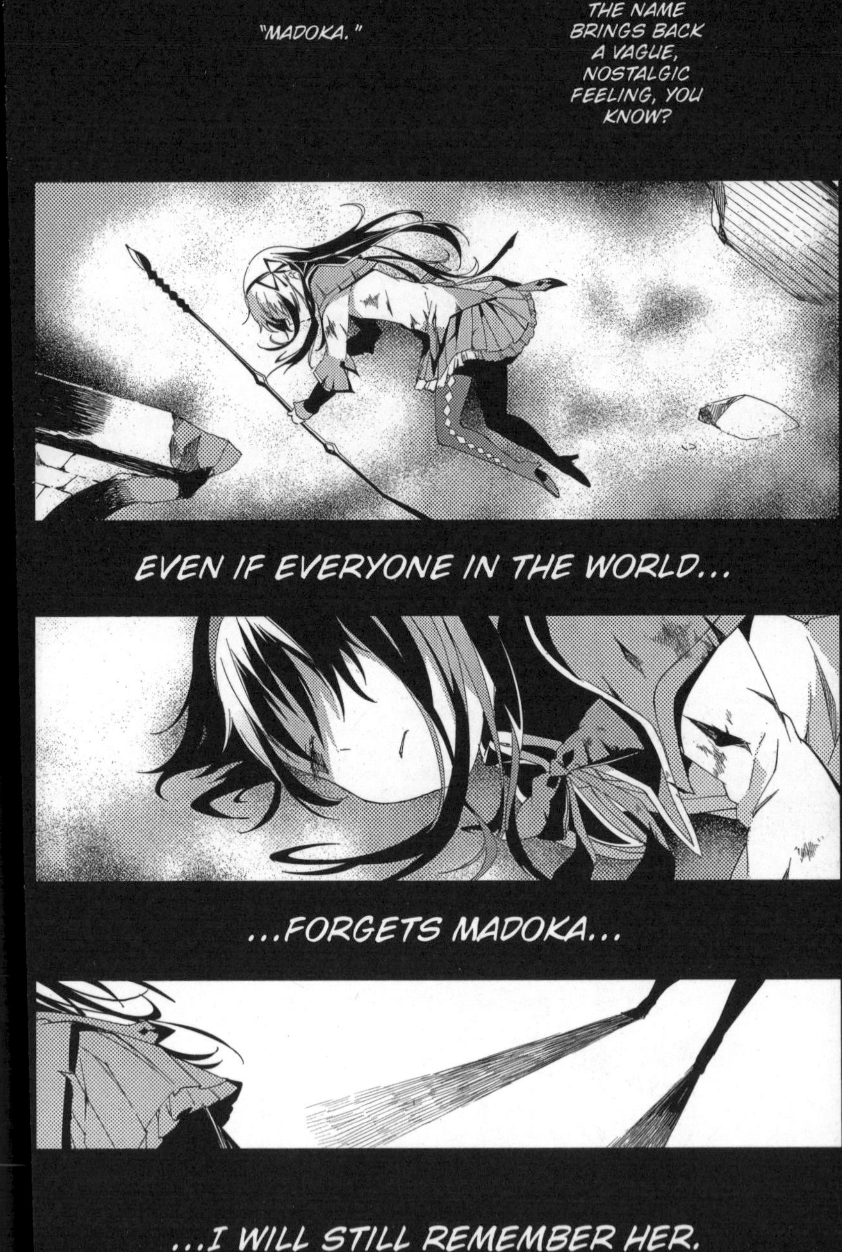
THE NAME BRINGS BACK A VAGUE, NOSTALGIC FEELING, YOU KNOW?
"MADOKA."
EVEN IF EVERYONE IN THE WORLD...
...FORGETS MADOKA...
...I WILL STILL REMEMBER HER.

UNTIL OUR FINAL DAY COMES...

...WE AWAIT THE LAW OF CYCLES TO LEAD US OFF....

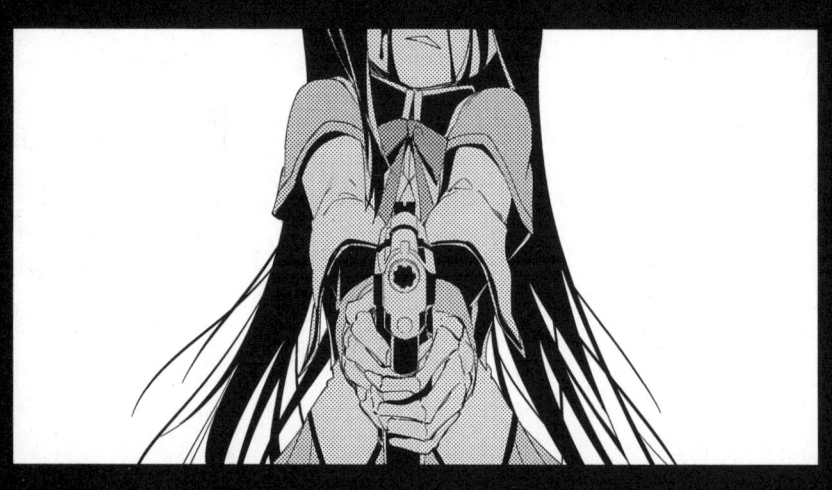

...DREAMING OF THAT FAMILIAR, SMILING FACE...

...THAT WE HOPE TO ONE DAY MEET AGAIN

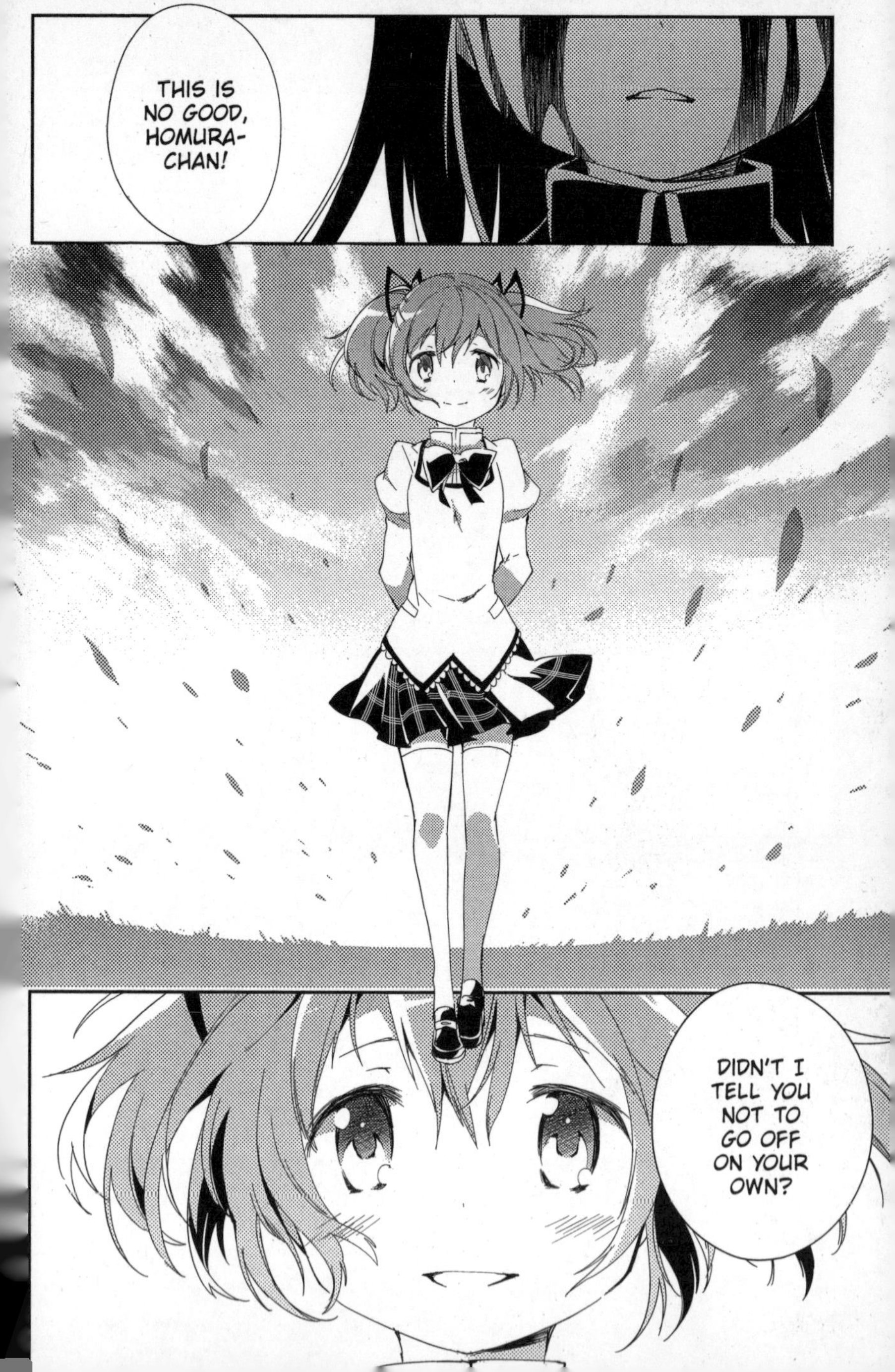
THIS IS NO GOOD, HOMURA-CHAN!
DIDN'T I TELL YOU NOT TO GO OFF ON YOUR OWN?

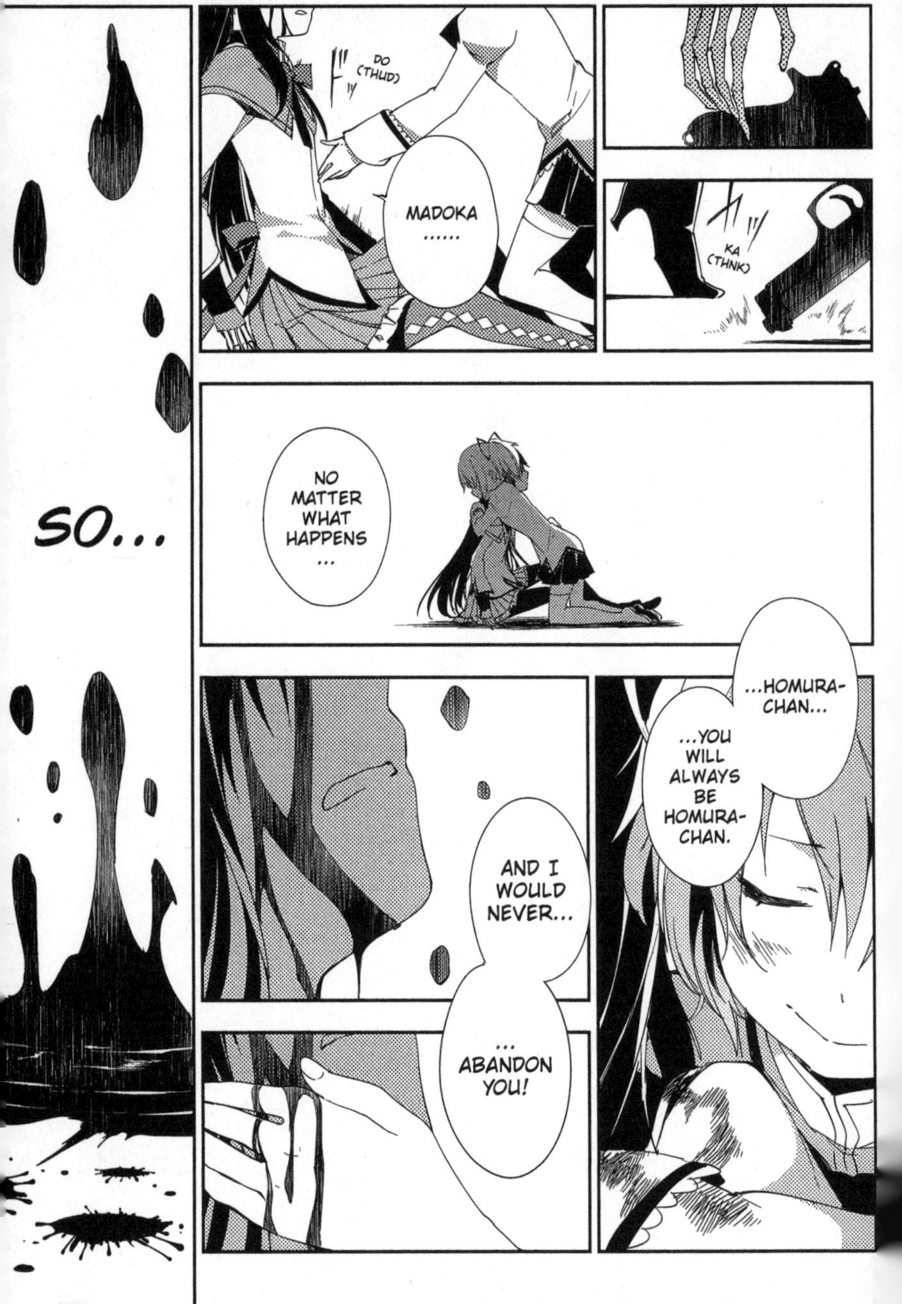
KA (THNK)
DO (THUD)
MADOKA ......
NO MATTER WHAT HAPPENS ...
...HOMURA-CHAN...
...YOU WILL ALWAYS BE HOMURA-CHAN.
AND I WOULD NEVER...
... ABANDON YOU!
SO...

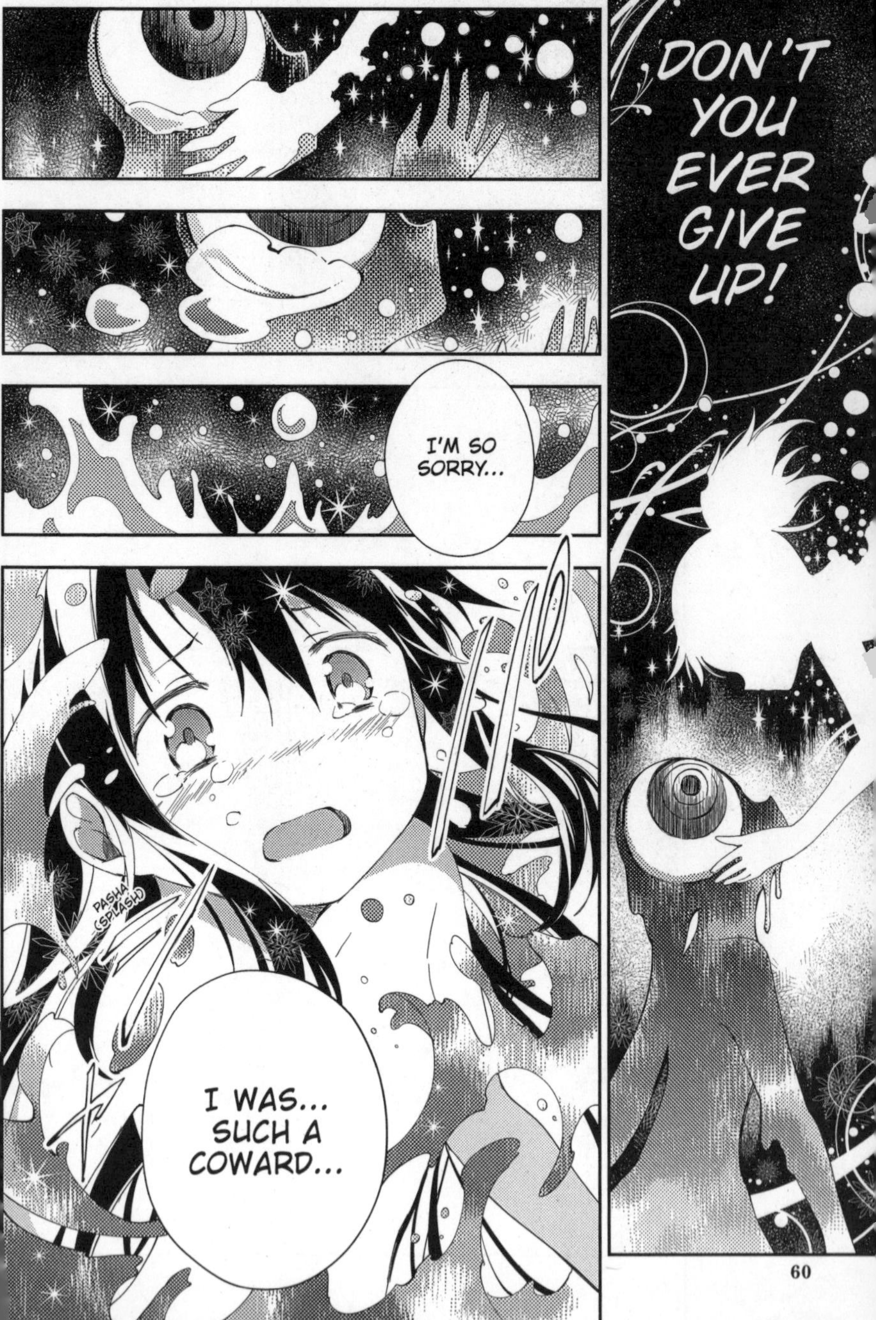
DON'T YOU EVER GIVE UP!
I'M SO SORRY...
PASHA (SPLASH)
I WAS... SUCH A COWARD...

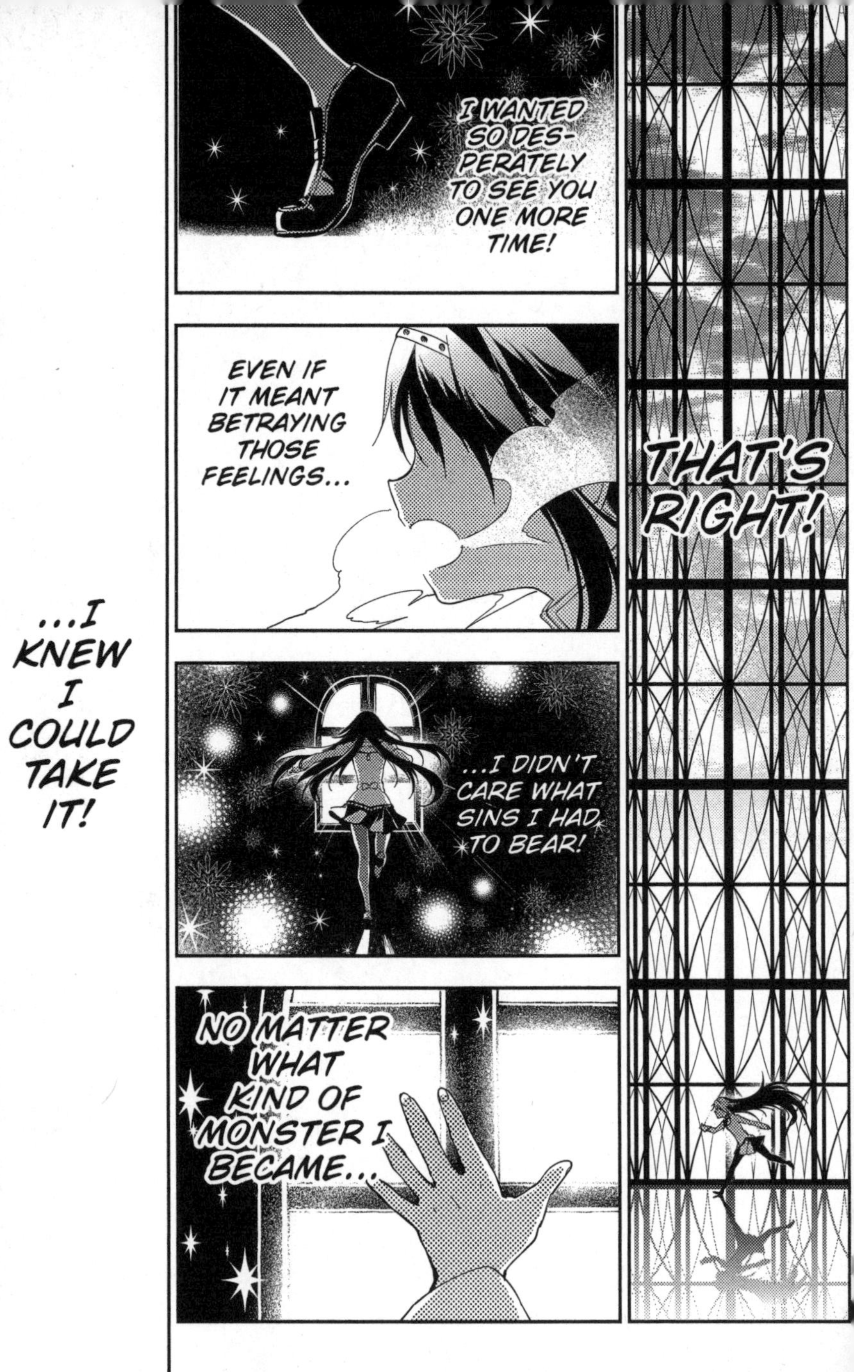
THAT'S RIGHT!
I WANTED SO DES-PERATELY TO SEE YOU ONE MORE TIME!
EVEN IF IT MEANT BETRAYING THOSE FEELINGS...
...I DIDN'T CARE WHAT SINS I HAD TO BEAR!
NO MATTER WHAT KIND OF MONSTER I BECAME...
...I KNEW I COULD TAKE IT!

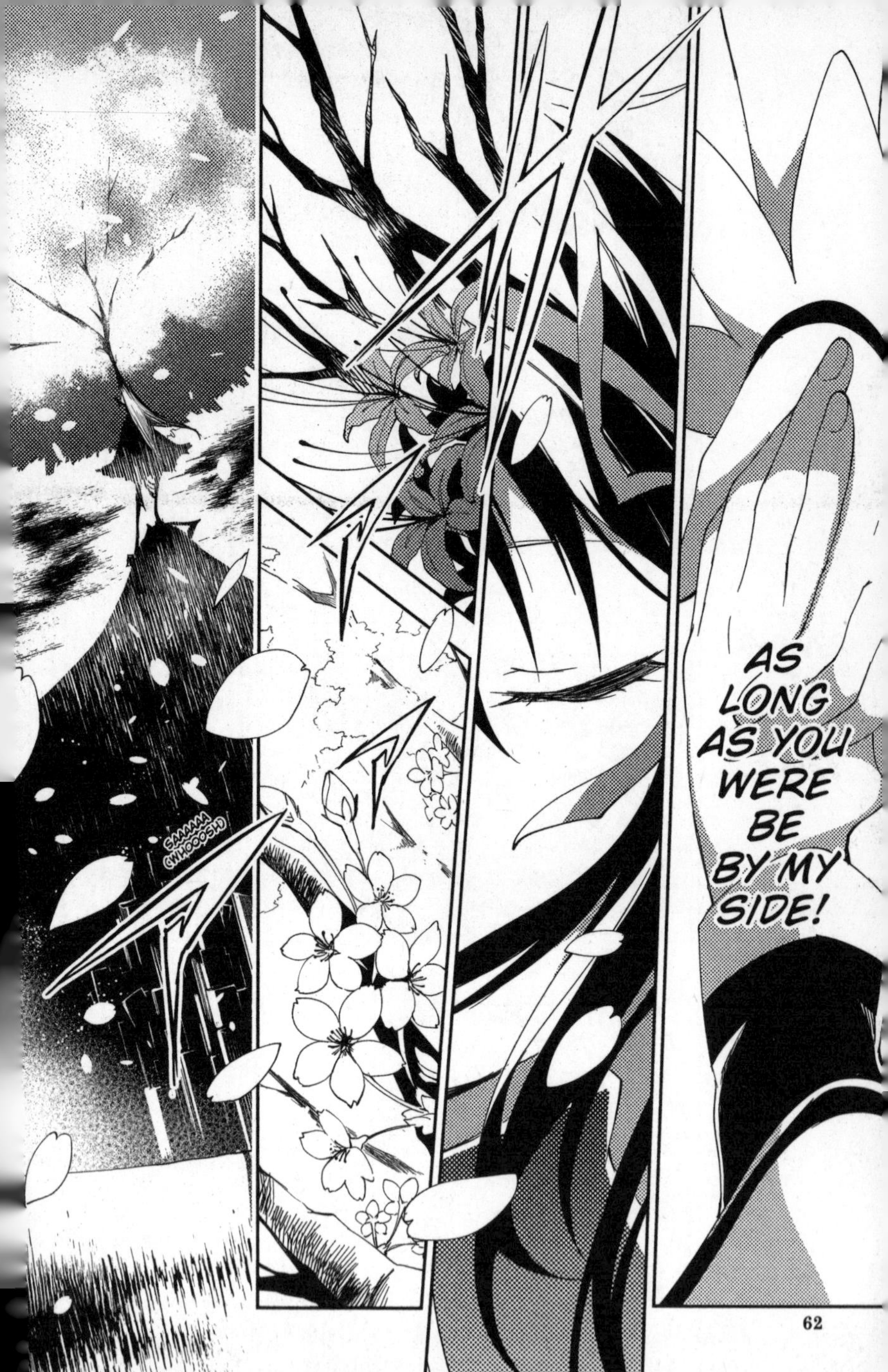
AS LONG AS YOU WERE BE BY MY SIDE!
SAAAAAA (WHOOOSH)

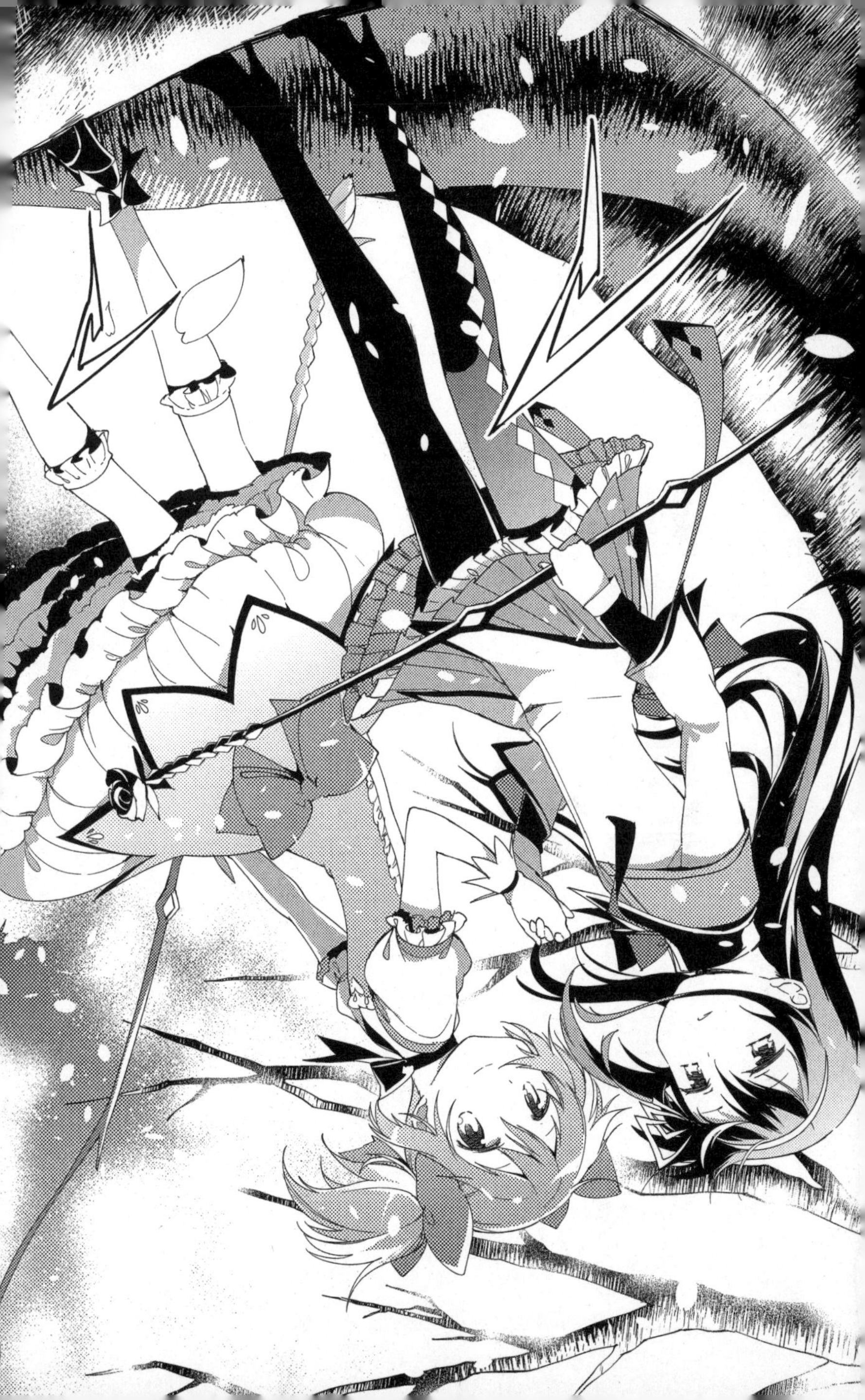

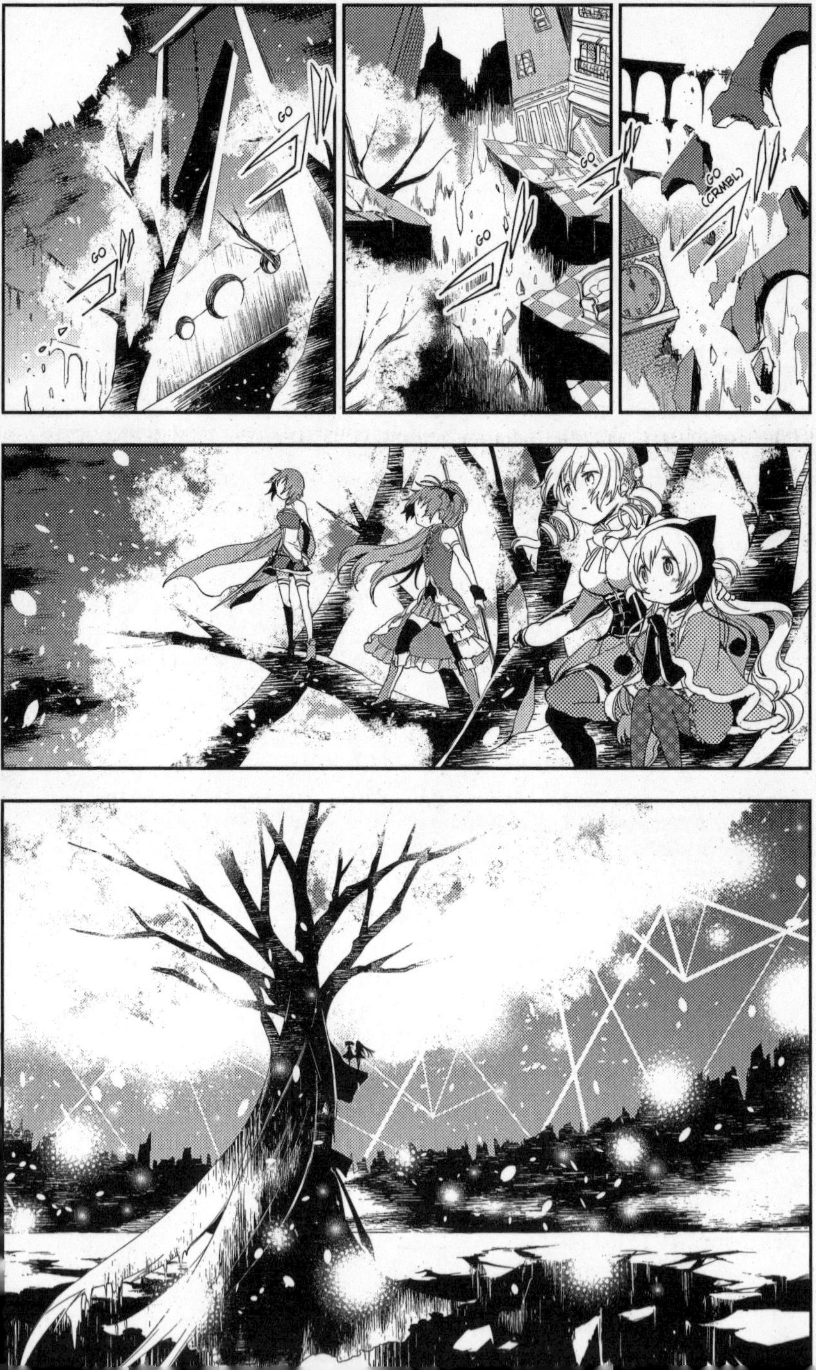
GO (CRMBL)
GO
GO
GO
GO

...HOMURA-CHAN...

...NOW...

...LET'S DO THIS TOGETHER...

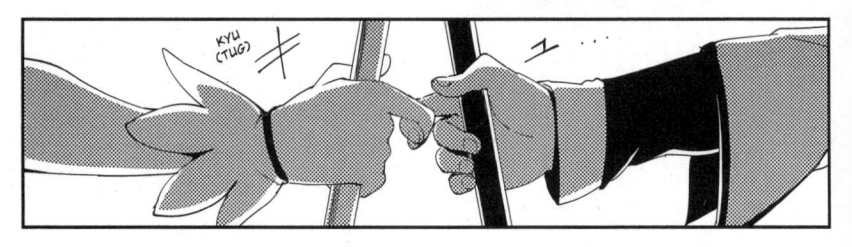

KYU
(TUG)

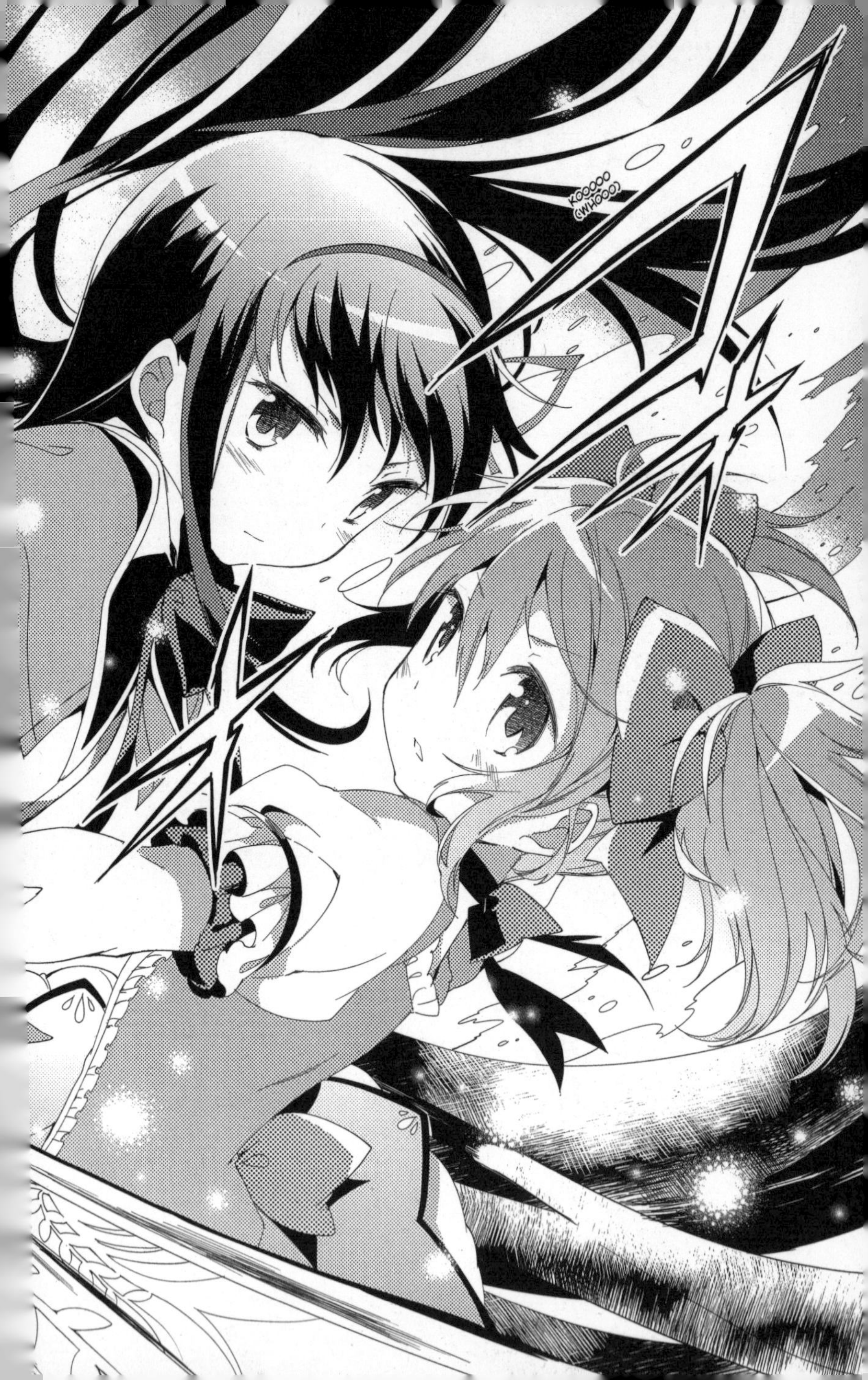
KOOOOO
(WHOOO)

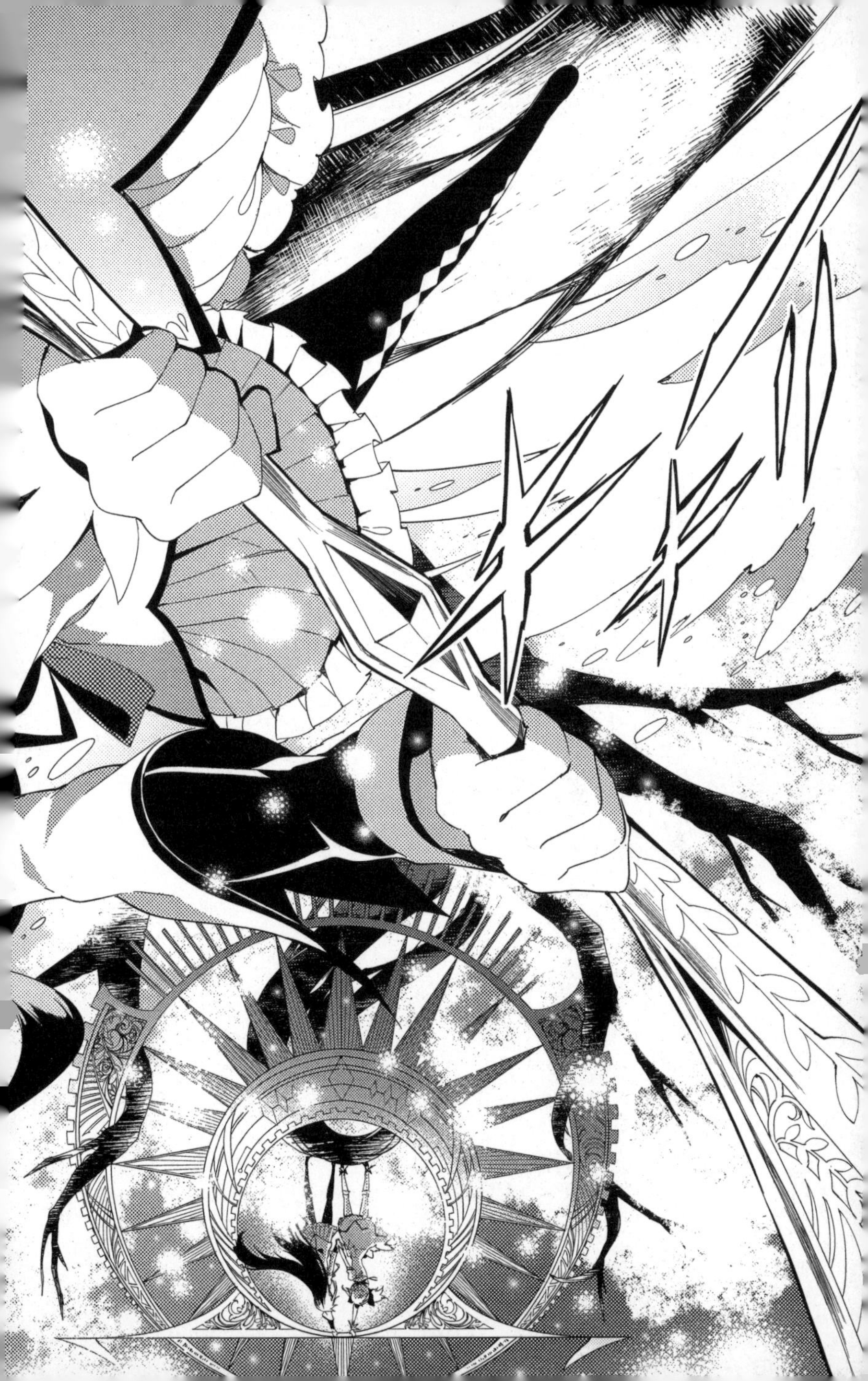

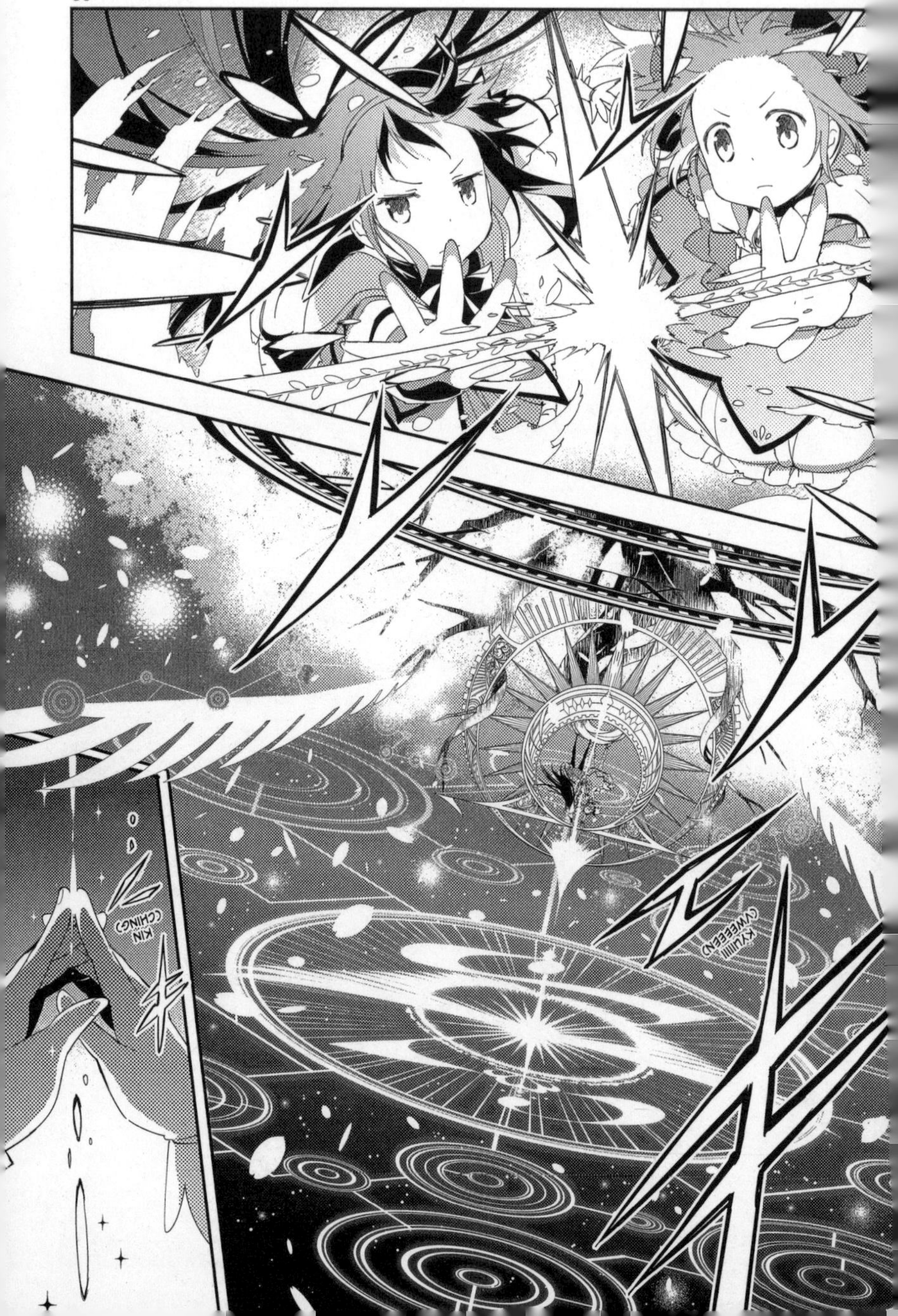
KYUIIIII
(VWEEEEN)
KIN
(CHING)

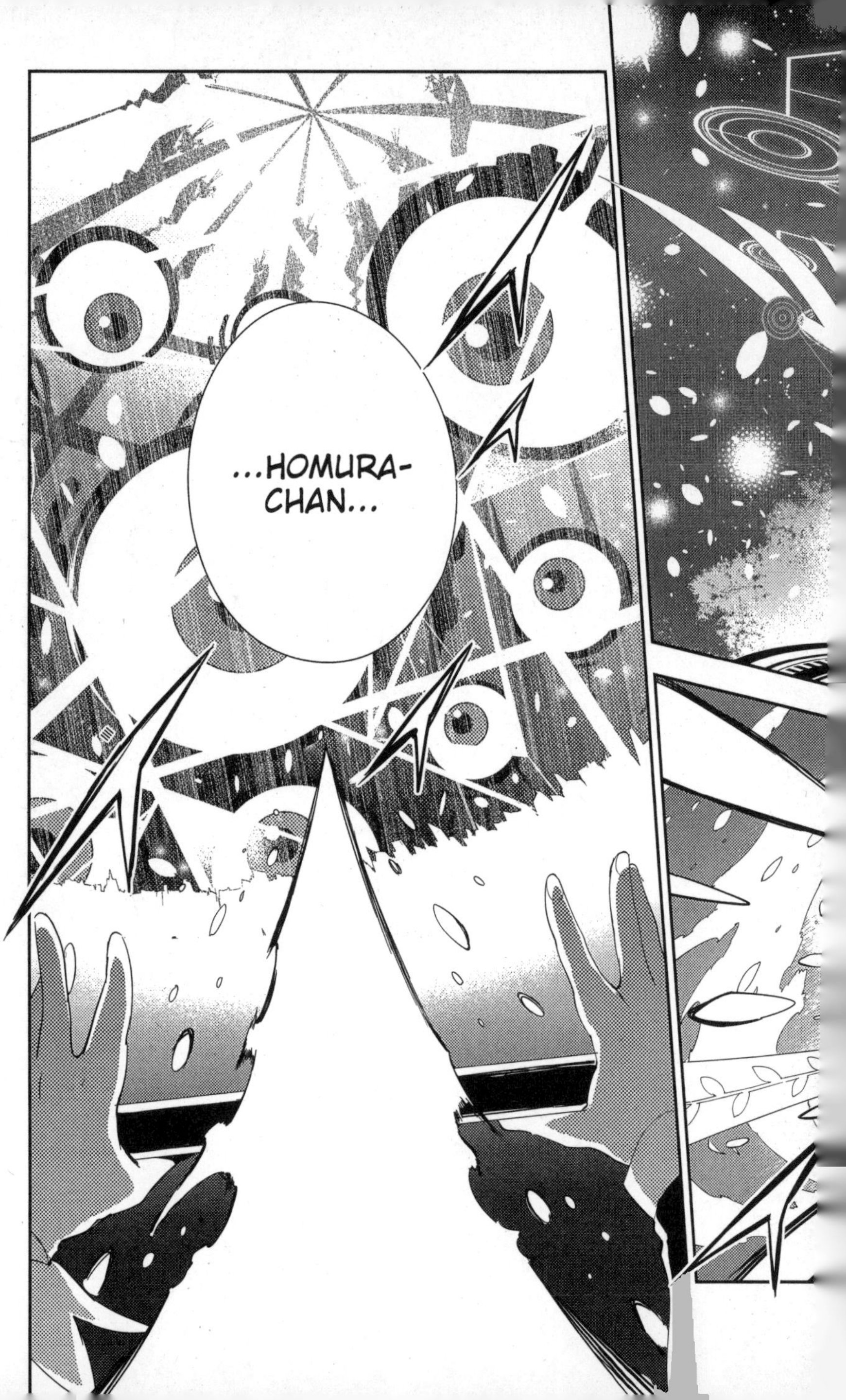
...HOMURA-CHAN...

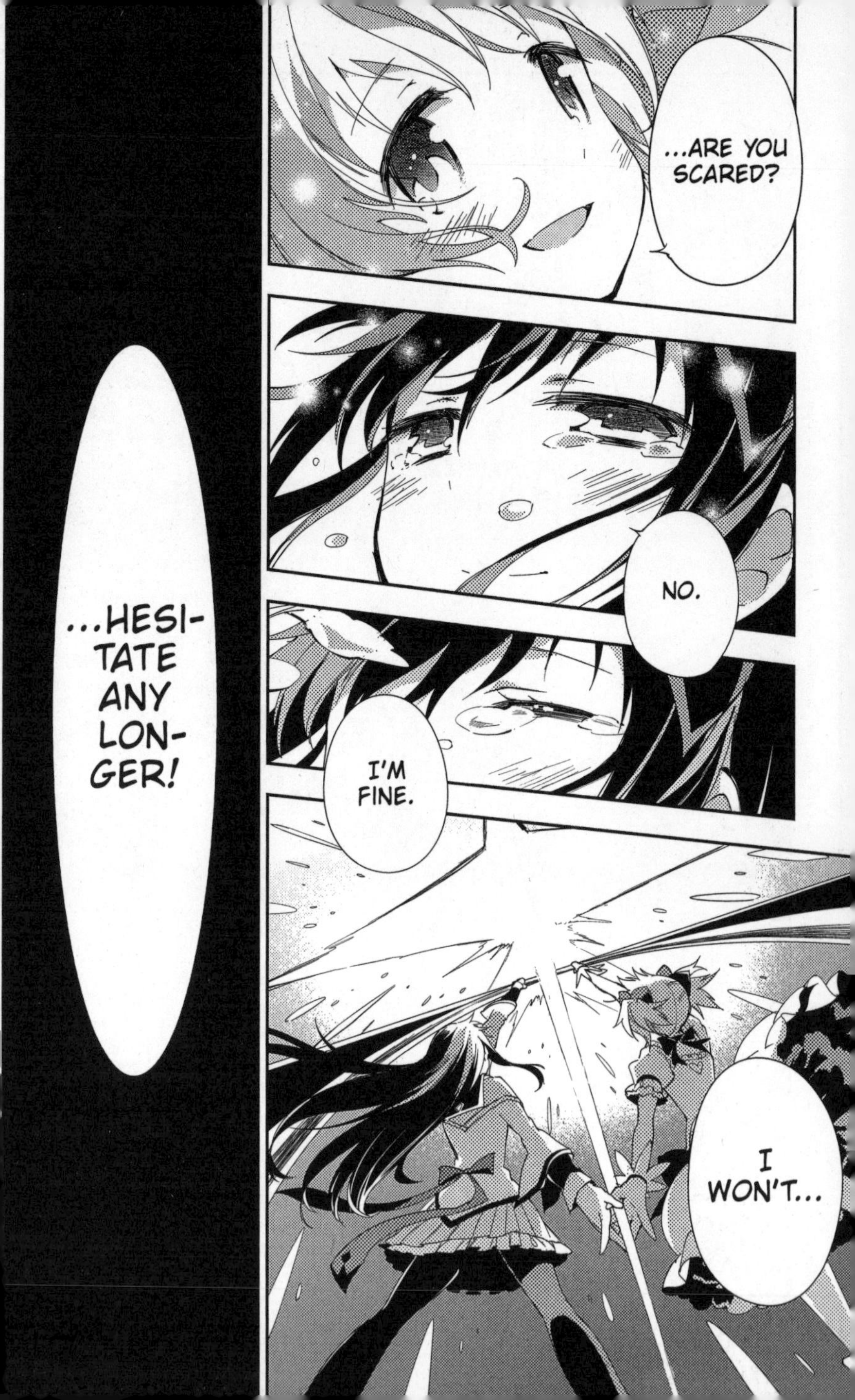
...ARE YOU SCARED?
NO.
I'M FINE.
I WON'T...
...HESITATE ANY LONGER!

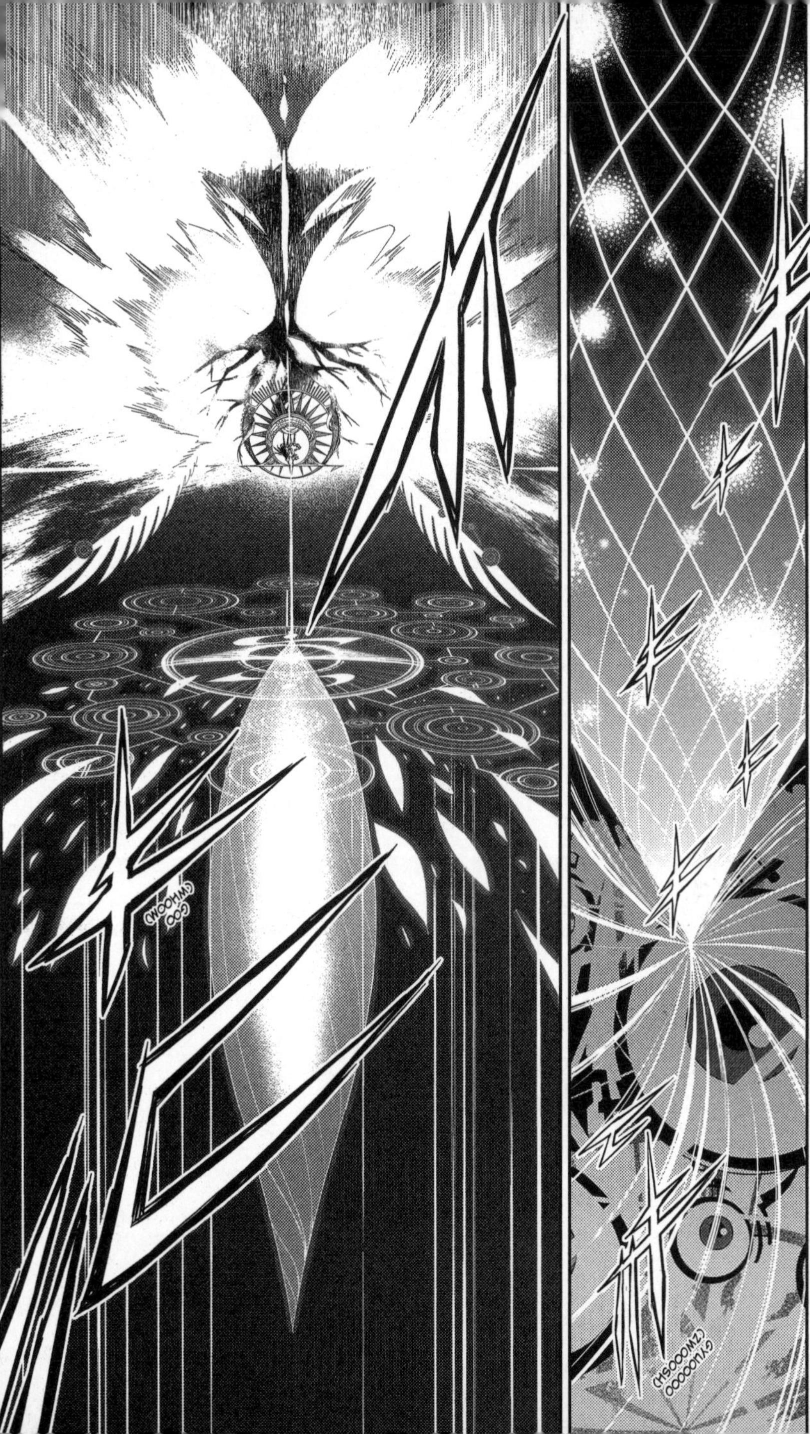
GYUOOOO (ZWOOOSH)
GOO (WHOOM)

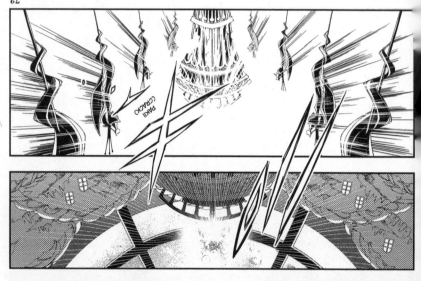

PAKI
(CRAAK)

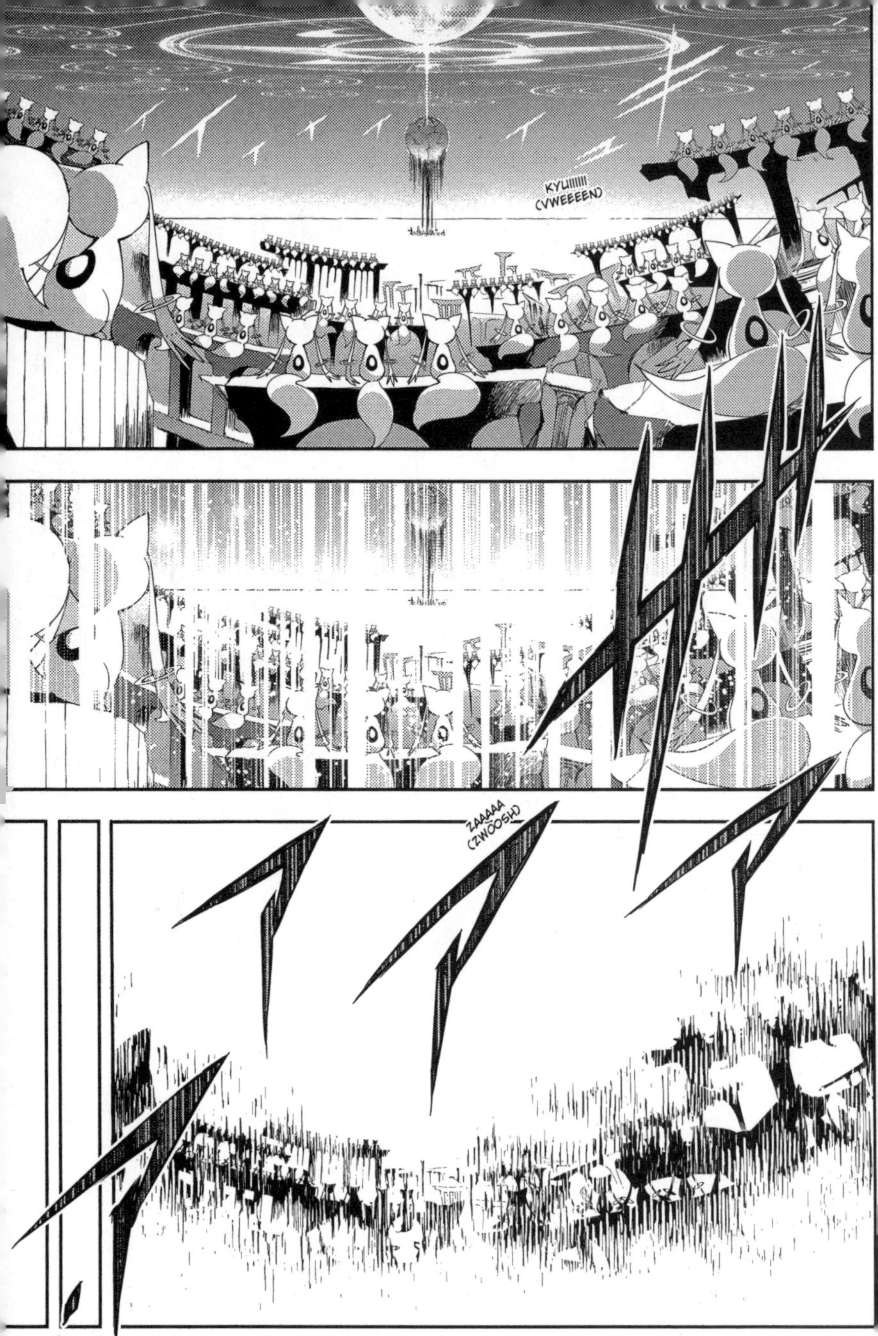
KYUIIIIII
(VWEEEEN)
ZAAAAA
(ZWOOSH)

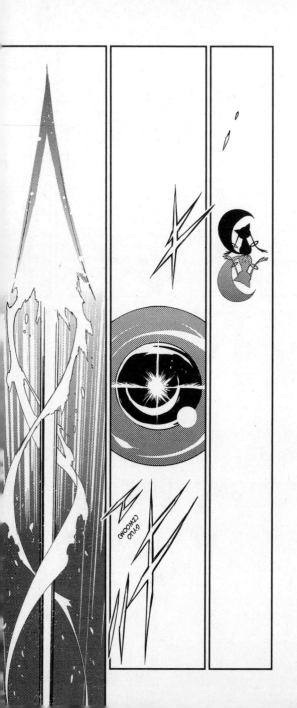

(VWOOM)

"...YOU HUMANS MAKE NO SENSE."

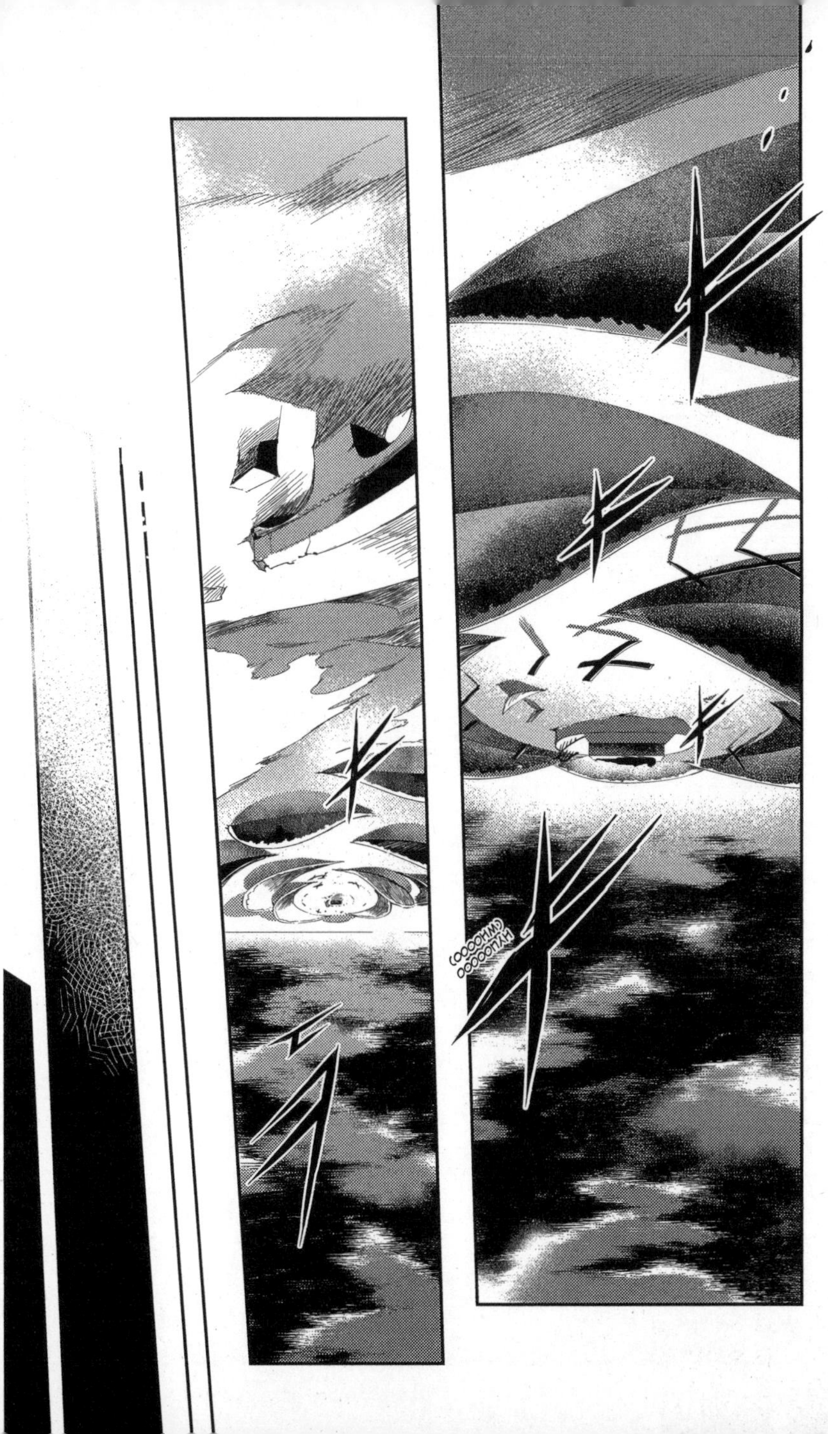
HYUOOOOO
GWHOOOO)

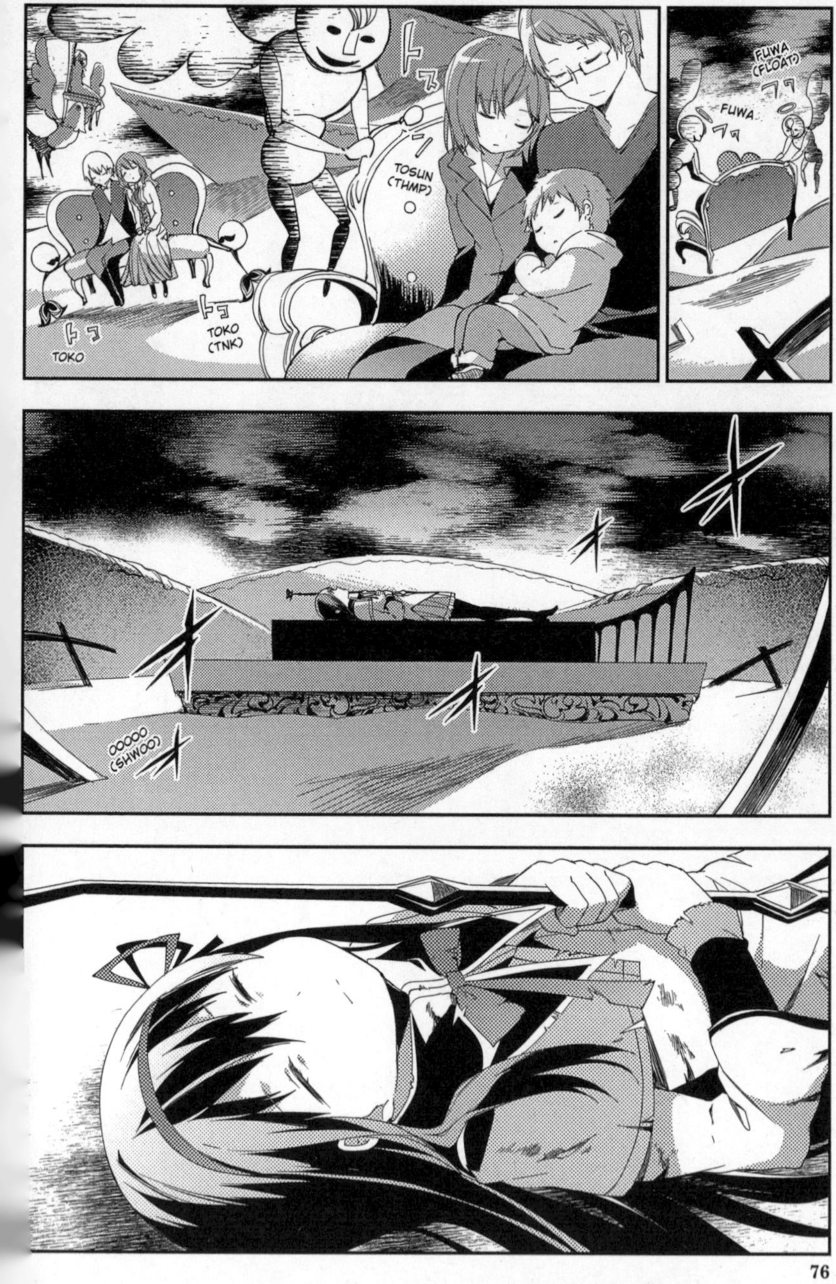
FUWA (FLOAT)
FUWA
TOSUN (THMP)
TOKO (TNK)
TOKO
OOOOO (SHWOO)

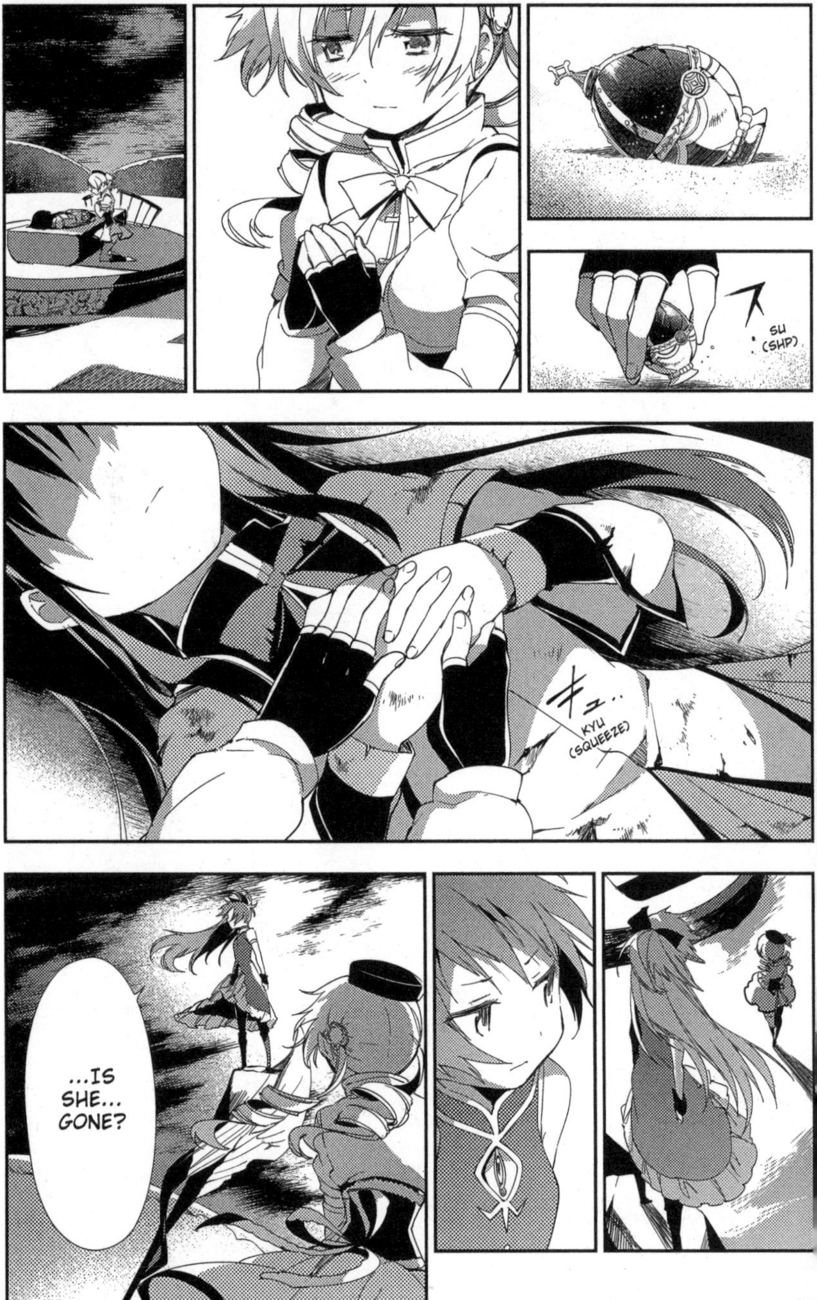
SU
(SHP)
KYU
(SQUEEZE)
...IS
SHE...
GONE?

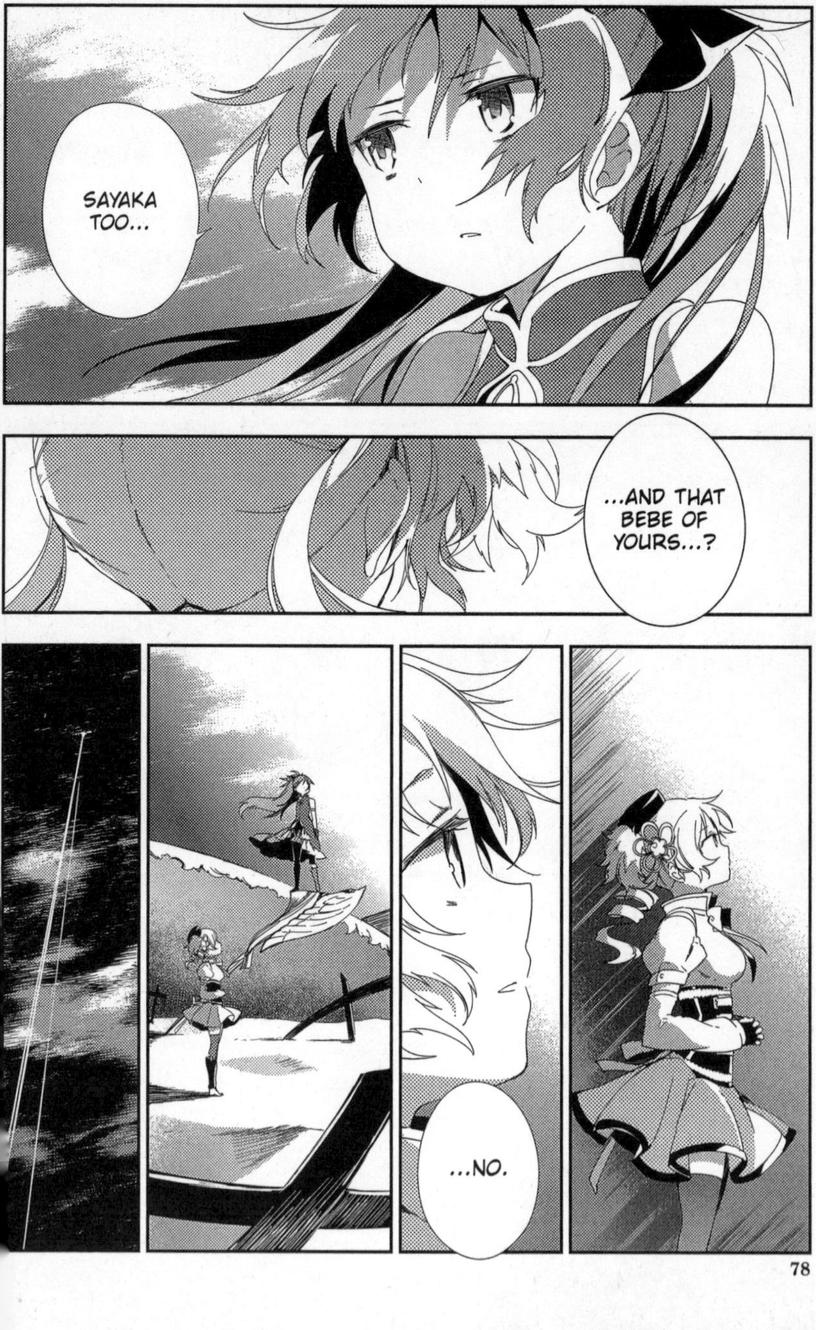
SAYAKA TOO...
...AND THAT BEBE OF YOURS...?
...NO.

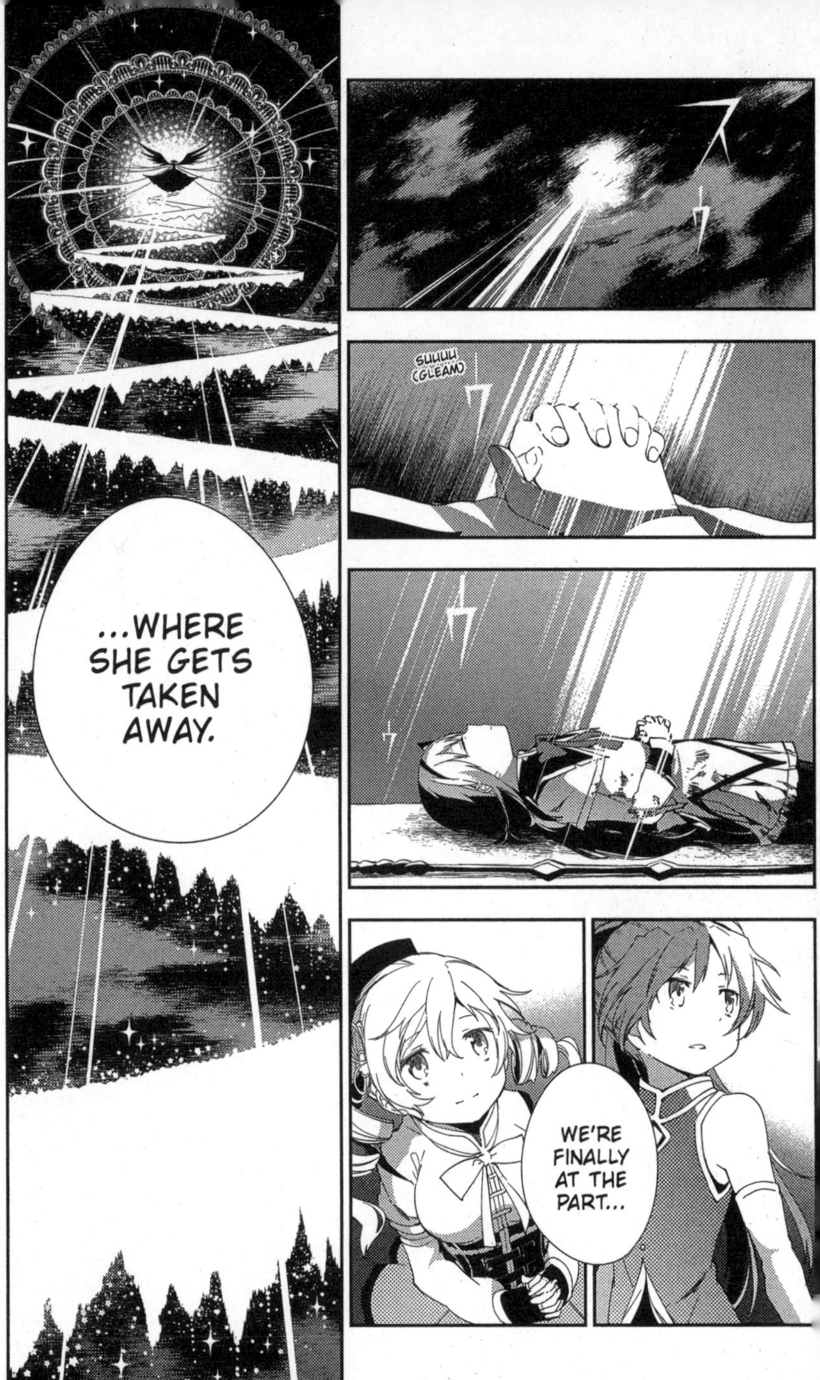
SUUUU (GLEAM)
WE'RE FINALLY AT THE PART...
...WHERE SHE GETS TAKEN AWAY.

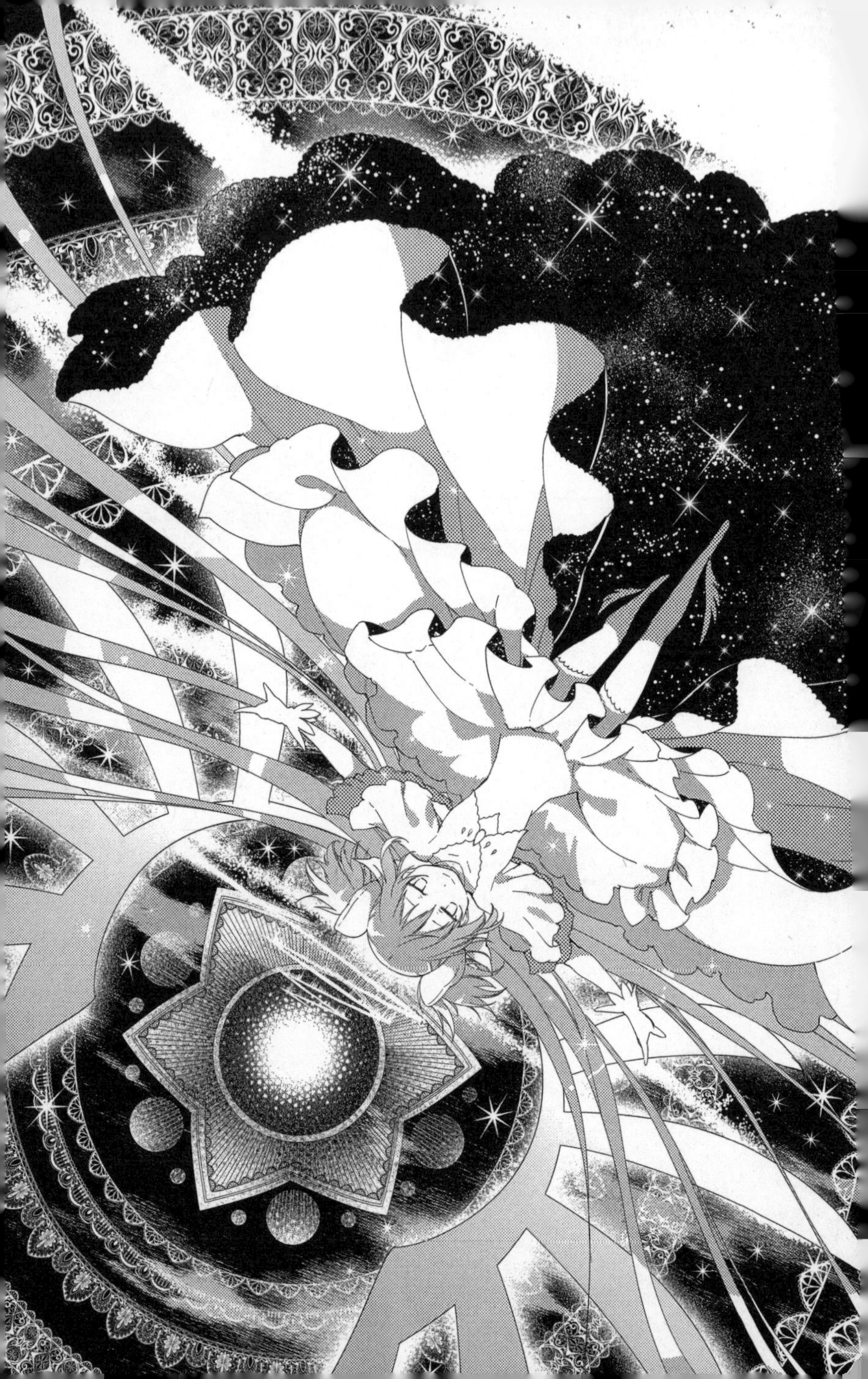

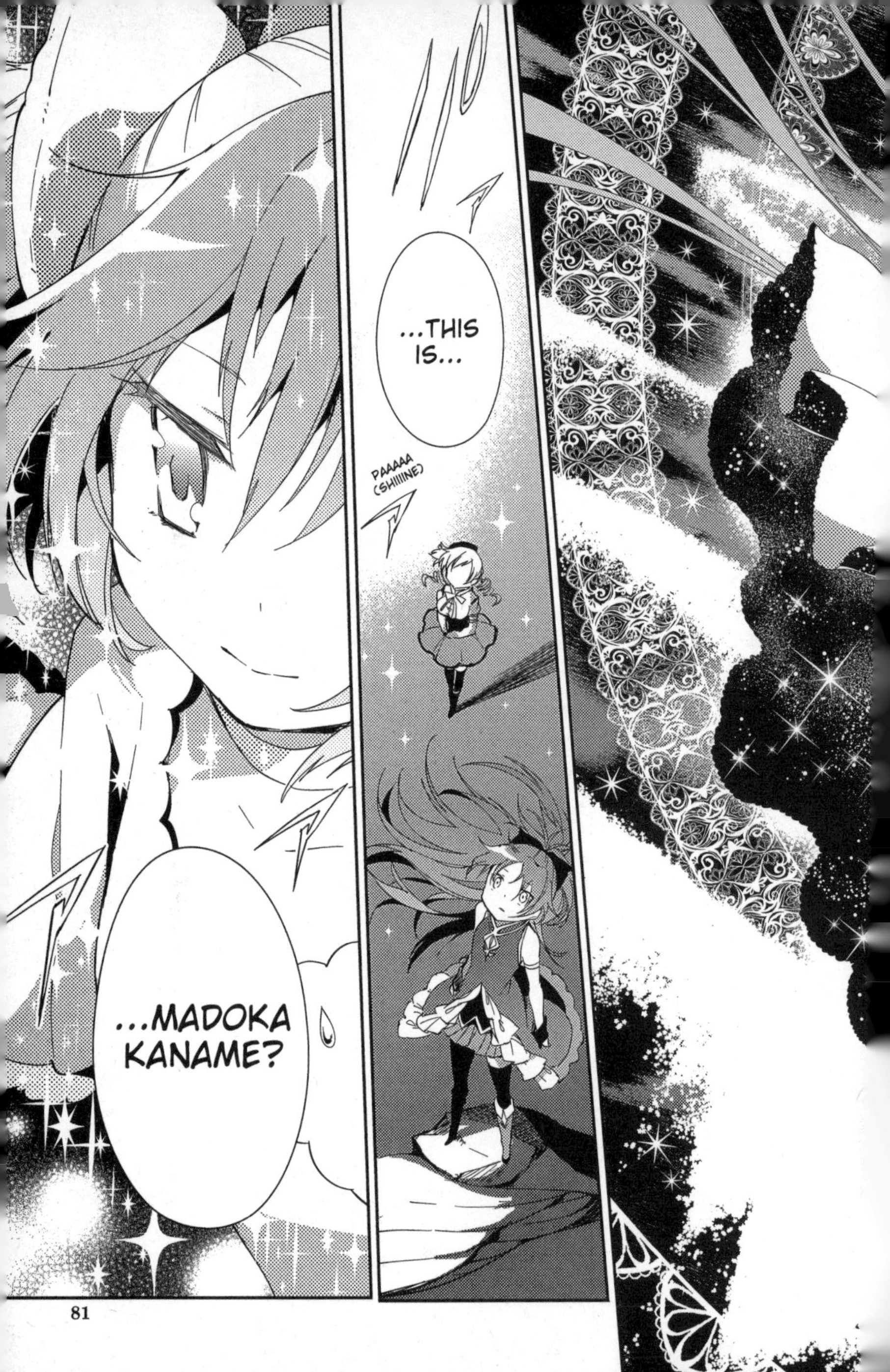
...THIS IS...
PAAAAA (SHIIIINE)
...MADOKA KANAME?

THE LAW OF CYCLES...
SOMEDAY THIS WILL GUIDE US AWAY AS WELL...
YES.
I CAME HERE FOR HOMURA-CHAN...
...I REMEMBER NOW.
HOW COULD I FORGET SOME-THING SO IMPORT-ANT...?

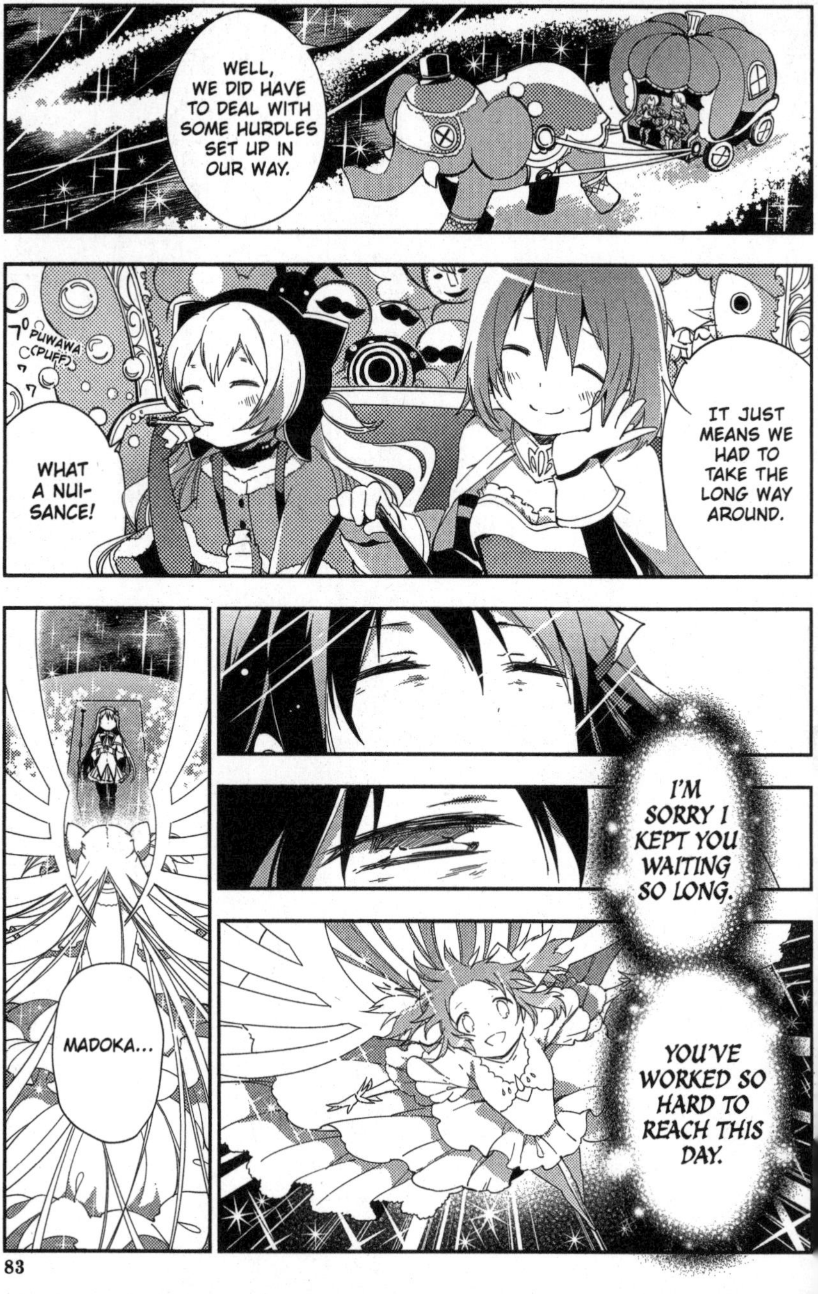
WELL, WE DID HAVE TO DEAL WITH SOME HURDLES SET UP IN OUR WAY.
IT JUST MEANS WE HAD TO TAKE THE LONG WAY AROUND.
PUWAWA (PUFF)
WHAT A NUI-SANCE!
I'M SORRY I KEPT YOU WAITING SO LONG.
YOU'VE WORKED SO HARD TO REACH THIS DAY.
MADOKA...

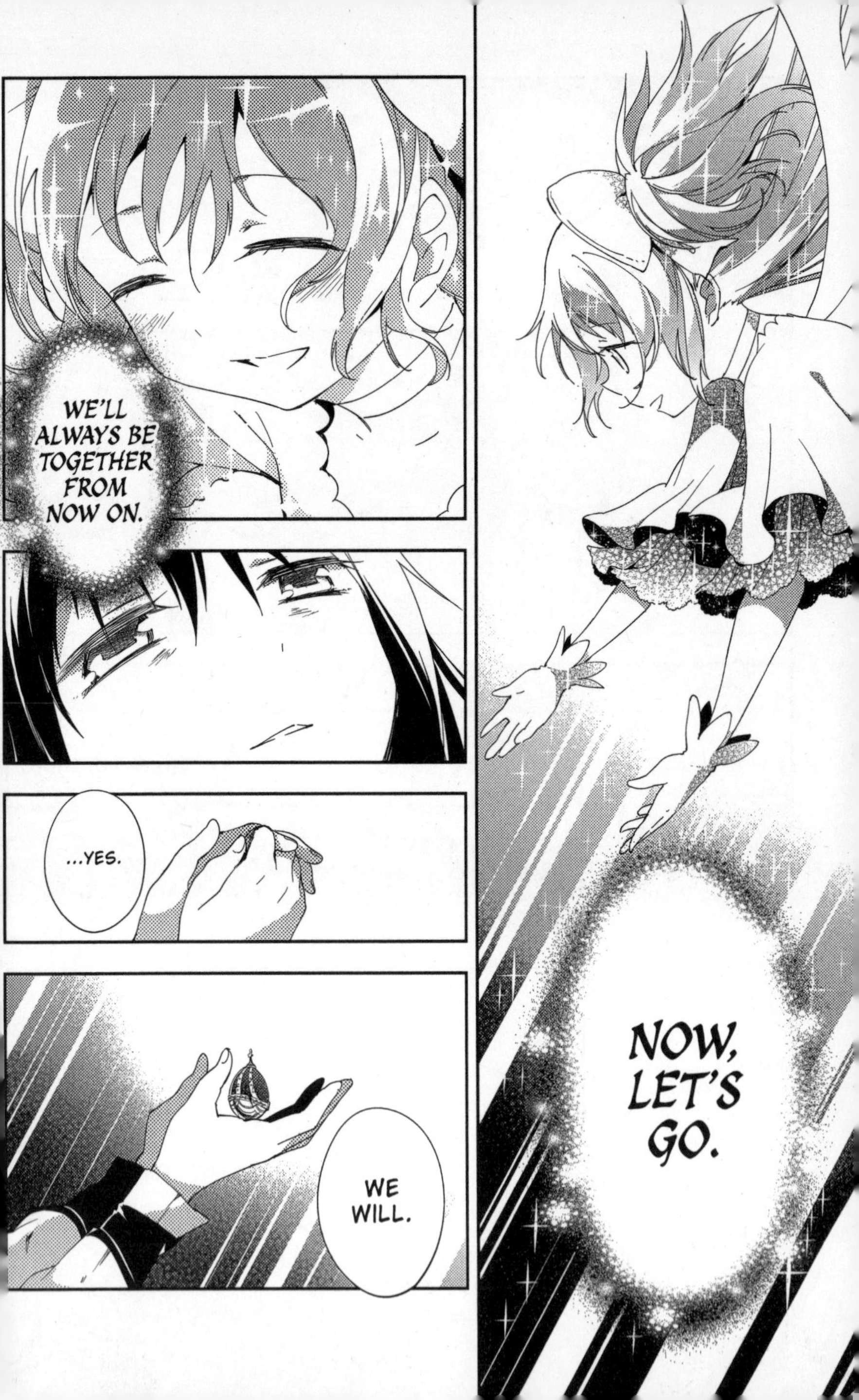
NOW, LET'S GO.
WE'LL ALWAYS BE TOGETHER FROM NOW ON.
...YES.
WE WILL.

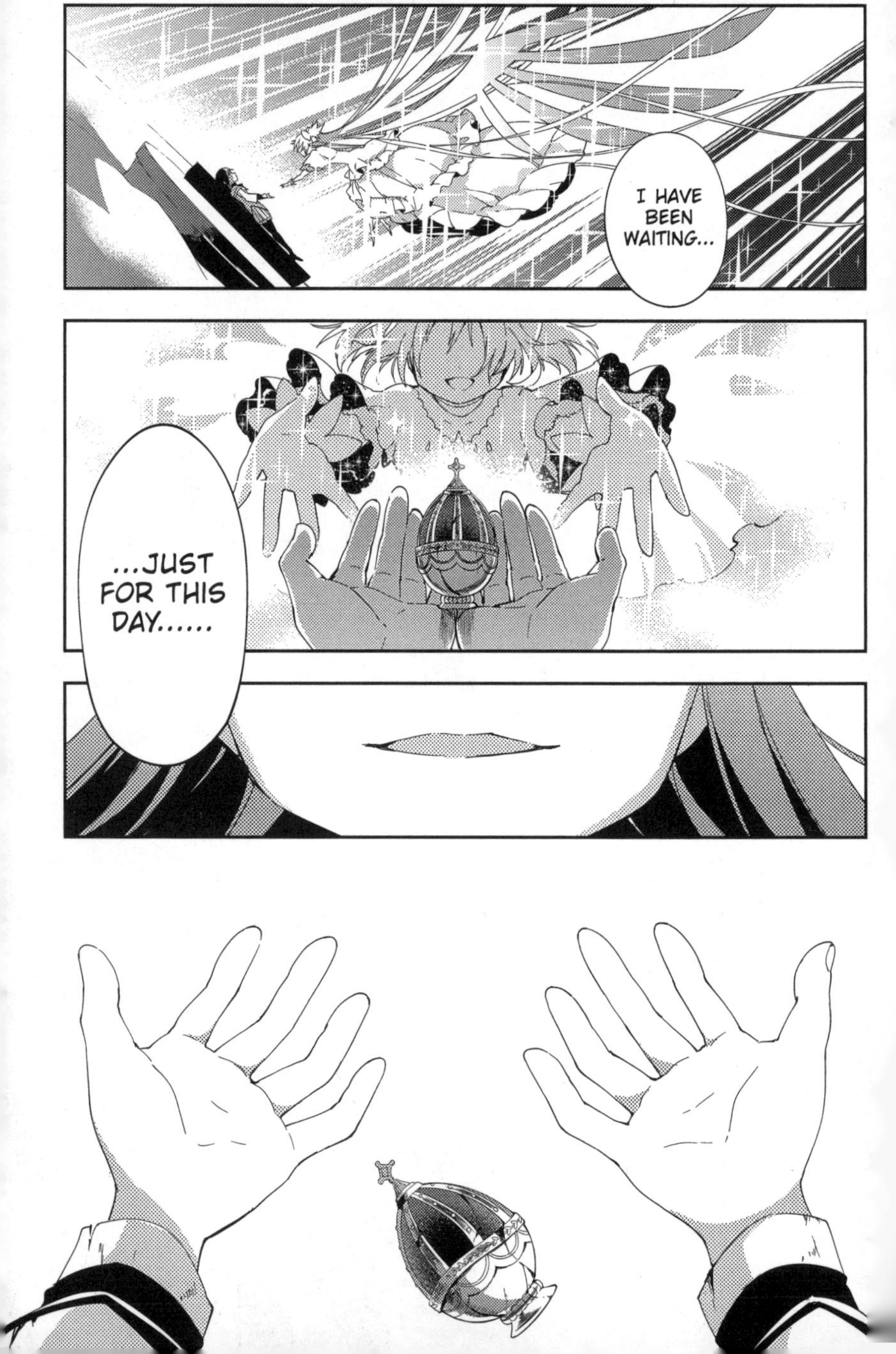
I HAVE BEEN WAITING...
...JUST FOR THIS DAY......

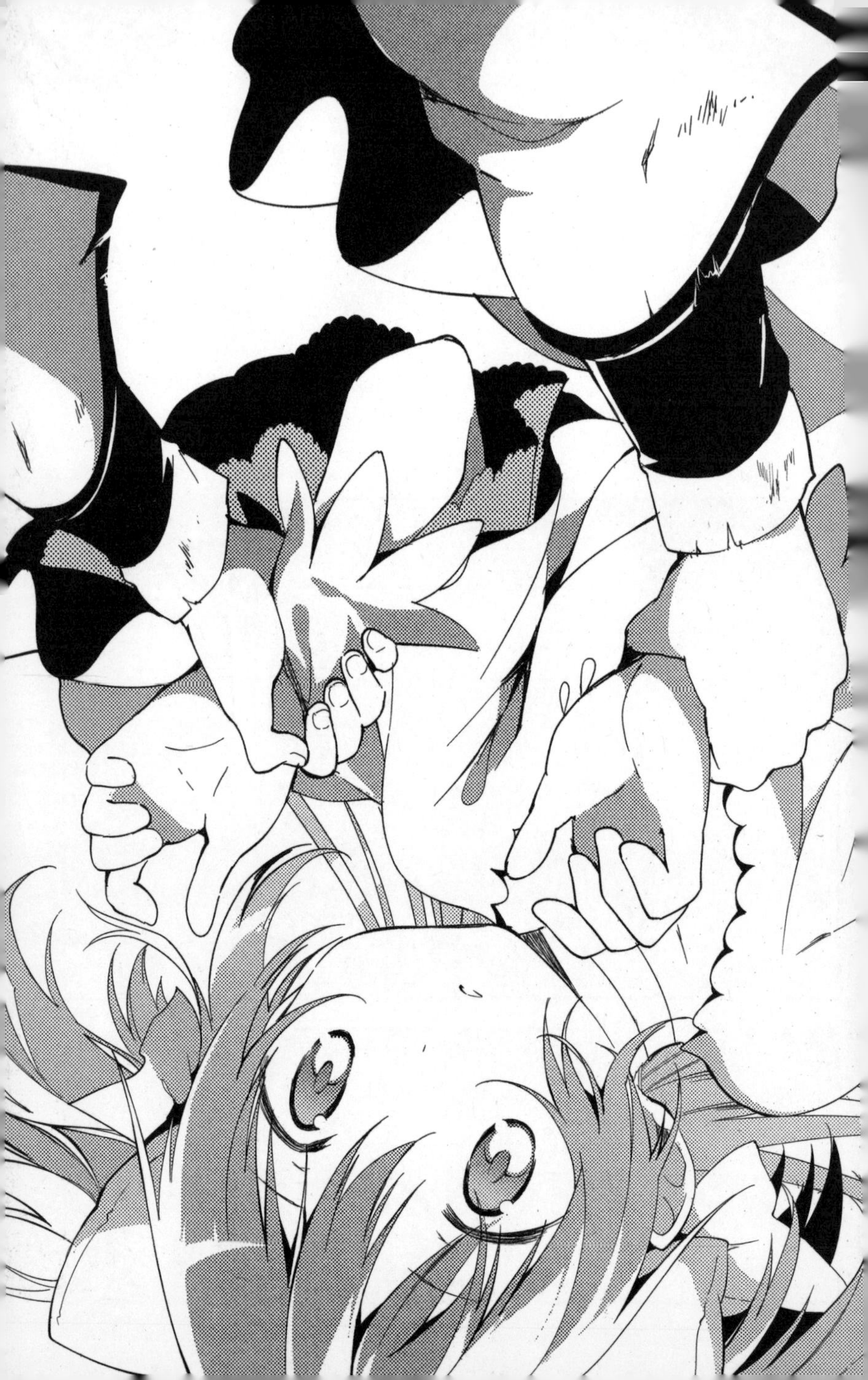

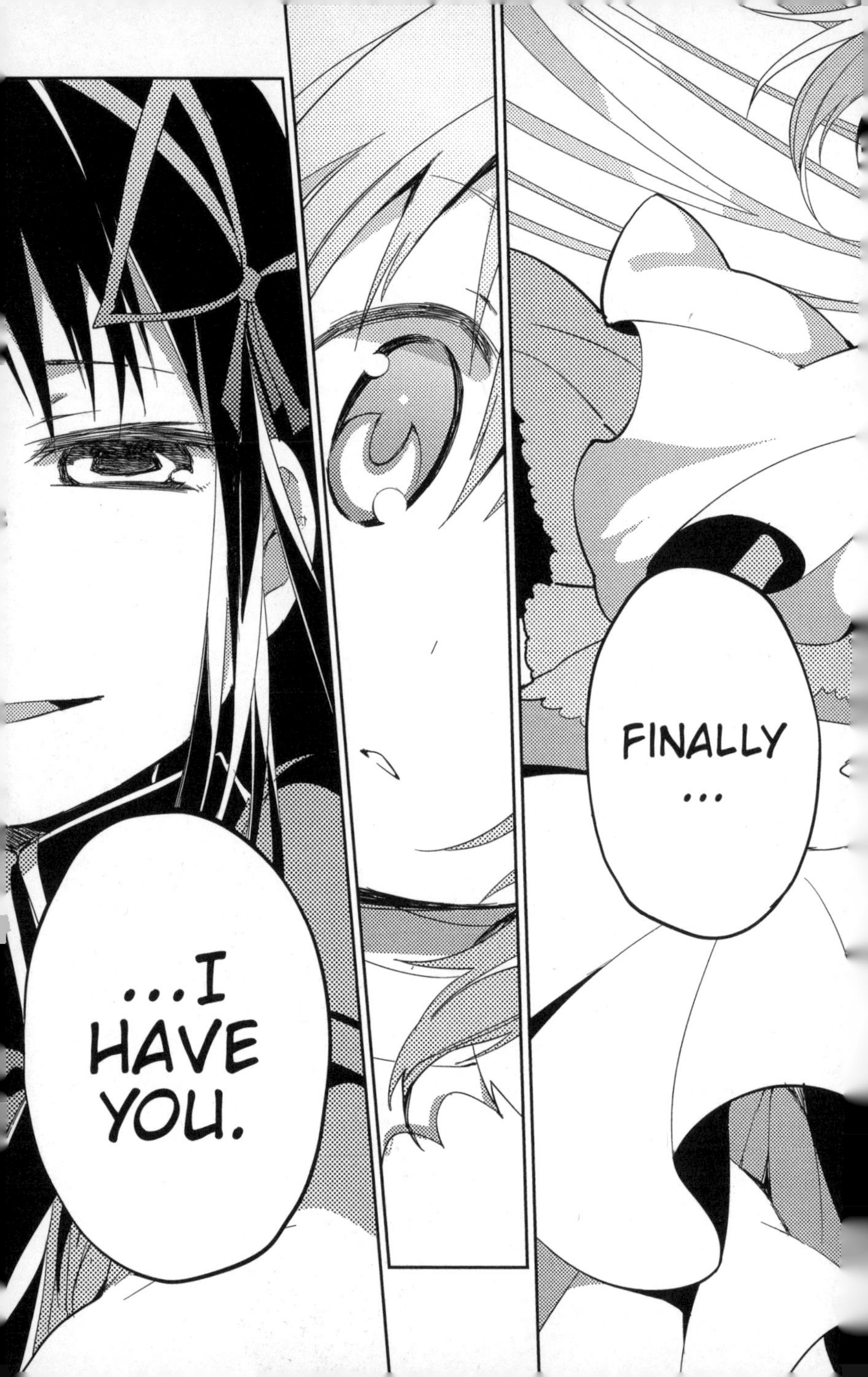
FINALLY ...
...I HAVE YOU.

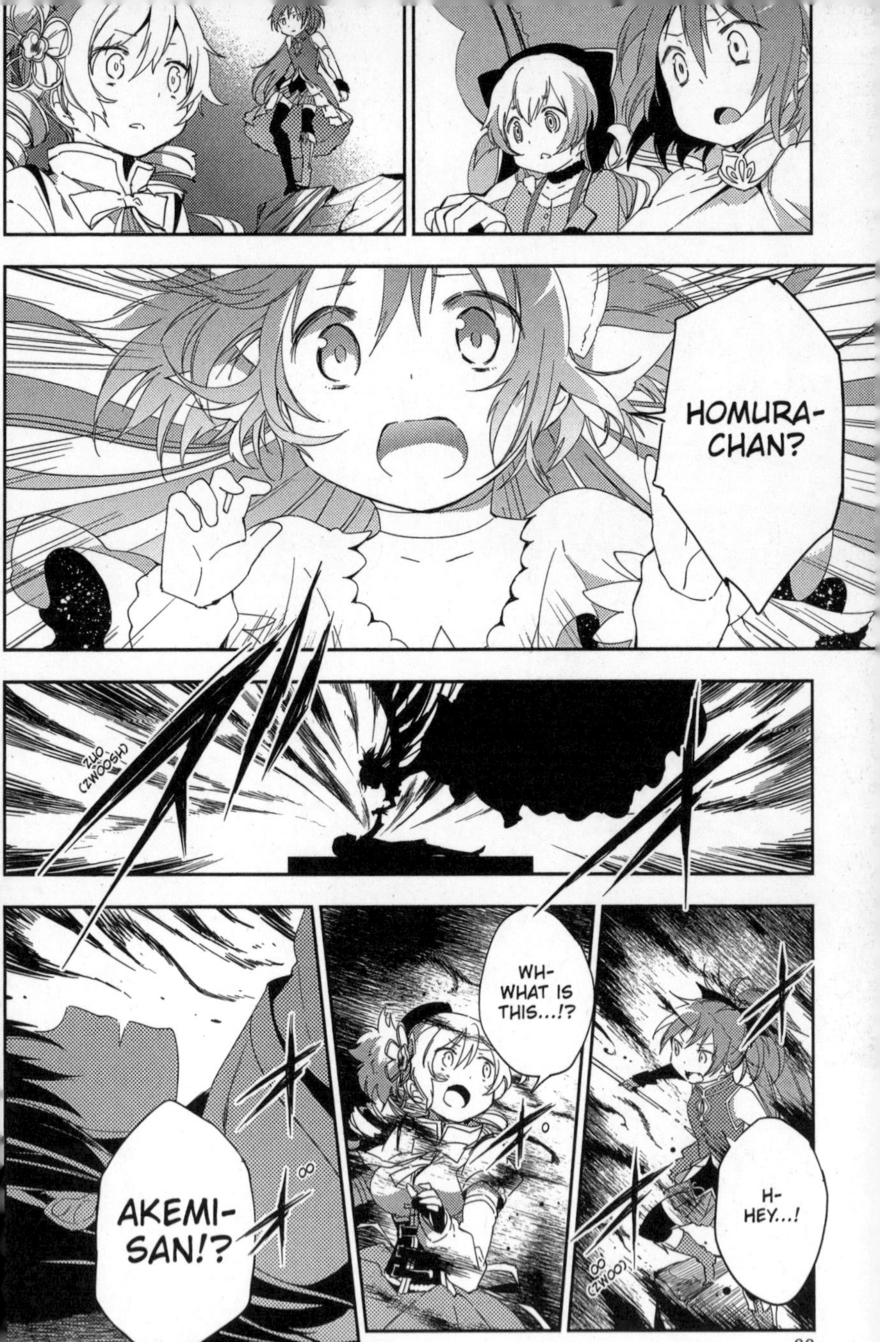
HOMURA-CHAN?
ZUO (ZWOOSH)
H-HEY...!
(ZWOO)
WH-WHAT IS THIS...!?
AKEMI-SAN!?

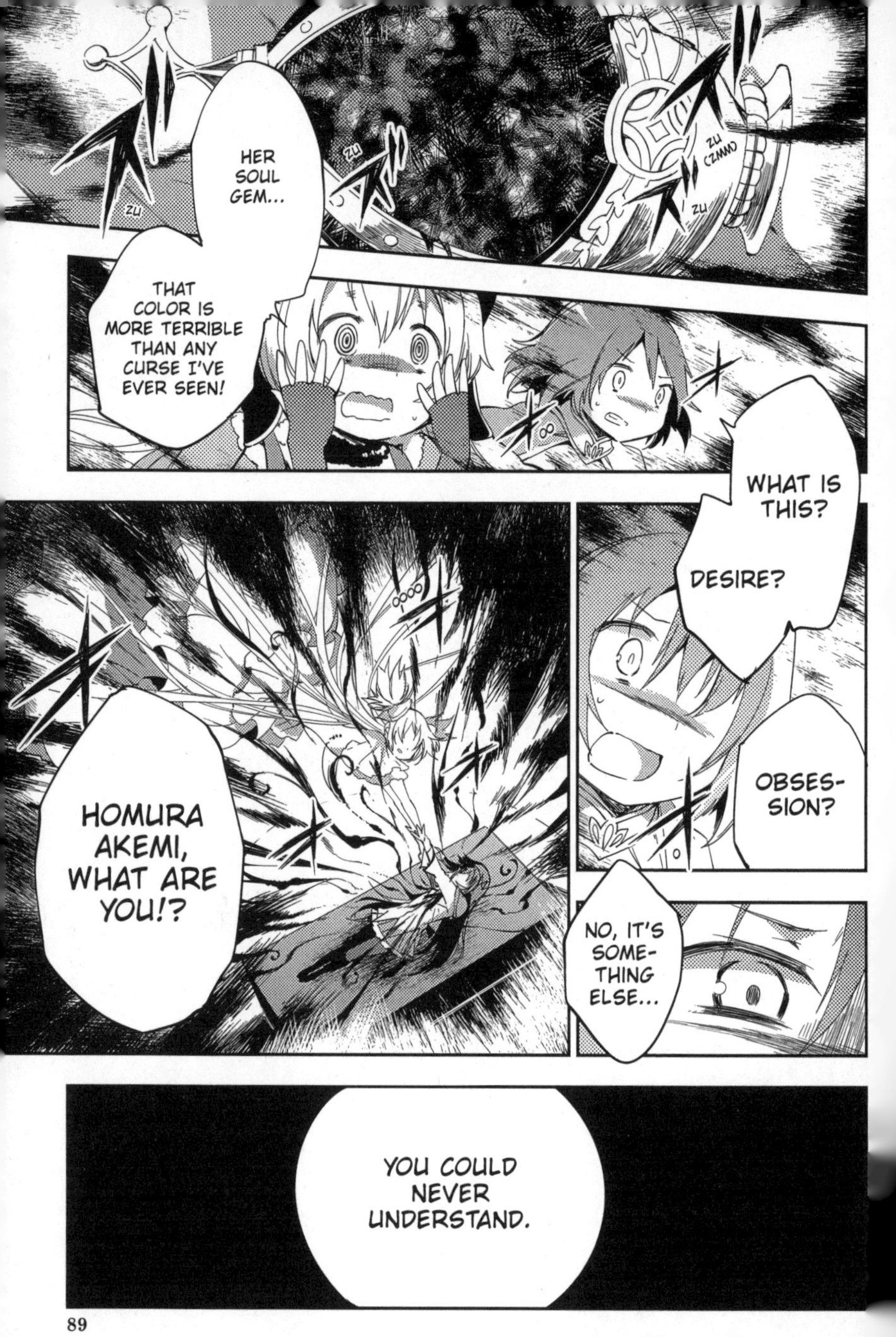
ZU (ZMMM)
ZU
HER SOUL GEM...
ZU
ZU
THAT COLOR IS MORE TERRIBLE THAN ANY CURSE I'VE EVER SEEN!
WHAT IS THIS?
DESIRE?
OBSESSION?
NO, IT'S SOMETHING ELSE...
HOMURA AKEMI, WHAT ARE YOU!?
YOU COULD NEVER UNDERSTAND.

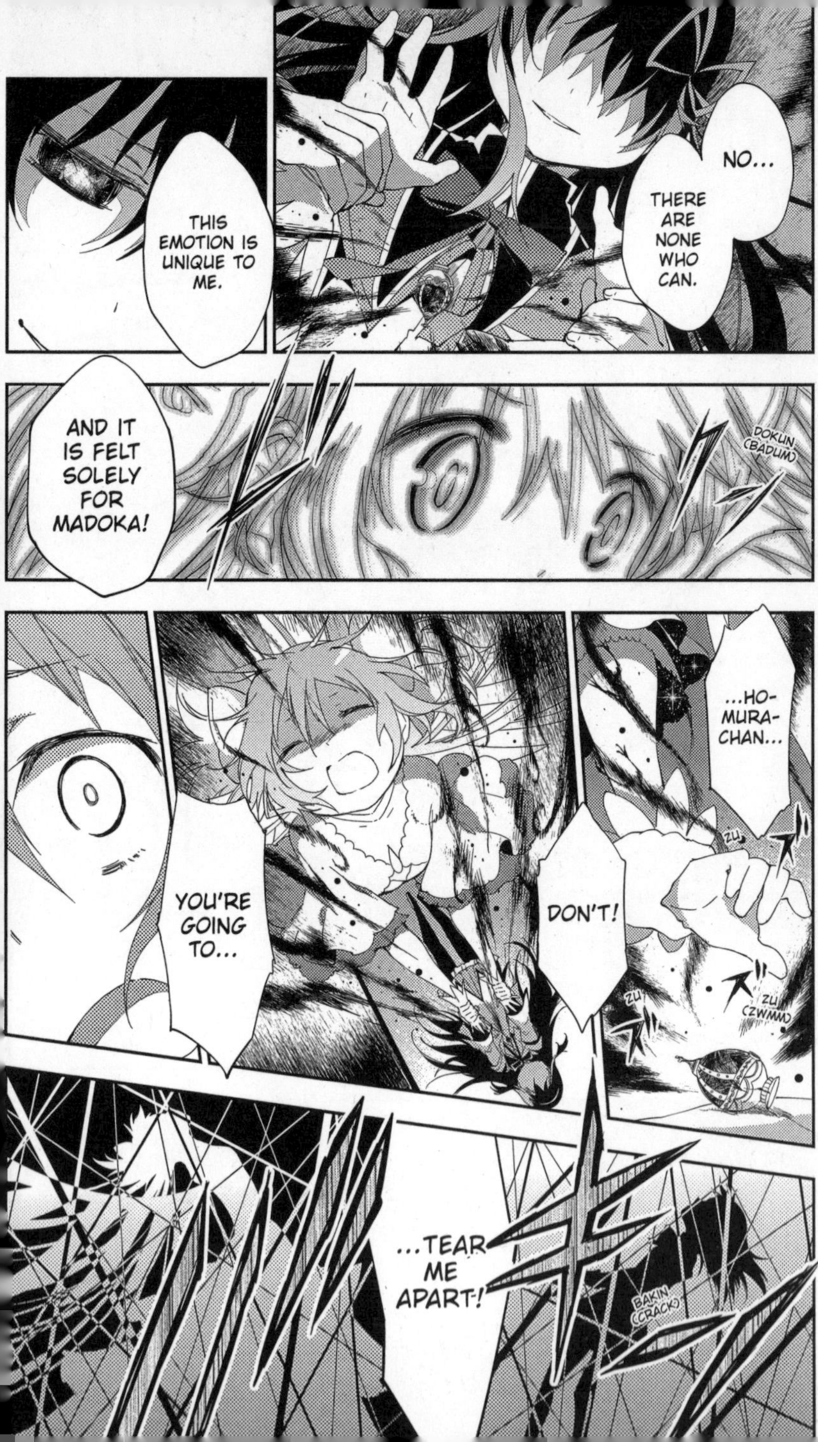
NO...
THERE ARE NONE WHO CAN.
THIS EMOTION IS UNIQUE TO ME.
DOKUN (BADUM)
AND IT IS FELT SOLELY FOR MADOKA!
...HO-MURA-CHAN...
ZU
DON'T!
ZU (ZWMM)
ZU
YOU'RE GOING TO...
BAKIN (CRACK)
...TEAR ME APART!

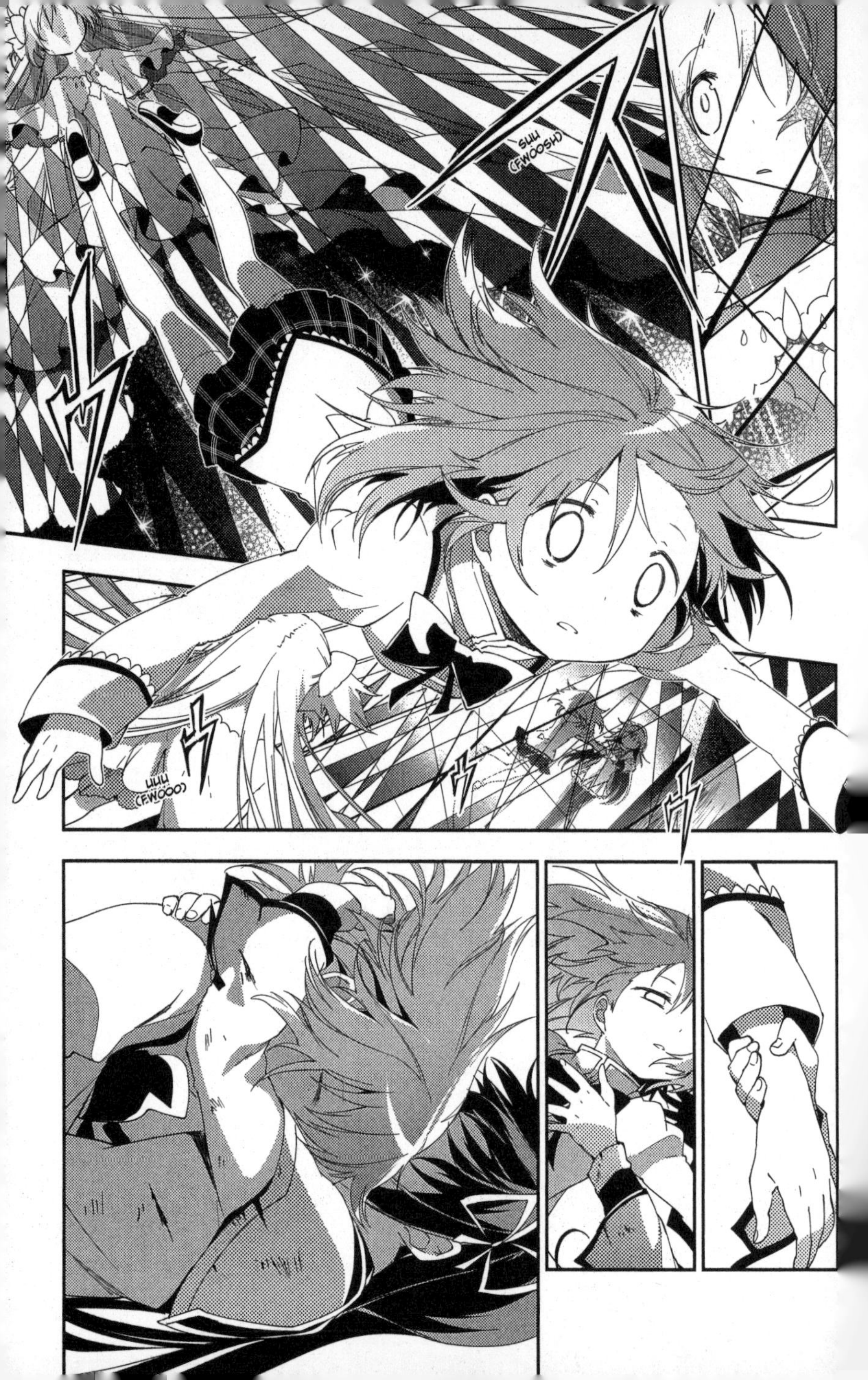
SUU (FWOOSH)
UUU (FWOOO)

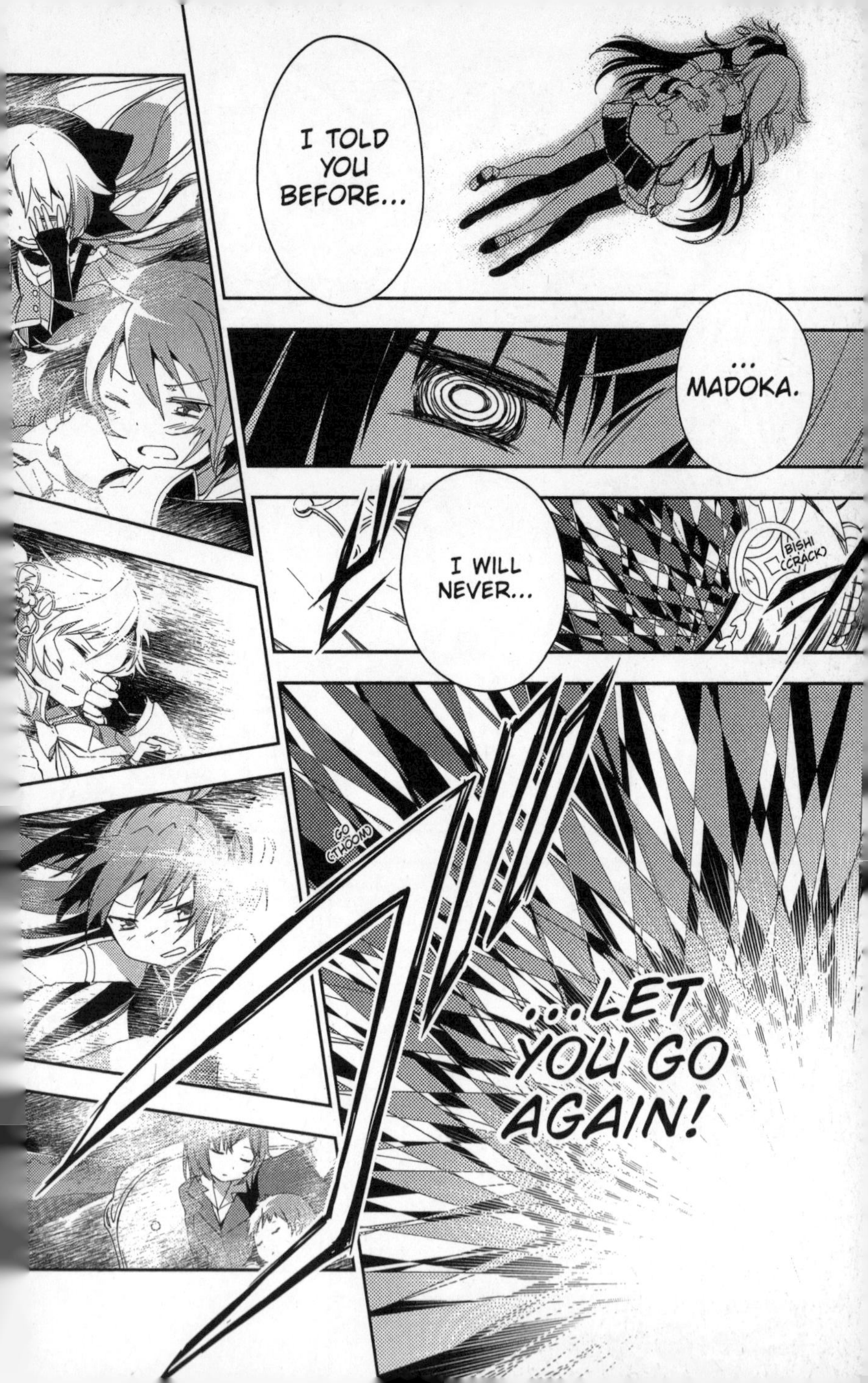
I TOLD YOU BEFORE...
... MADOKA.
I WILL NEVER...
BISHI (CRACK)
GO (THOOM)
...LET YOU GO AGAIN!

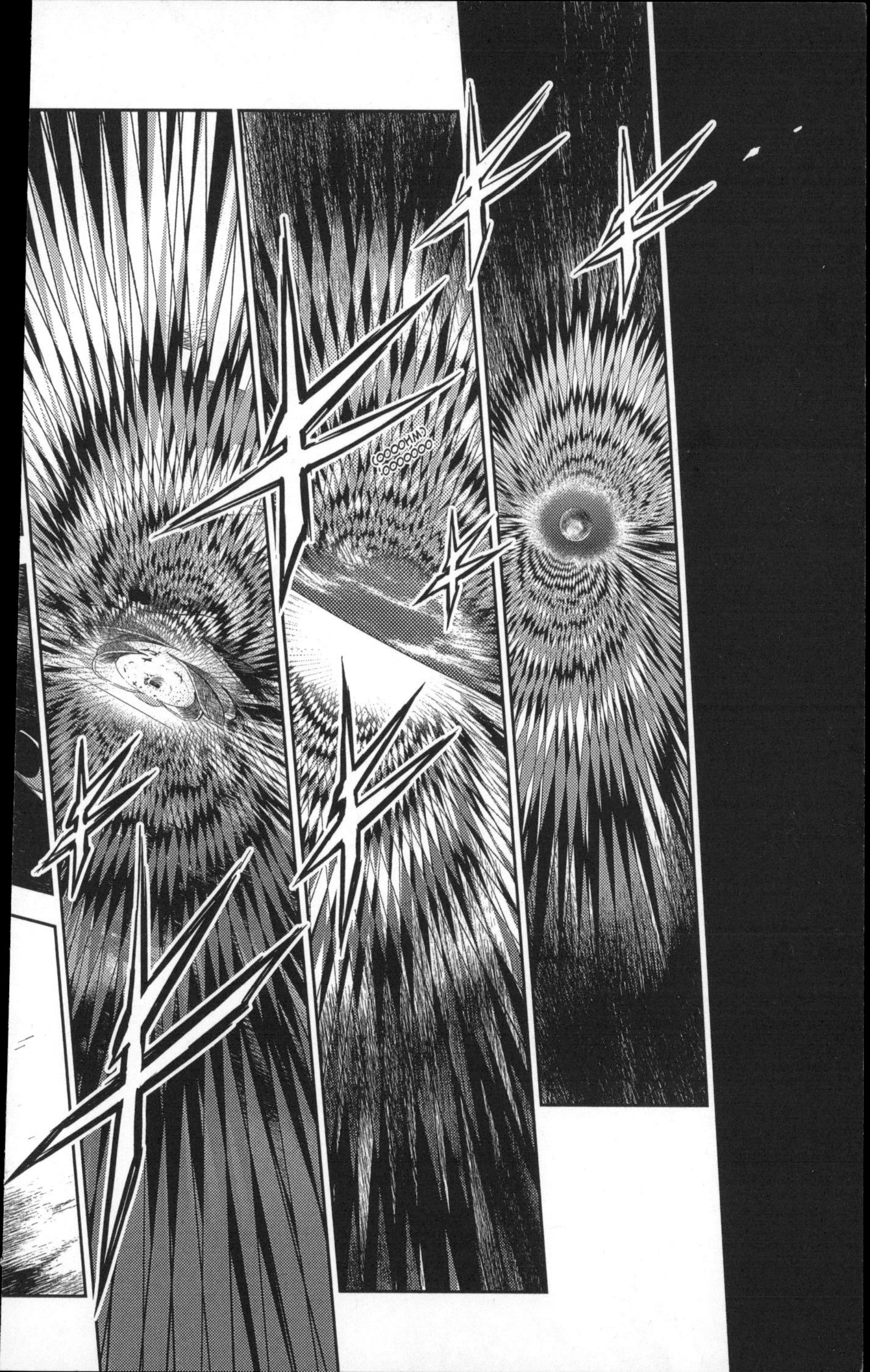
(WHOOOO OOOOOOO)

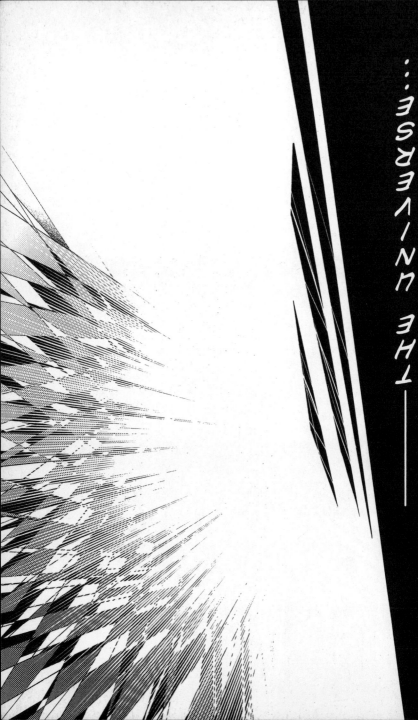

...THE UNIVERSE——

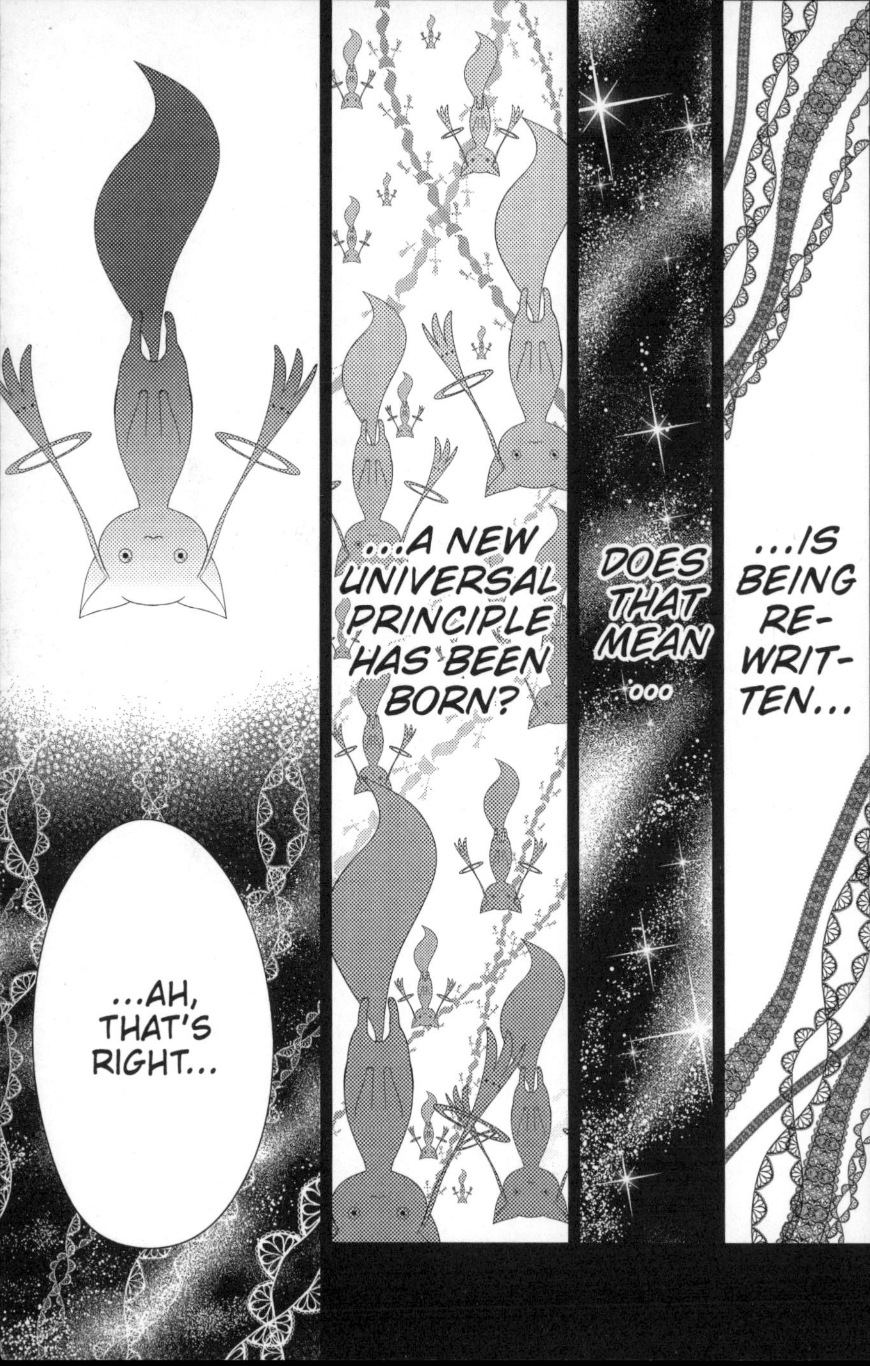
...IS BEING RE-WRIT-TEN...
DOES THAT MEAN...
...A NEW UNIVERSAL PRINCIPLE HAS BEEN BORN?
...AH, THAT'S RIGHT...

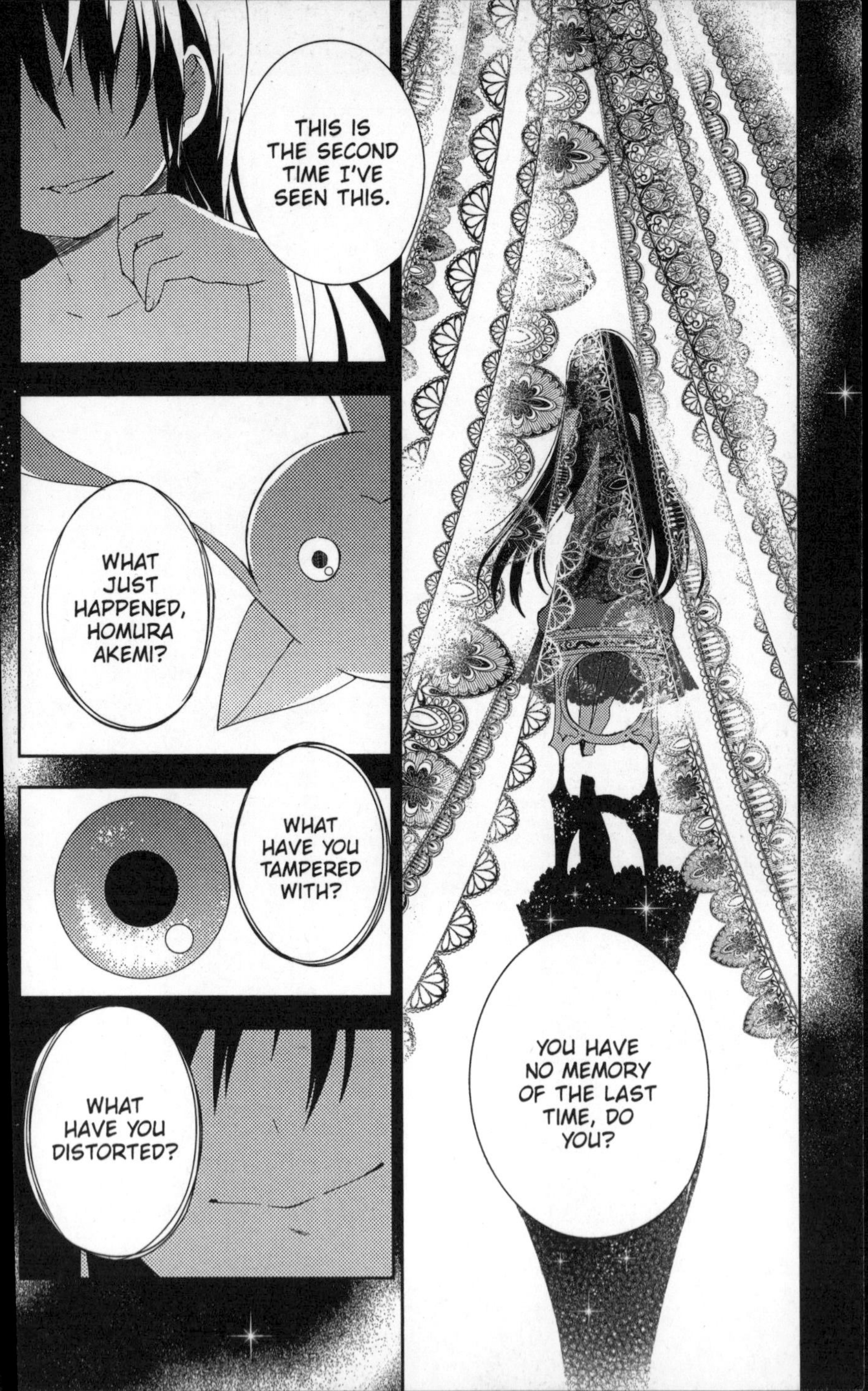
YOU HAVE NO MEMORY OF THE LAST TIME, DO YOU?
THIS IS THE SECOND TIME I'VE SEEN THIS.
WHAT JUST HAPPENED, HOMURA AKEMI?
WHAT HAVE YOU TAMPERED WITH?
WHAT HAVE YOU DISTORTED?

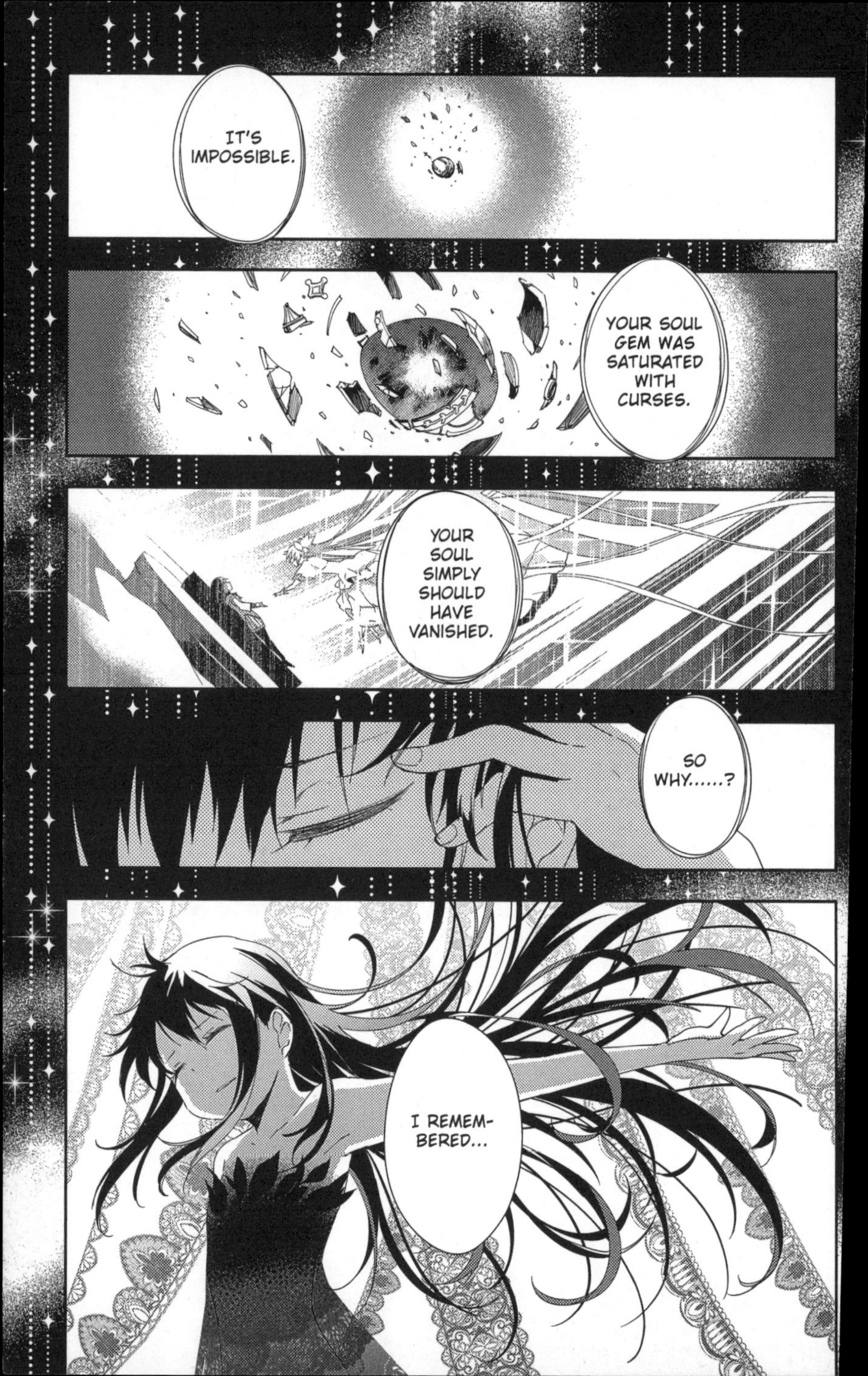
IT'S IMPOSSIBLE.
YOUR SOUL GEM WAS SATURATED WITH CURSES.
YOUR SOUL SIMPLY SHOULD HAVE VANISHED.
SO WHY......?
I REMEMBERED...

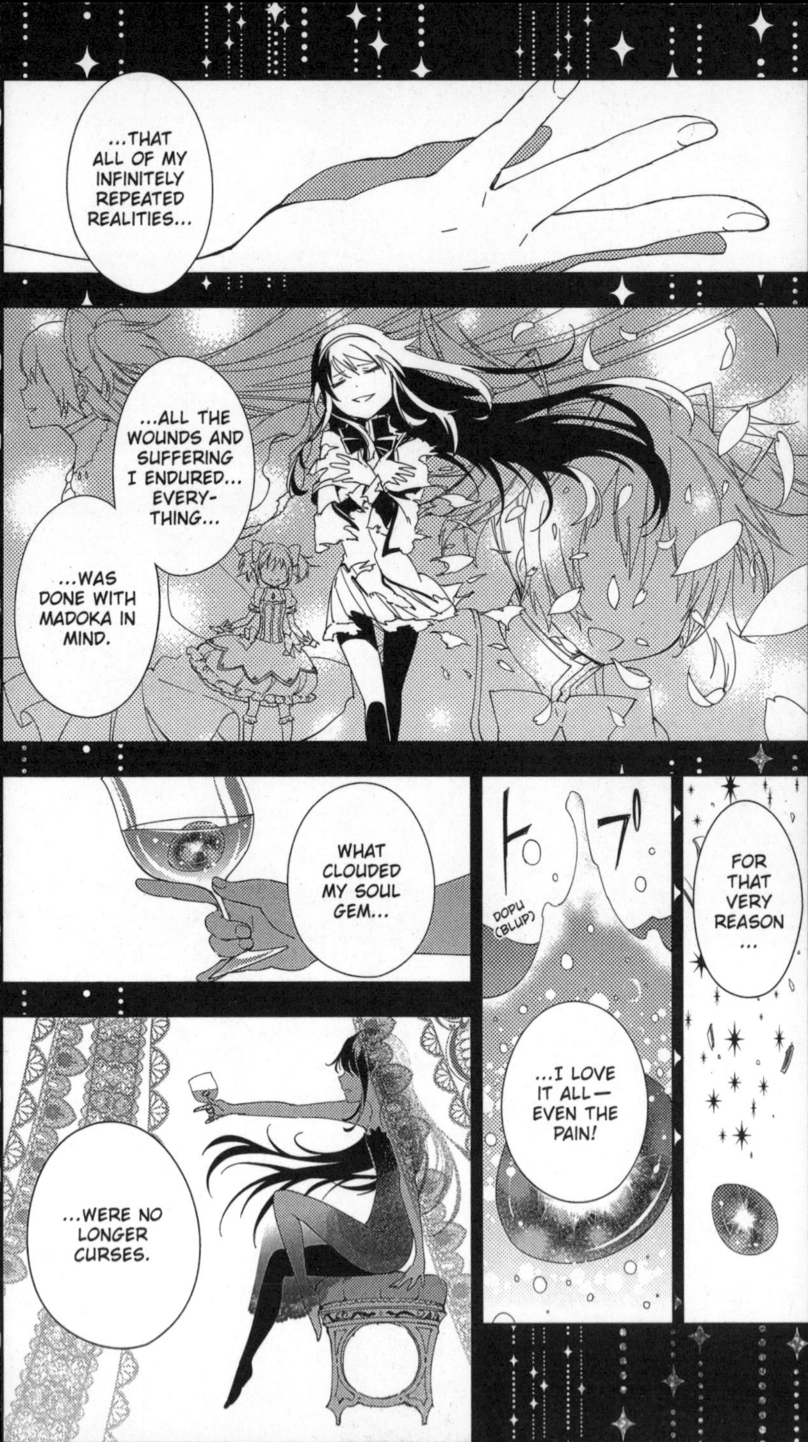
...THAT ALL OF MY INFINITELY REPEATED REALITIES...
...ALL THE WOUNDS AND SUFFERING I ENDURED... EVERY-THING...
...WAS DONE WITH MADOKA IN MIND.
FOR THAT VERY REASON ...
DOPU (BLUP)
...I LOVE IT ALL— EVEN THE PAIN!
WHAT CLOUDED MY SOUL GEM...
...WERE NO LONGER CURSES.

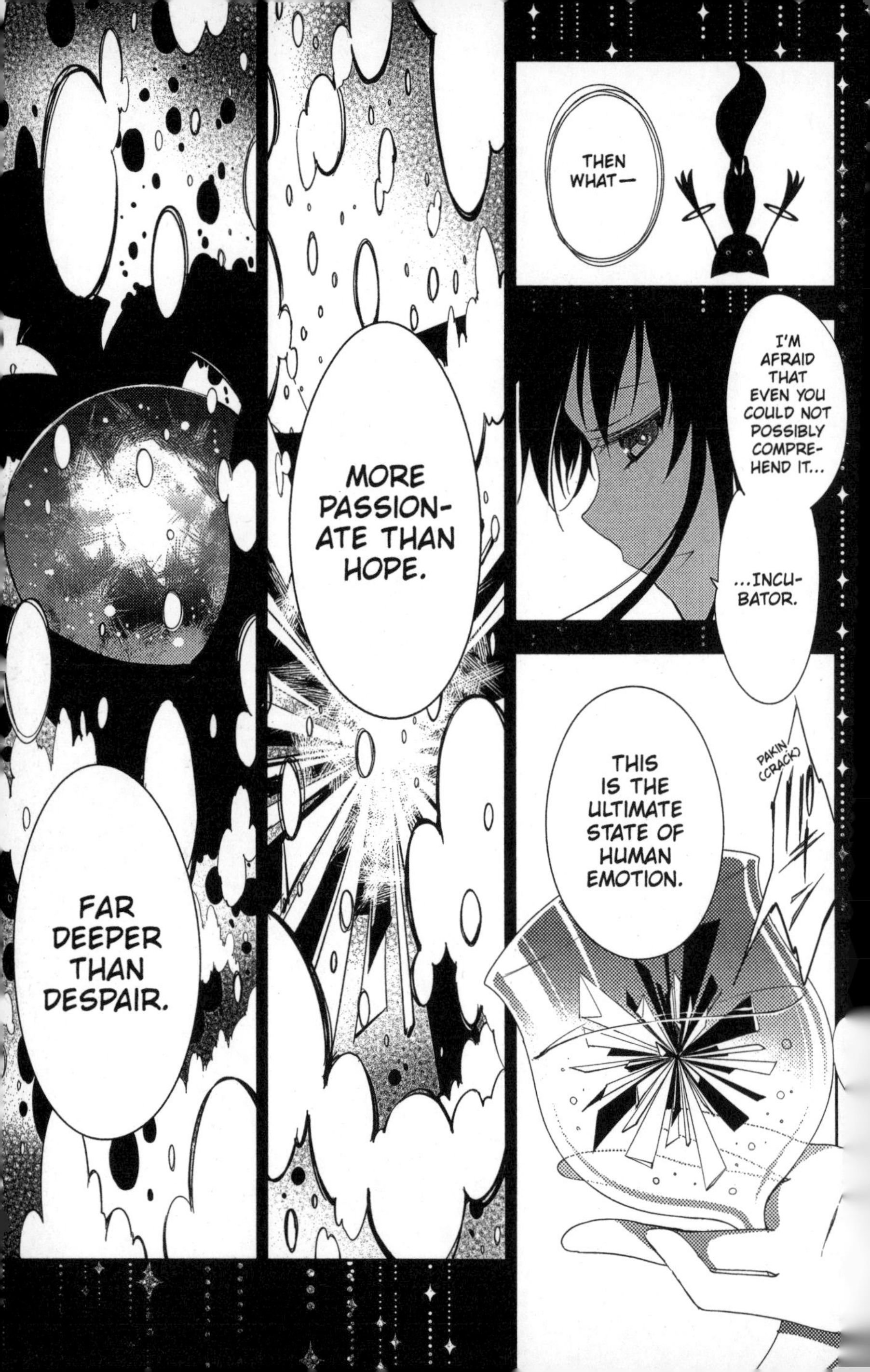
THEN WHAT—
I'M AFRAID THAT EVEN YOU COULD NOT POSSIBLY COMPRE-HEND IT...
...INCU-BATOR.
PAKIN (CRACK)
THIS IS THE ULTIMATE STATE OF HUMAN EMOTION.
MORE PASSION-ATE THAN HOPE.
FAR DEEPER THAN DESPAIR.

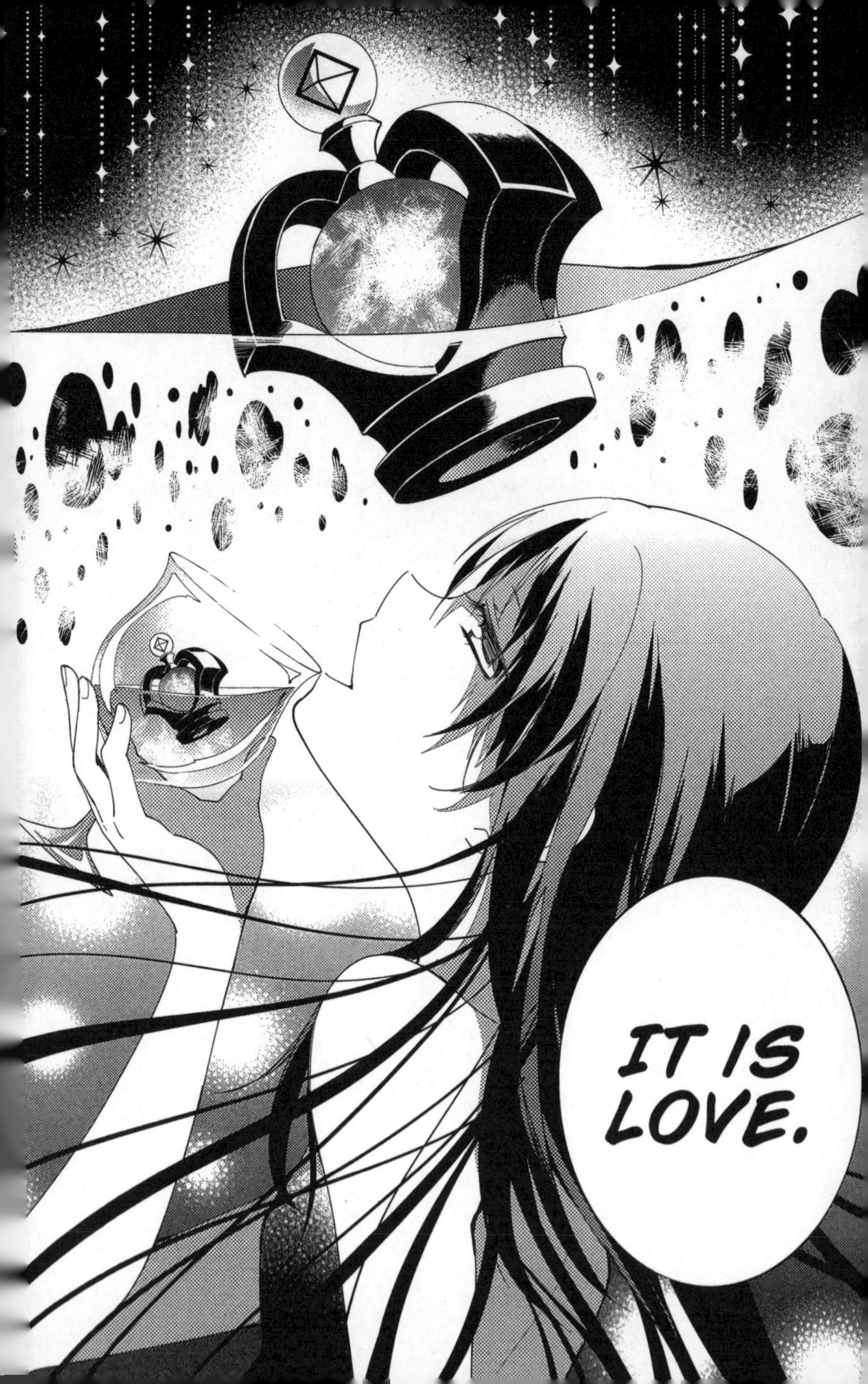
IT IS LOVE.

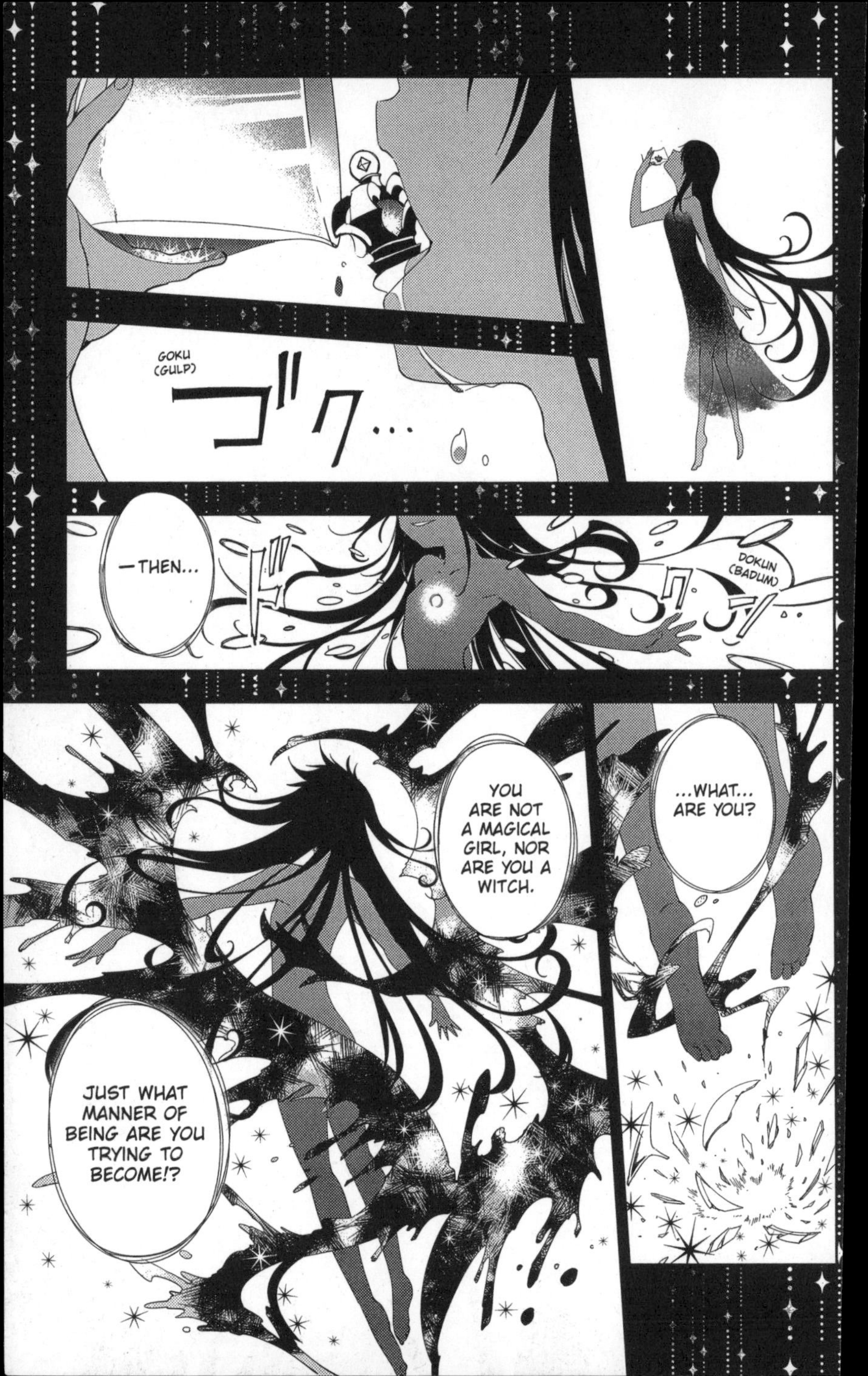
GOKU (GULP)
ゴク…
DOKUN (BADUM)
ドクン
—THEN…
…WHAT… ARE YOU?
YOU ARE NOT A MAGICAL GIRL, NOR ARE YOU A WITCH.
JUST WHAT MANNER OF BEING ARE YOU TRYING TO BECOME!?

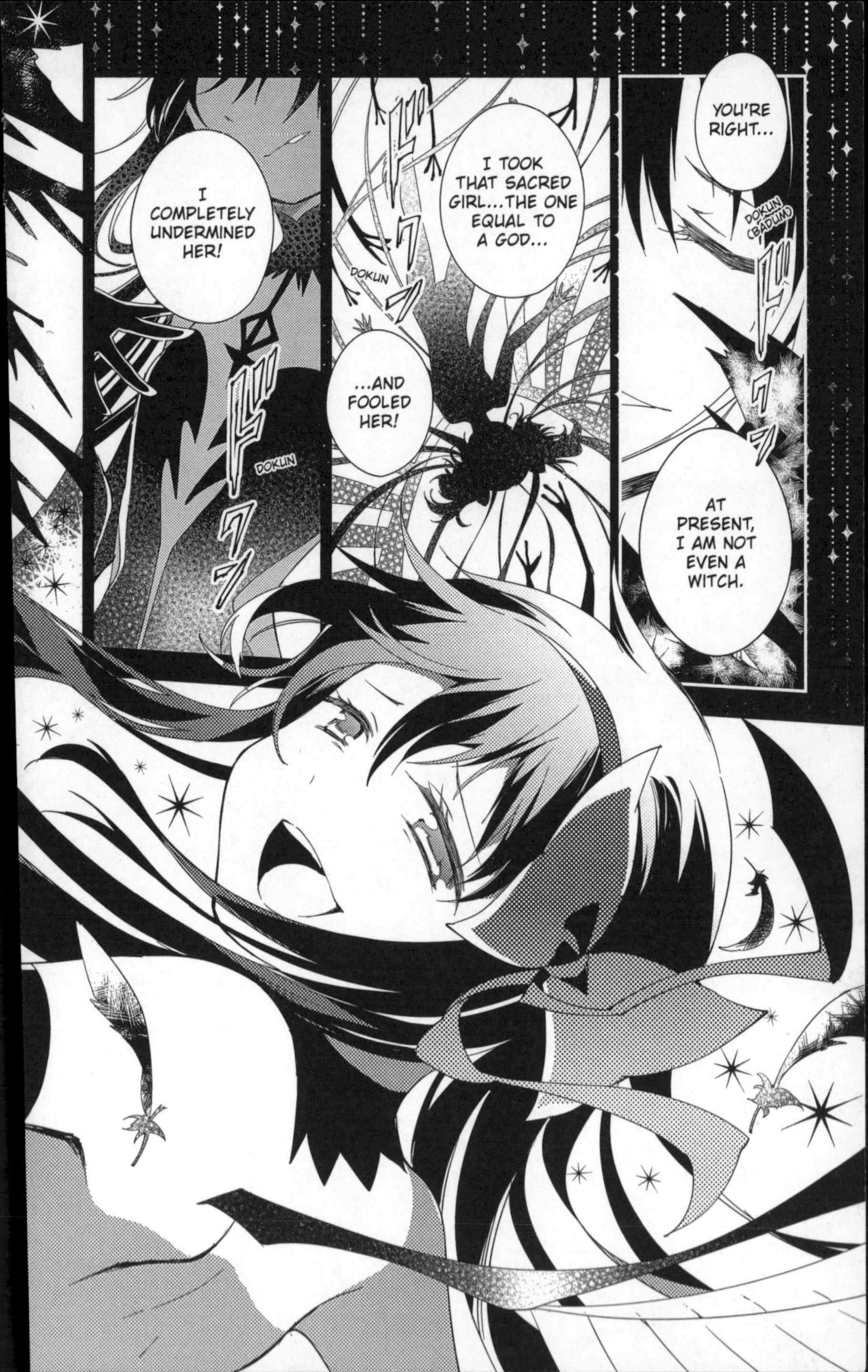
YOU'RE RIGHT...
DOKUN (BADUM)
AT PRESENT, I AM NOT EVEN A WITCH.
I TOOK THAT SACRED GIRL...THE ONE EQUAL TO A GOD...
DOKUN
...AND FOOLED HER!
I COMPLETELY UNDERMINED HER!
DOKUN

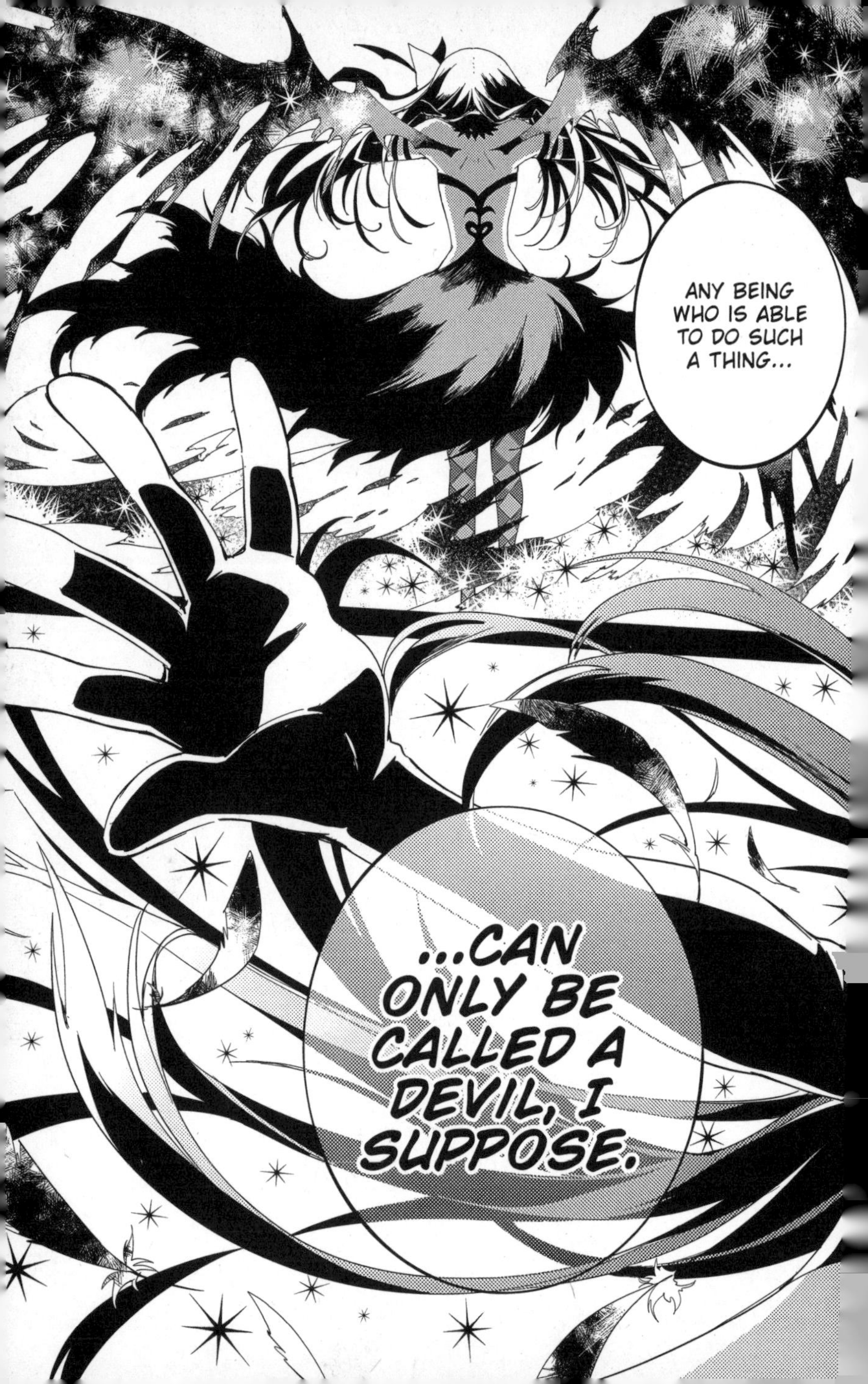
ANY BEING WHO IS ABLE TO DO SUCH A THING...
...CAN ONLY BE CALLED A DEVIL, I SUPPOSE.

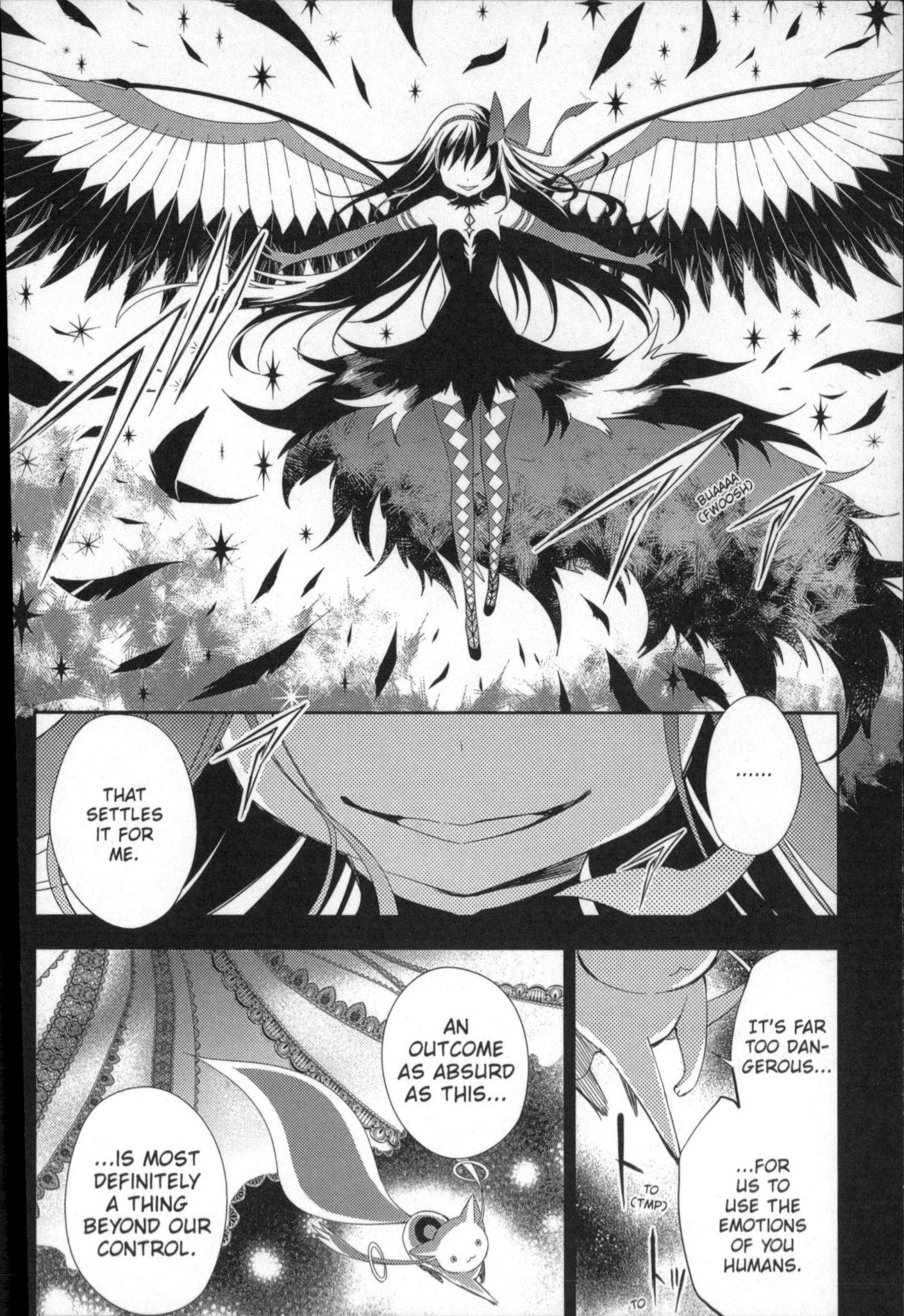
BUAAAA (FWOOSH)
......
THAT SETTLES IT FOR ME.
IT'S FAR TOO DAN-GEROUS...
TO (TMP)
...FOR US TO USE THE EMOTIONS OF YOU HUMANS.
TO
AN OUTCOME AS ABSURD AS THIS...
...IS MOST DEFINITELY A THING BEYOND OUR CONTROL.

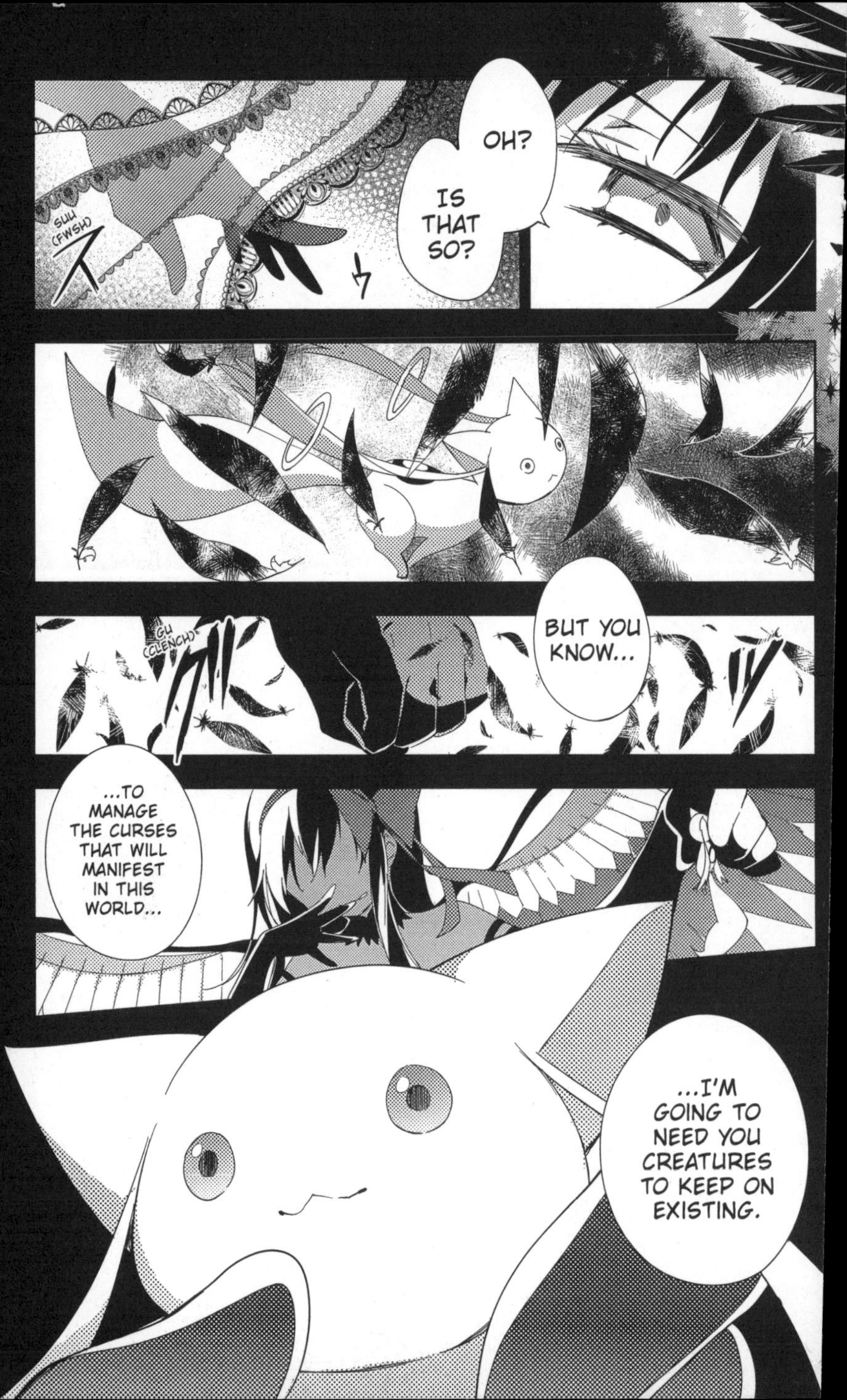
OH?
IS THAT SO?
SUU (FWSH)
BUT YOU KNOW...
GU (CLENCH)
...TO MANAGE THE CURSES THAT WILL MANIFEST IN THIS WORLD...
...I'M GOING TO NEED YOU CREATURES TO KEEP ON EXISTING.

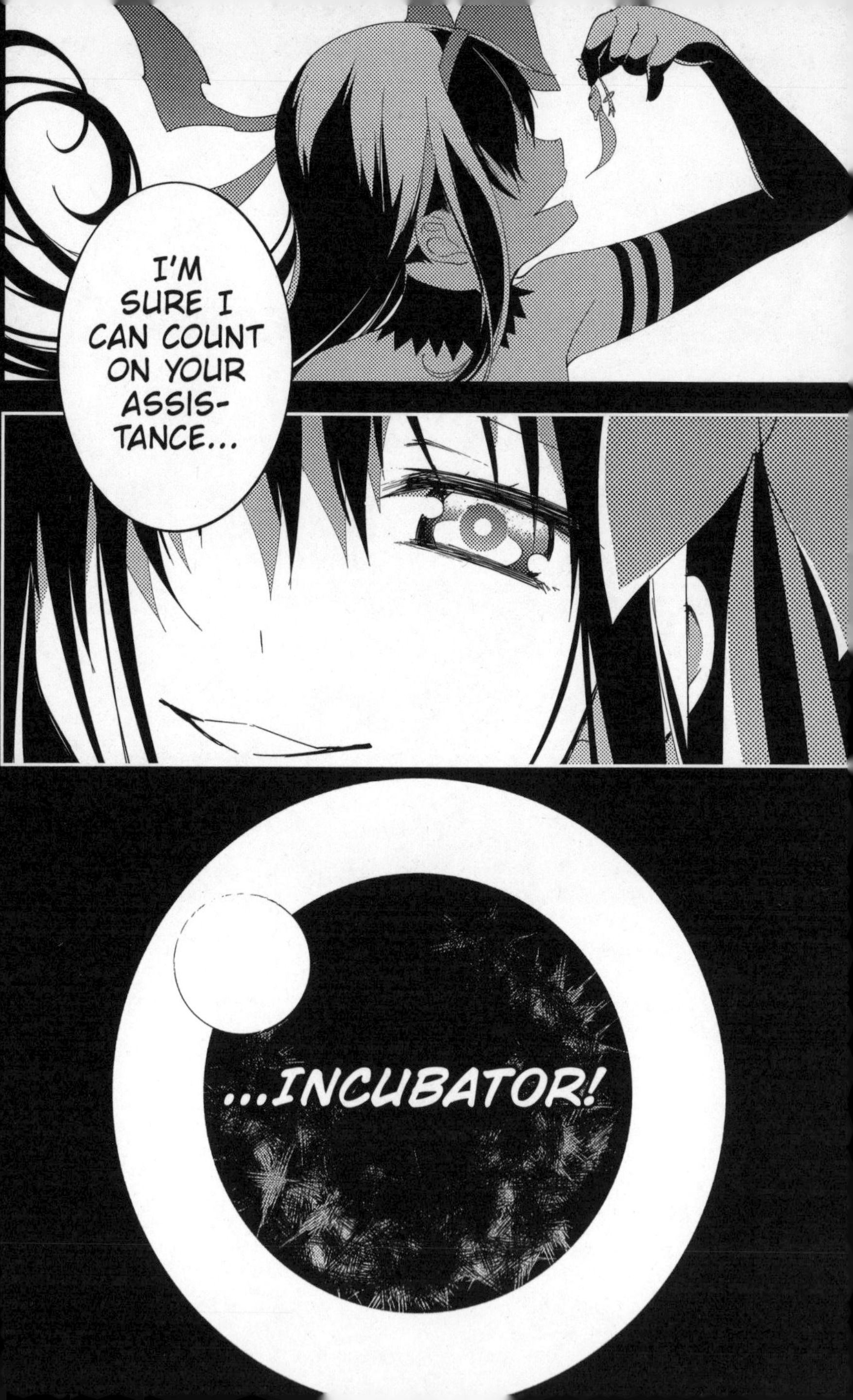
I'M SURE I CAN COUNT ON YOUR ASSIS-TANCE...
...INCUBATOR!

PUELLA MAGI
MADOKA★MAGICA
THE MOVIE -REBELLION-

FINAL CHAPTER

PASHA

PASHA
(SPLASH)

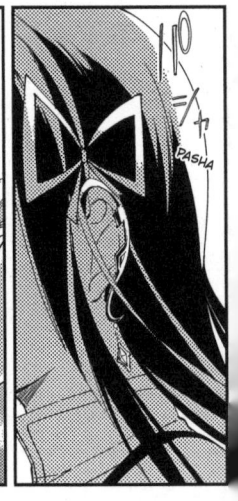

PASHA

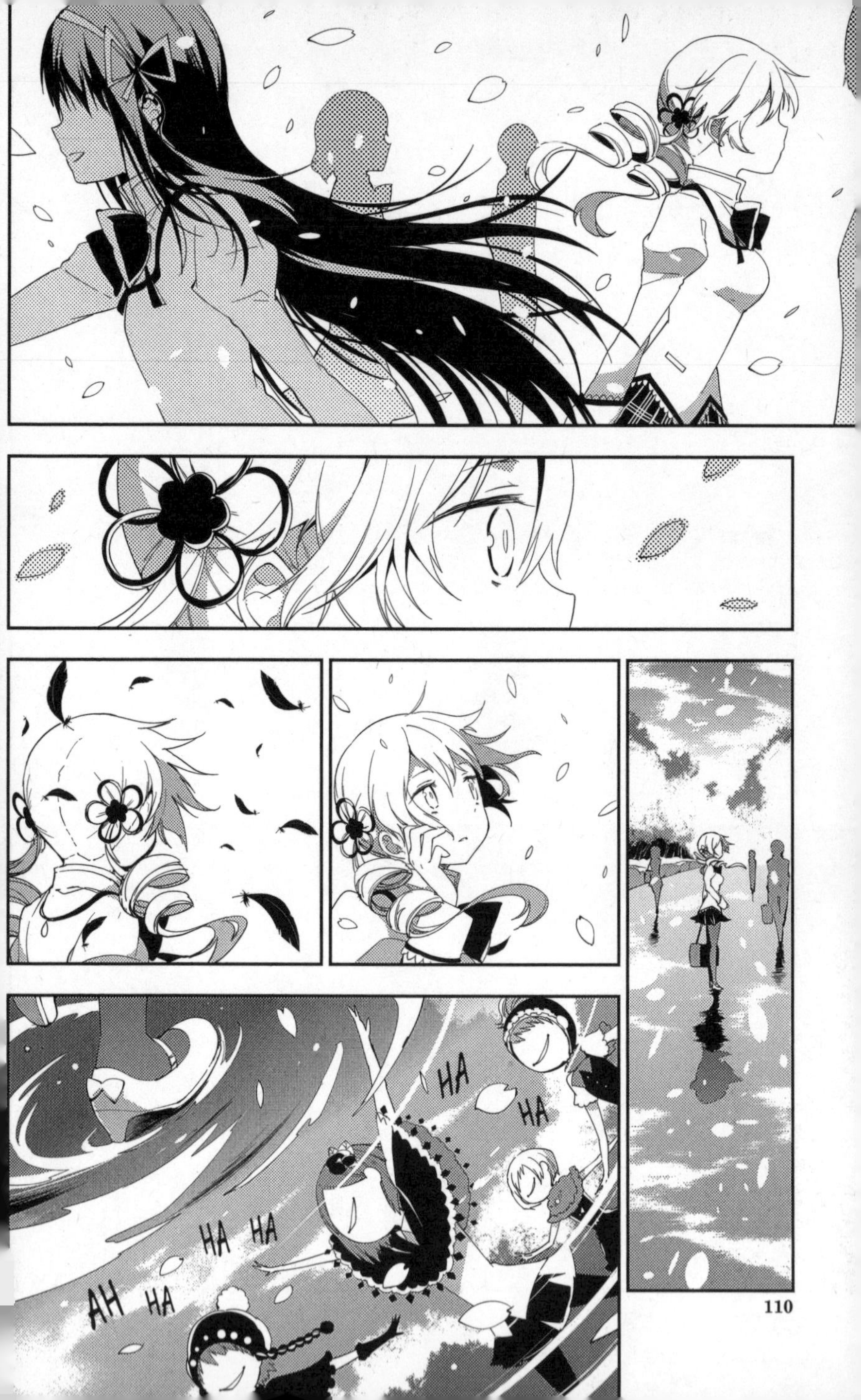
HA
HA
HA HA
AH HA

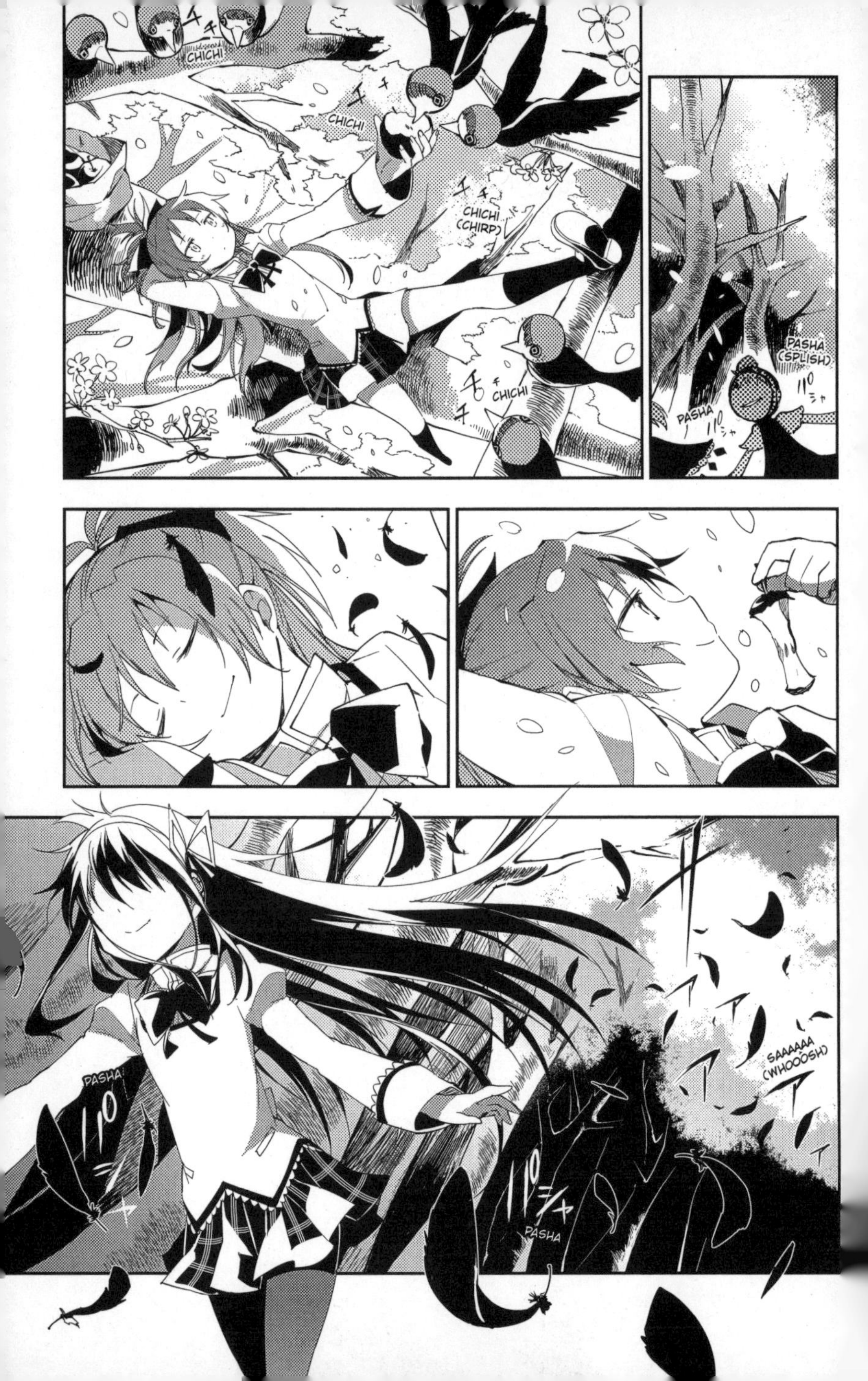
PASHA (SPLISH)
PASHA
CHICHI
CHICHI
CHICHI (CHIRP)
CHICHI
SAAAAAA (WHOOOSH)
PASHA
PASHA

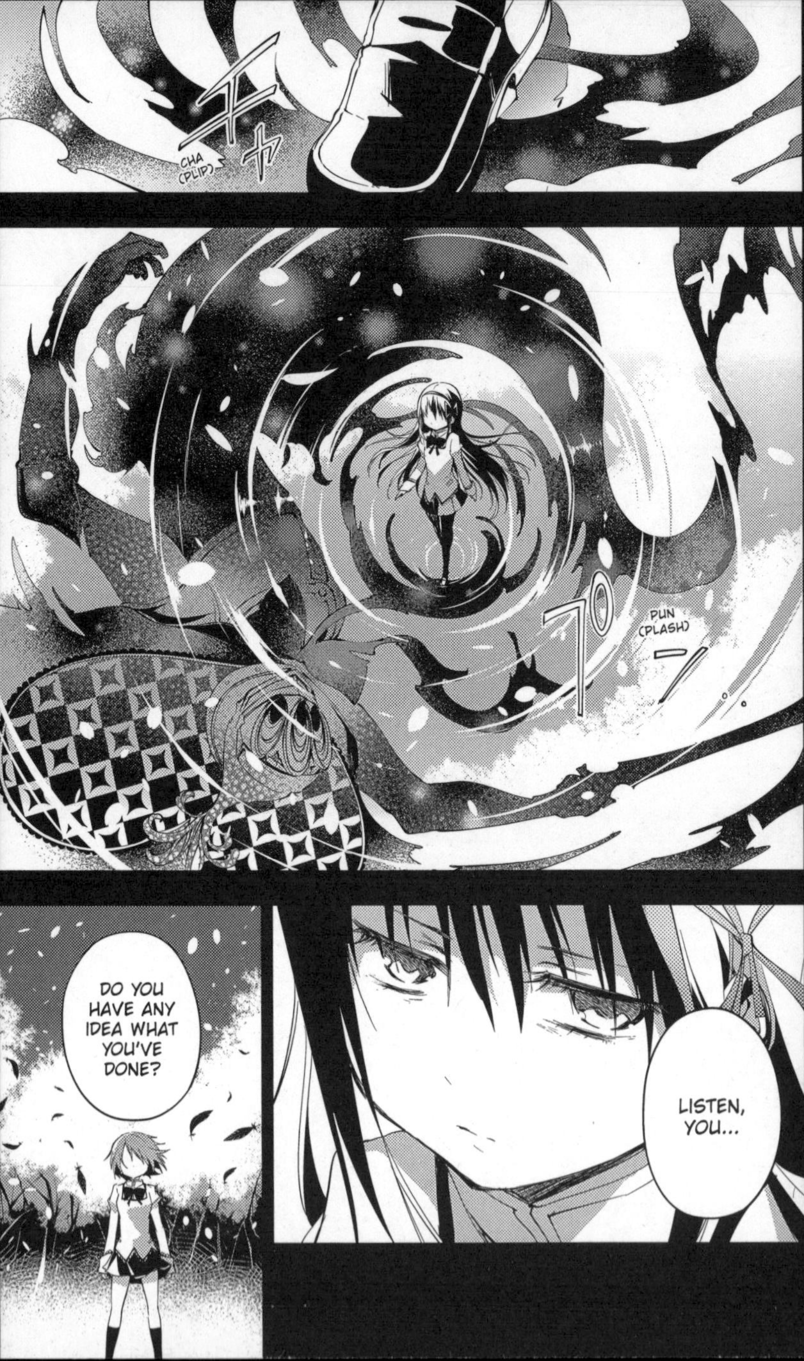
CHA (PLIP)
PUN (PLASH)
LISTEN, YOU...
DO YOU HAVE ANY IDEA WHAT YOU'VE DONE?

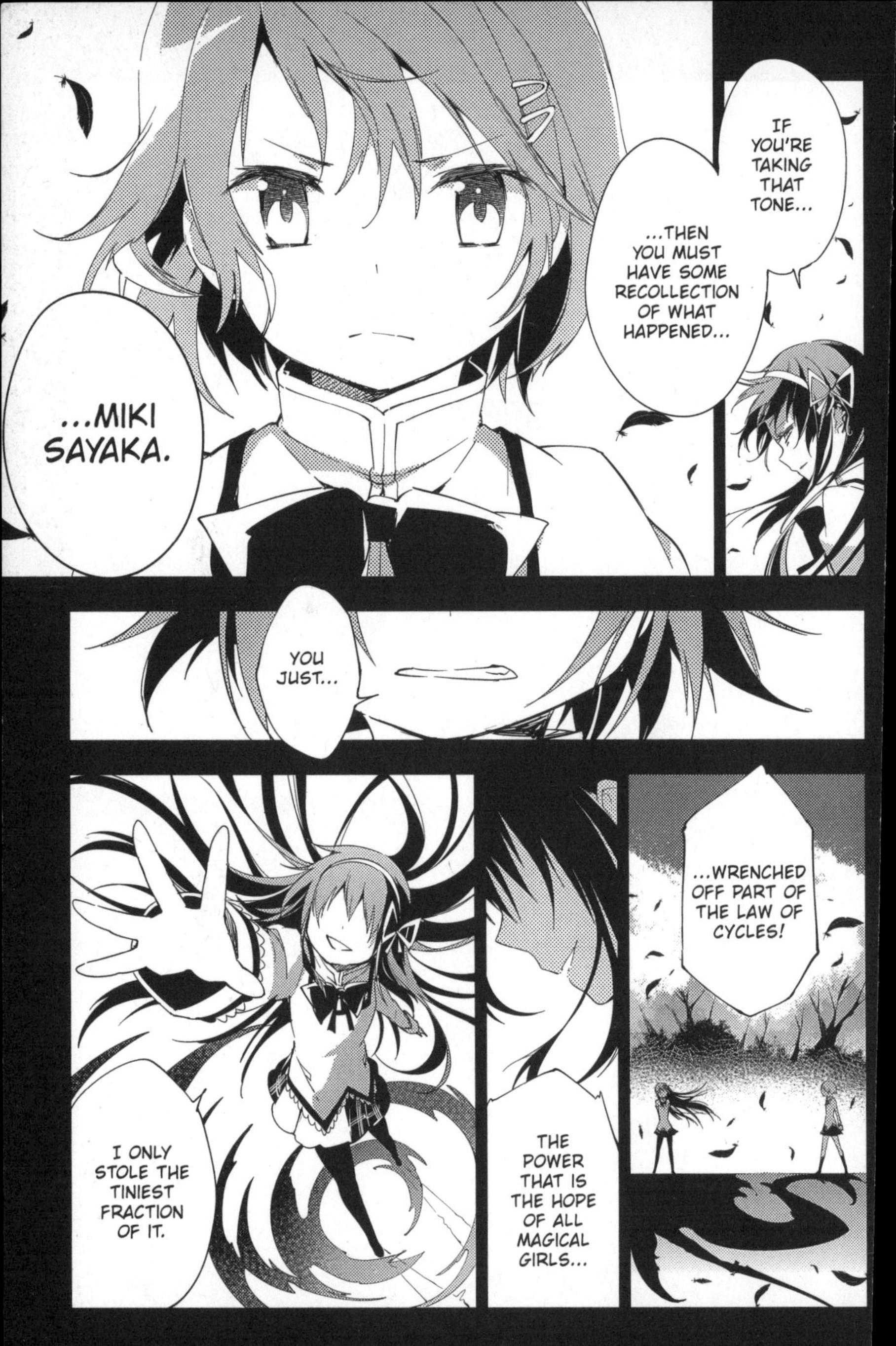
IF YOU'RE TAKING THAT TONE...
...THEN YOU MUST HAVE SOME RECOLLECTION OF WHAT HAPPENED...
...MIKI SAYAKA.
YOU JUST...
...WRENCHED OFF PART OF THE LAW OF CYCLES!
THE POWER THAT IS THE HOPE OF ALL MAGICAL GIRLS...
I ONLY STOLE THE TINIEST FRACTION OF IT.

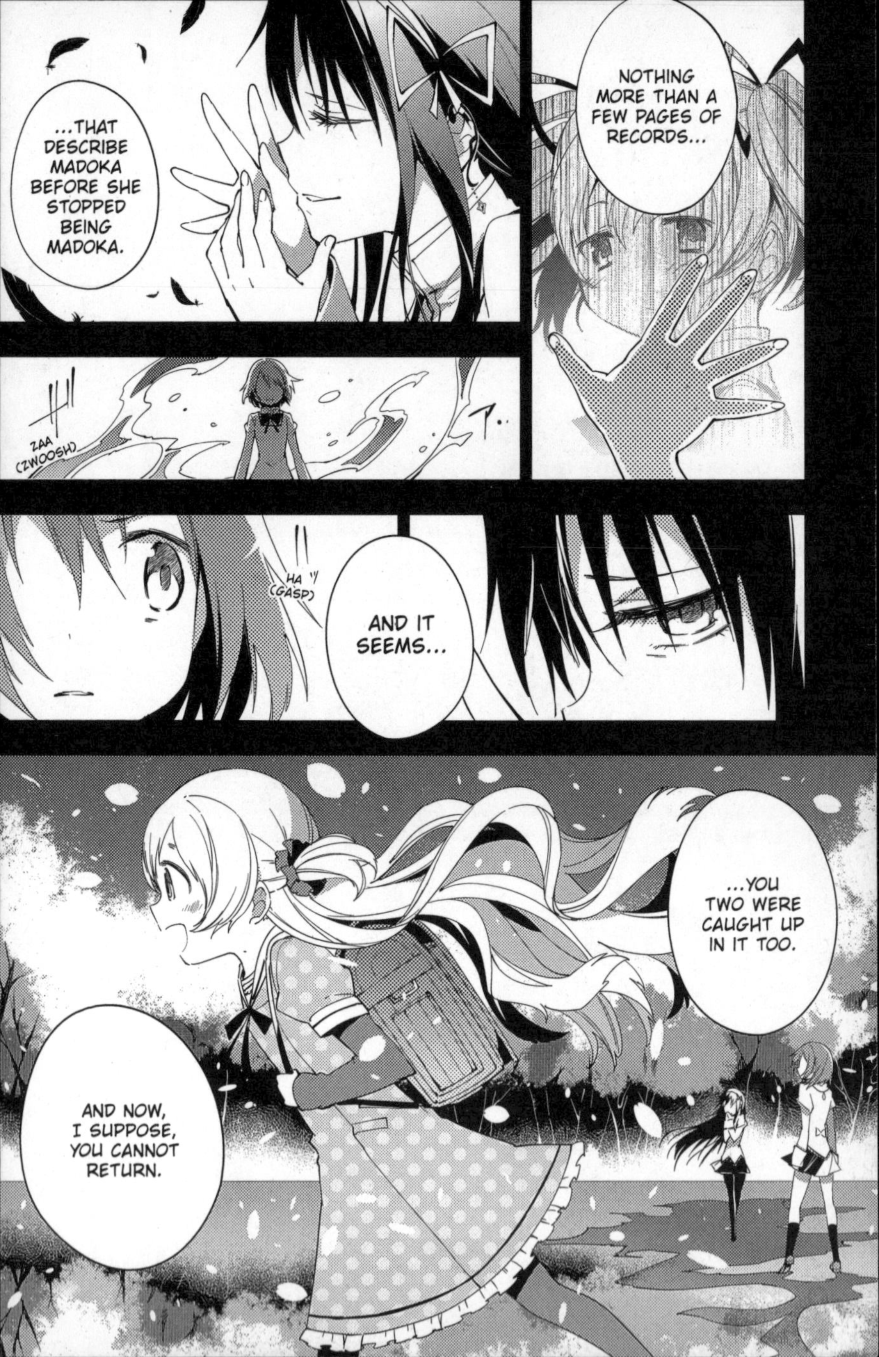
NOTHING MORE THAN A FEW PAGES OF RECORDS...
...THAT DESCRIBE MADOKA BEFORE SHE STOPPED BEING MADOKA.
ZAA (ZWOOSH)
AND IT SEEMS...
HA (GASP)
...YOU TWO WERE CAUGHT UP IN IT TOO.
AND NOW, I SUPPOSE, YOU CANNOT RETURN.

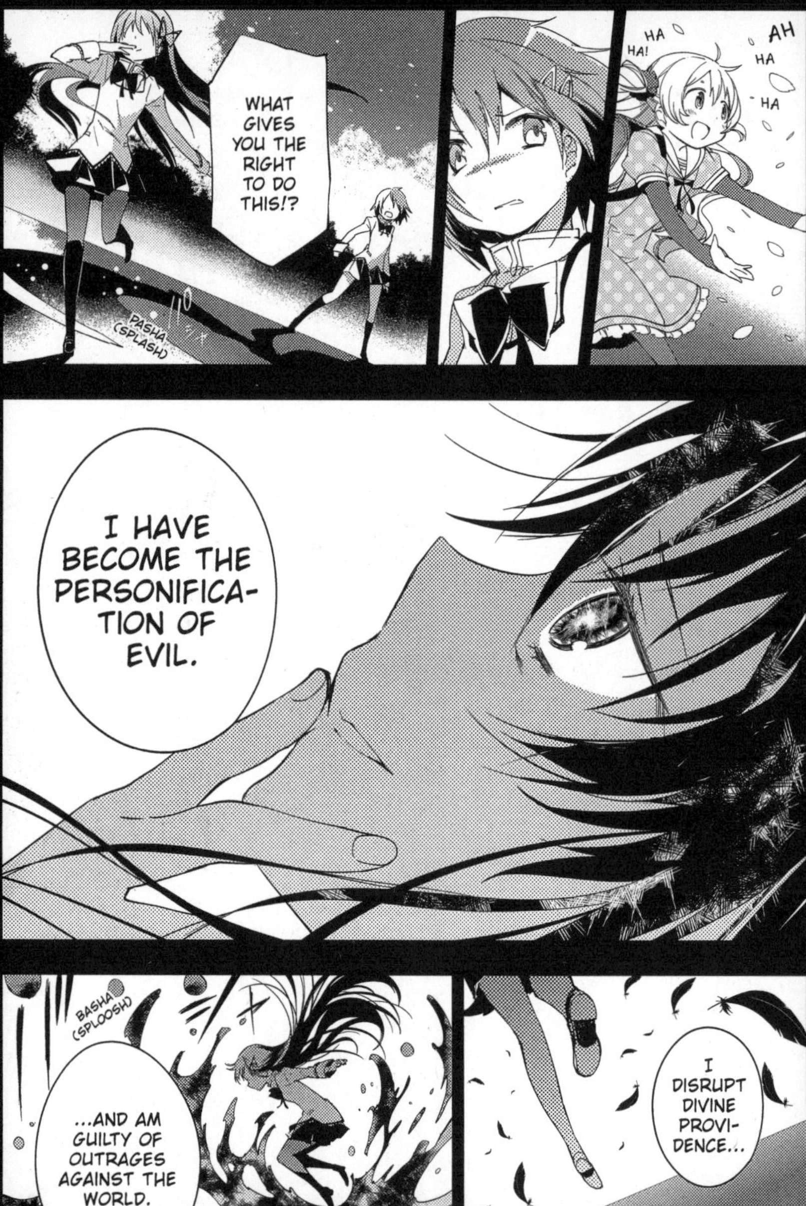
AH
HA
HA
HA
HA!
WHAT GIVES YOU THE RIGHT TO DO THIS!?
PASHA (SPLASH)
I HAVE BECOME THE PERSONIFICATION OF EVIL.
I DISRUPT DIVINE PROVIDENCE...
BASHA (SPLOOSH)
...AND AM GUILTY OF OUTRAGES AGAINST THE WORLD.

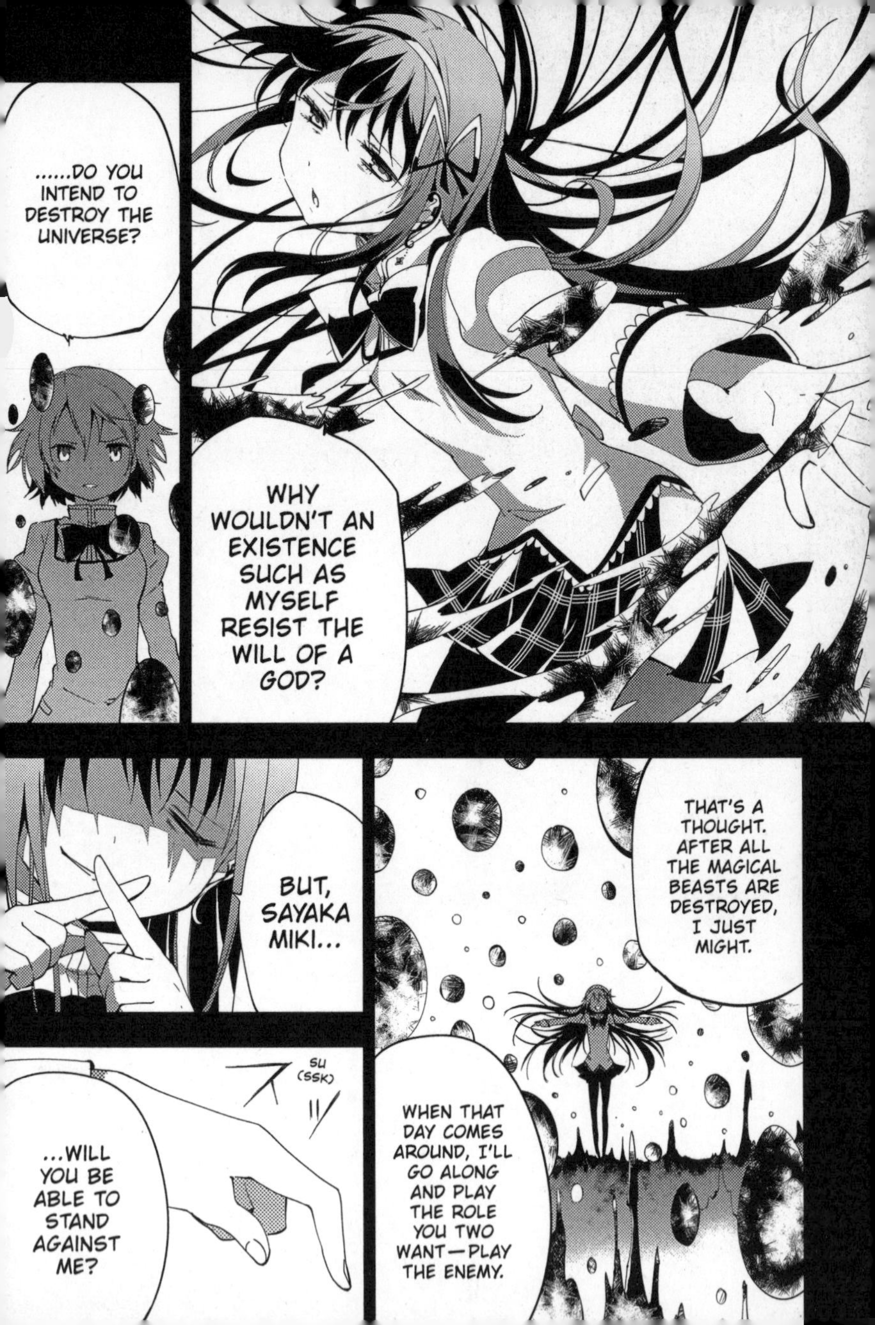
WHY WOULDN'T AN EXISTENCE SUCH AS MYSELF RESIST THE WILL OF A GOD?
......DO YOU INTEND TO DESTROY THE UNIVERSE?
THAT'S A THOUGHT. AFTER ALL THE MAGICAL BEASTS ARE DESTROYED, I JUST MIGHT.
WHEN THAT DAY COMES AROUND, I'LL GO ALONG AND PLAY THE ROLE YOU TWO WANT—PLAY THE ENEMY.
BUT, SAYAKA MIKI...
SU (SSK)
...WILL YOU BE ABLE TO STAND AGAINST ME?

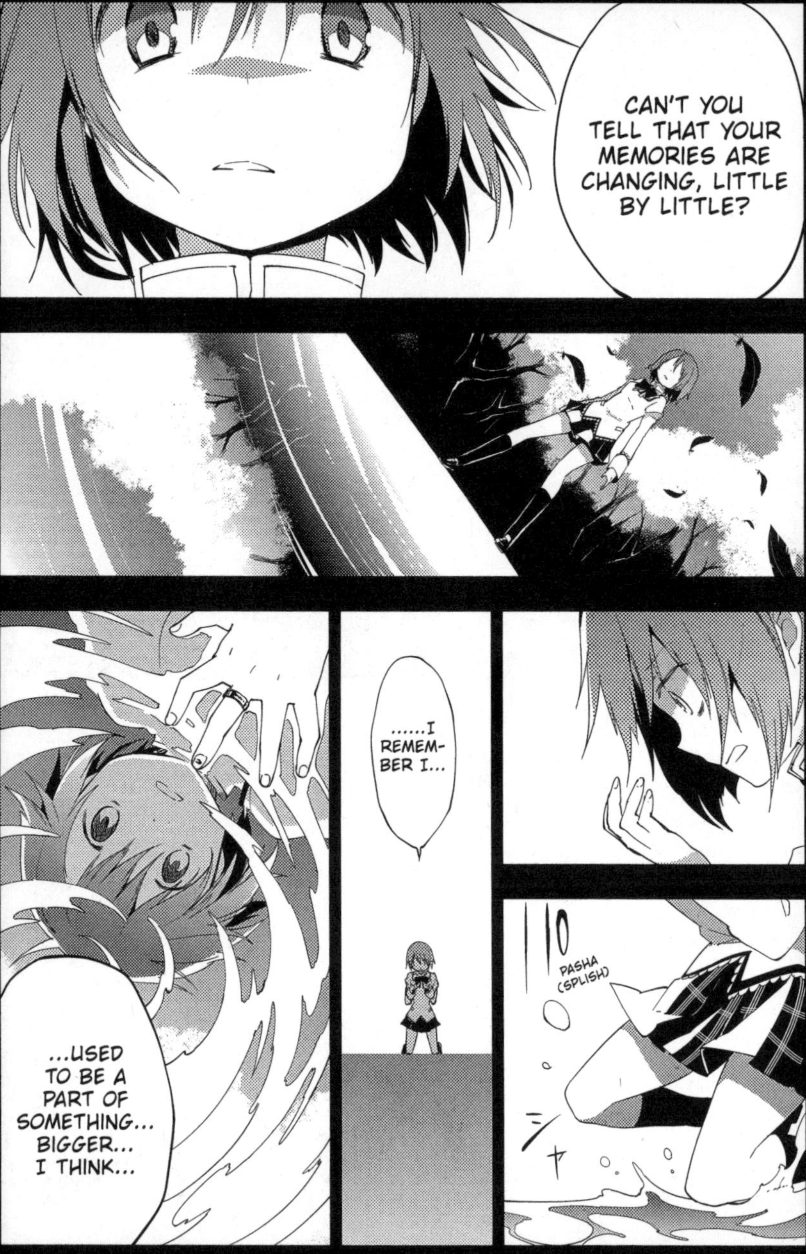
CAN'T YOU TELL THAT YOUR MEMORIES ARE CHANGING, LITTLE BY LITTLE?
PASHA (SPLISH)
......I REMEMBER I...
...USED TO BE A PART OF SOMETHING... BIGGER... I THINK...

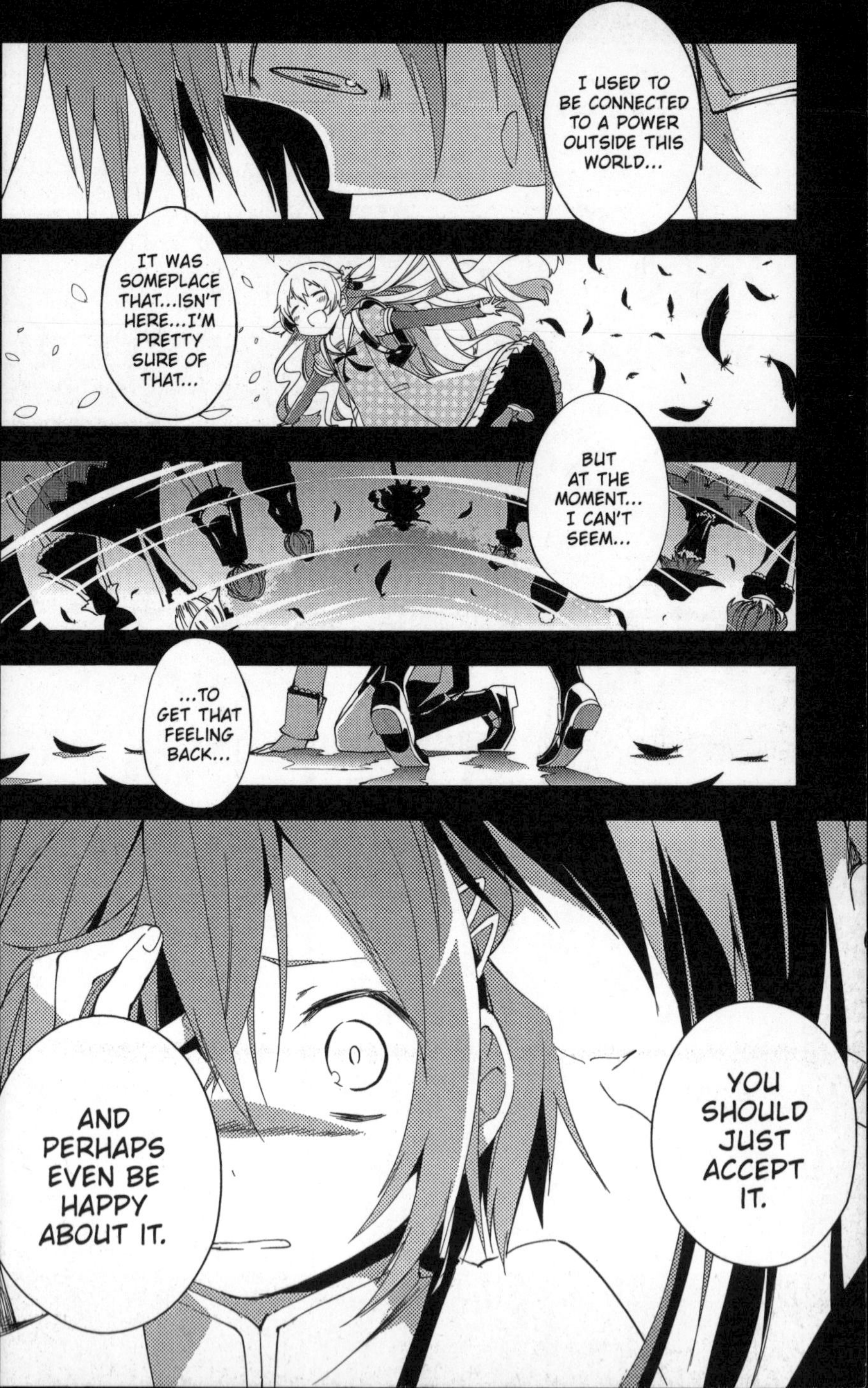
I USED TO BE CONNECTED TO A POWER OUTSIDE THIS WORLD...
IT WAS SOMEPLACE THAT...ISN'T HERE...I'M PRETTY SURE OF THAT...
BUT AT THE MOMENT... I CAN'T SEEM...
...TO GET THAT FEELING BACK...
YOU SHOULD JUST ACCEPT IT.
AND PERHAPS EVEN BE HAPPY ABOUT IT.

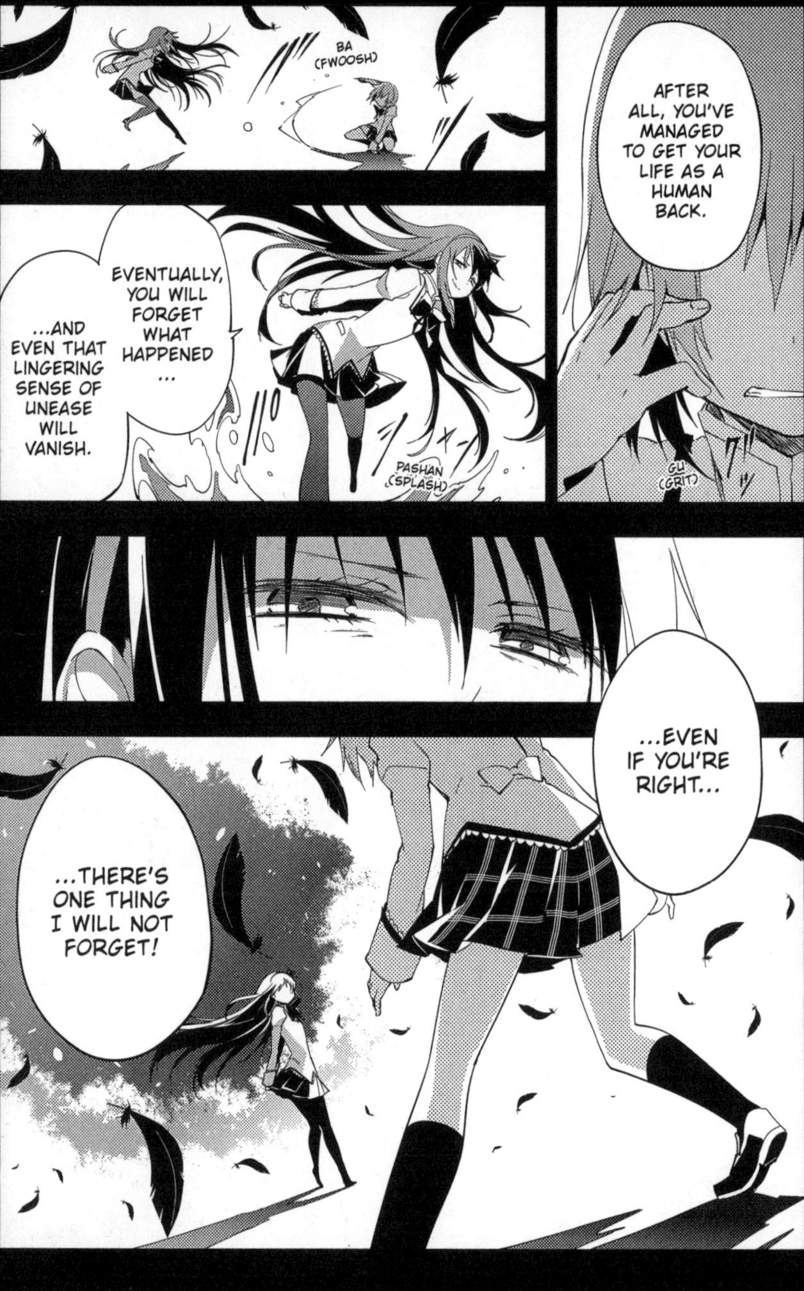
AFTER ALL, YOU'VE MANAGED TO GET YOUR LIFE AS A HUMAN BACK.
GU (GRIT)
BA (FWOOSH)
EVENTUALLY, YOU WILL FORGET WHAT HAPPENED ...
...AND EVEN THAT LINGERING SENSE OF UNEASE WILL VANISH.
PASHAN (SPLASH)
...EVEN IF YOU'RE RIGHT...
...THERE'S ONE THING I WILL NOT FORGET!

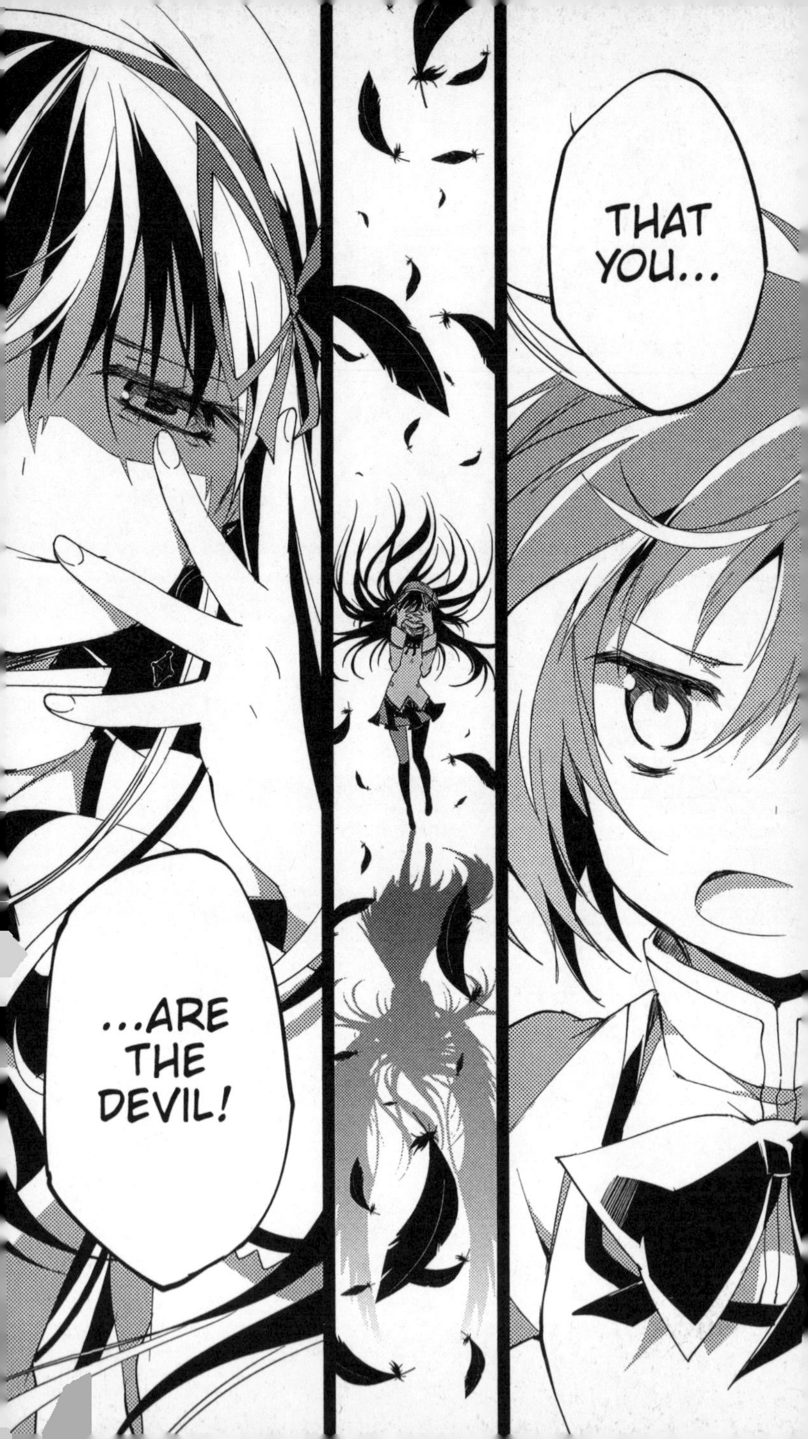
THAT YOU...
...ARE THE DEVIL!

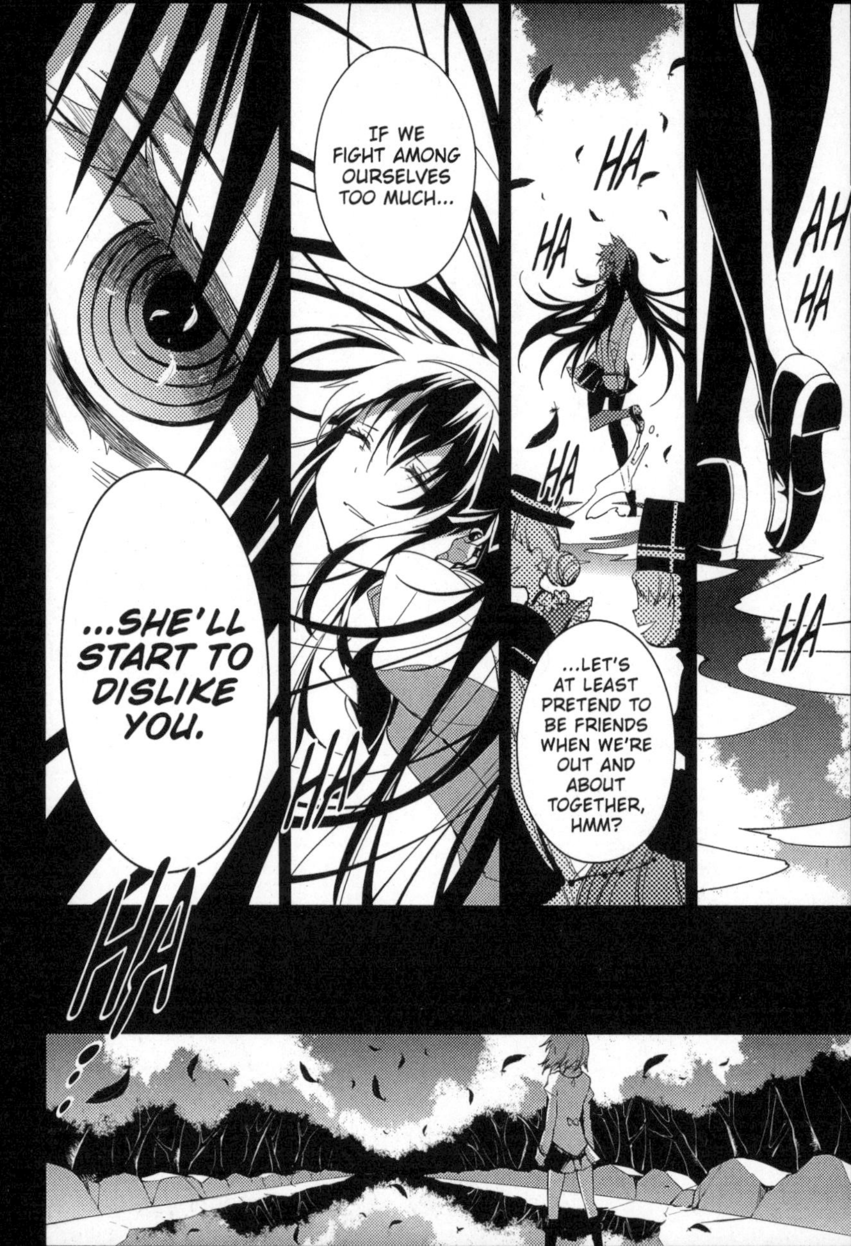
AH HA HA
HA
HA
HA
HA
...LET'S AT LEAST PRETEND TO BE FRIENDS WHEN WE'RE OUT AND ABOUT TOGETHER, HMM?
IF WE FIGHT AMONG OURSELVES TOO MUCH...
HA
...SHE'LL START TO DISLIKE YOU.
HA
...

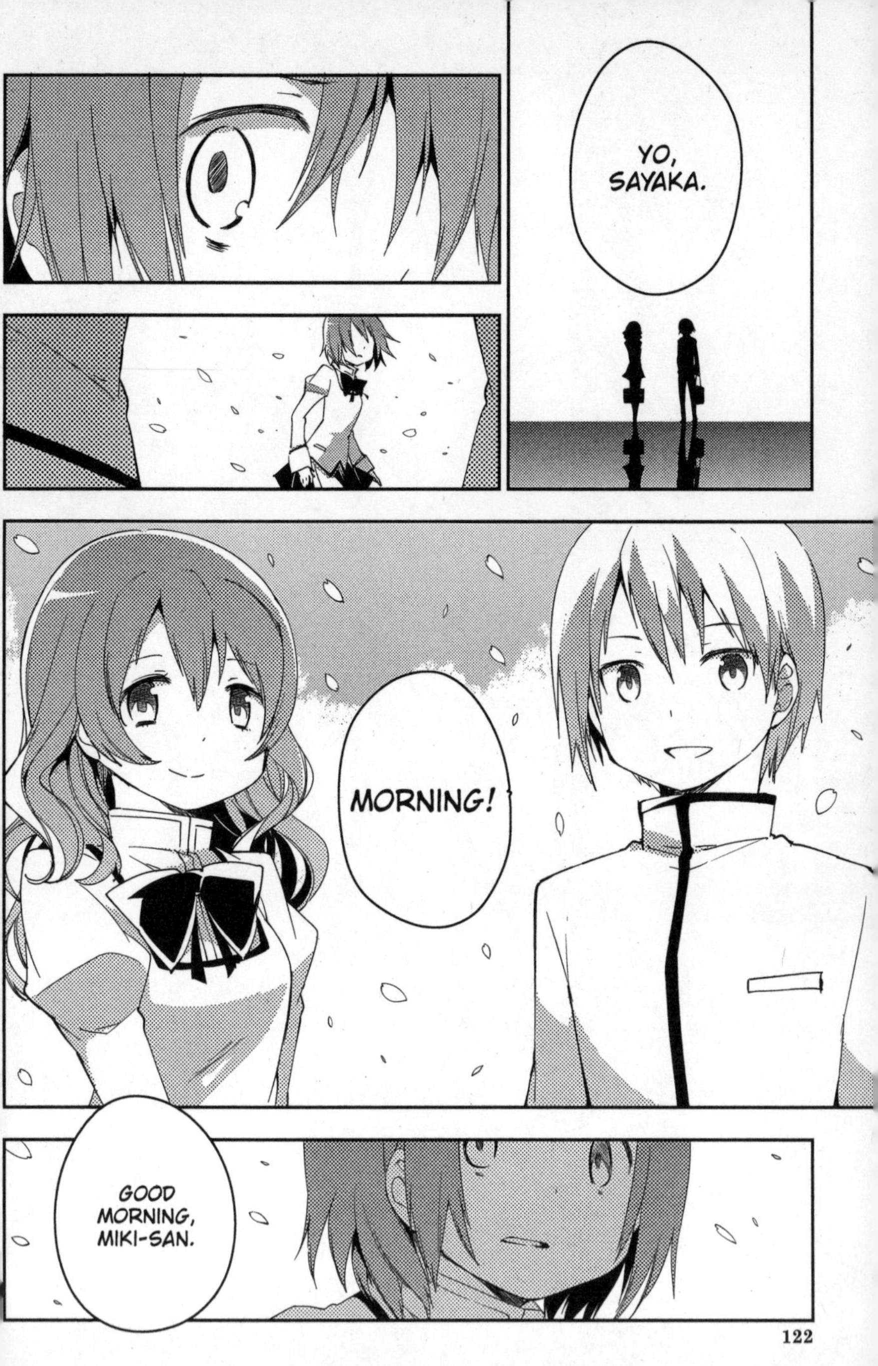
YO, SAYAKA.
MORNING!
GOOD MORNING, MIKI-SAN.

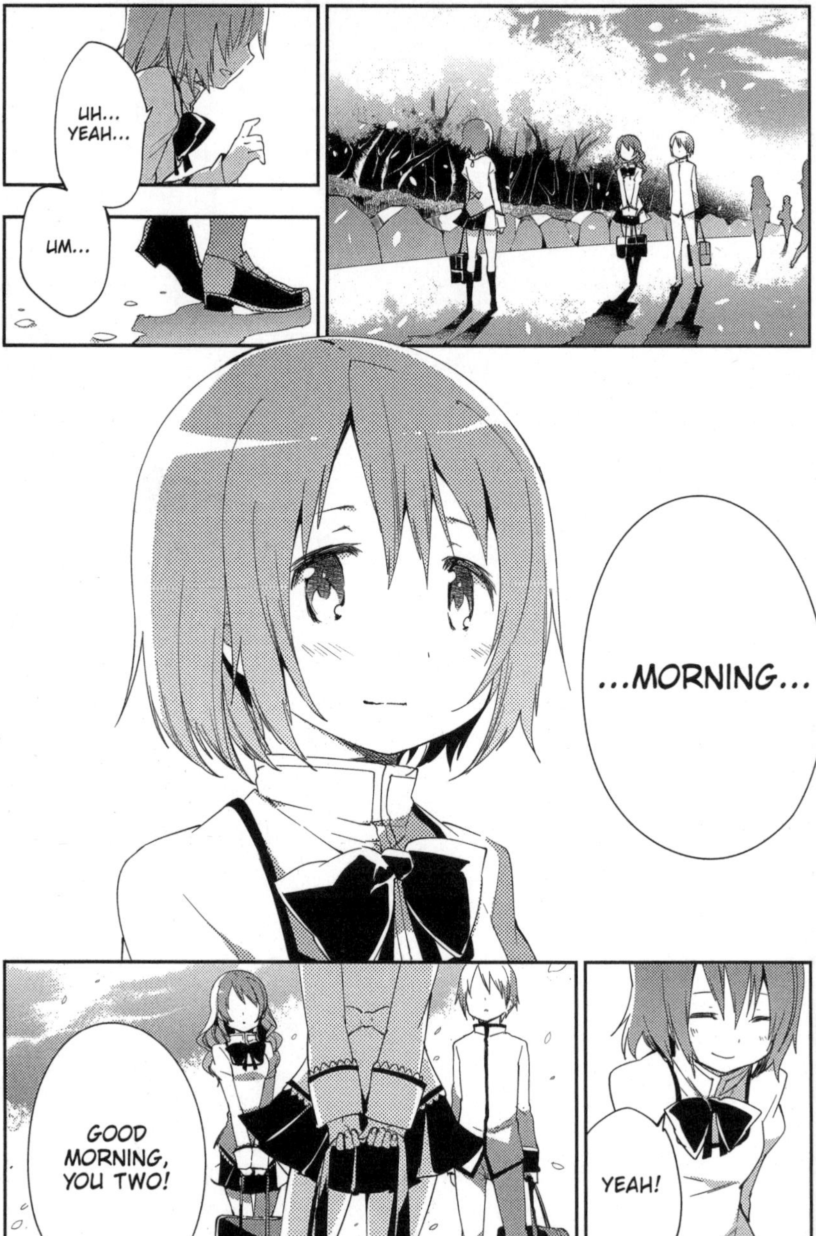
UH... YEAH...
UM...
...MORNING...
YEAH!
GOOD MORNING, YOU TWO!

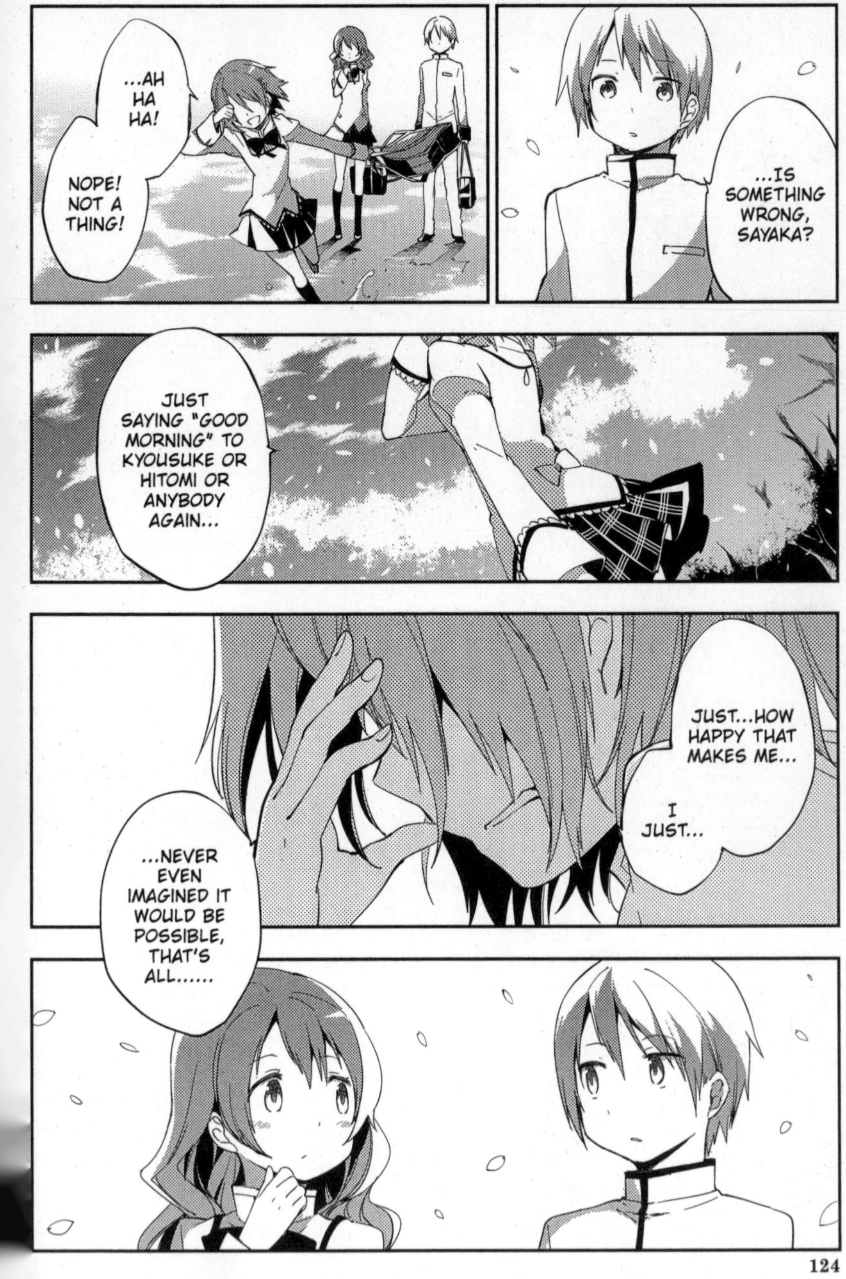
...IS SOMETHING WRONG, SAYAKA?
...AH HA HA!
NOPE! NOT A THING!
JUST SAYING "GOOD MORNING" TO KYOUSUKE OR HITOMI OR ANYBODY AGAIN...
JUST...HOW HAPPY THAT MAKES ME...
I JUST...
...NEVER EVEN IMAGINED IT WOULD BE POSSIBLE, THAT'S ALL......

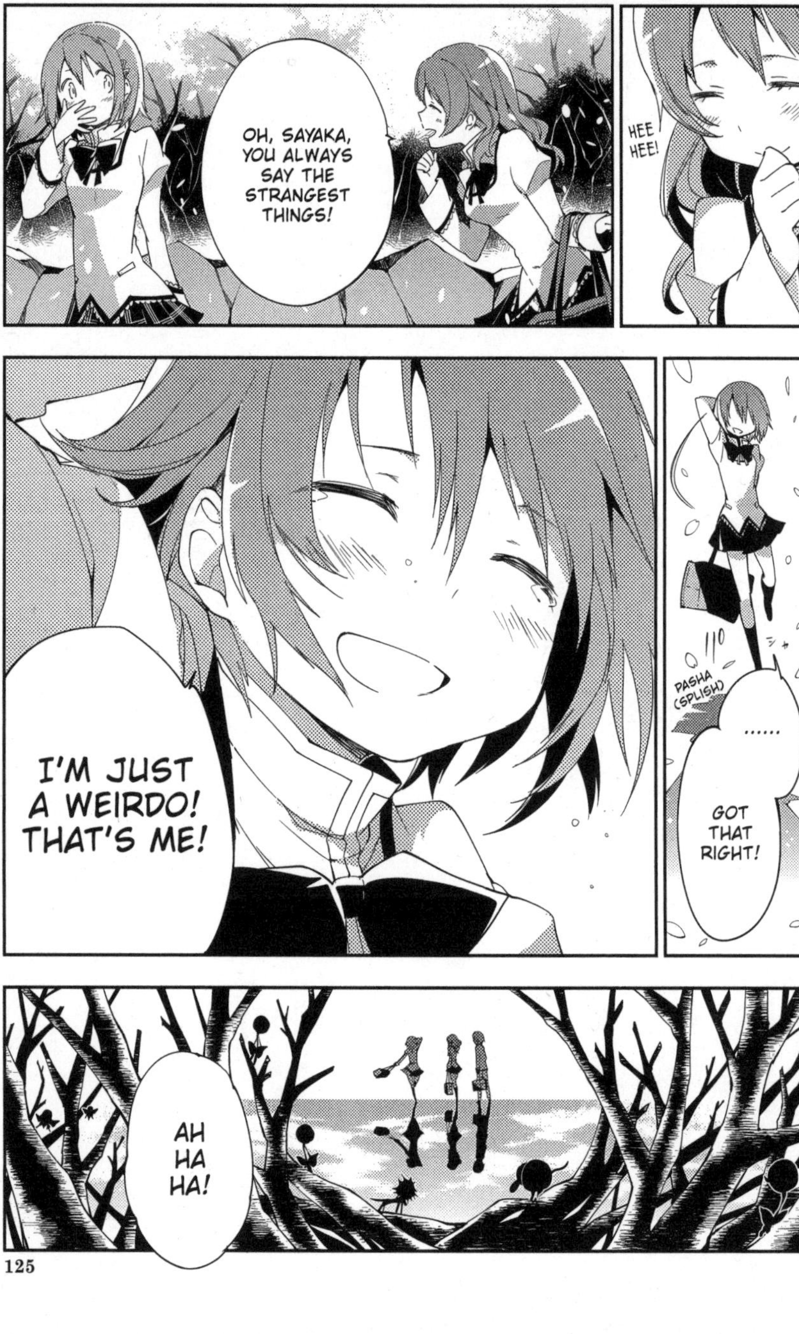
HEE HEE!
OH, SAYAKA, YOU ALWAYS SAY THE STRANGEST THINGS!
......
GOT THAT RIGHT!
PASHA (SPLISH)
シャ
I'M JUST A WEIRDO! THAT'S ME!
AH HA HA!

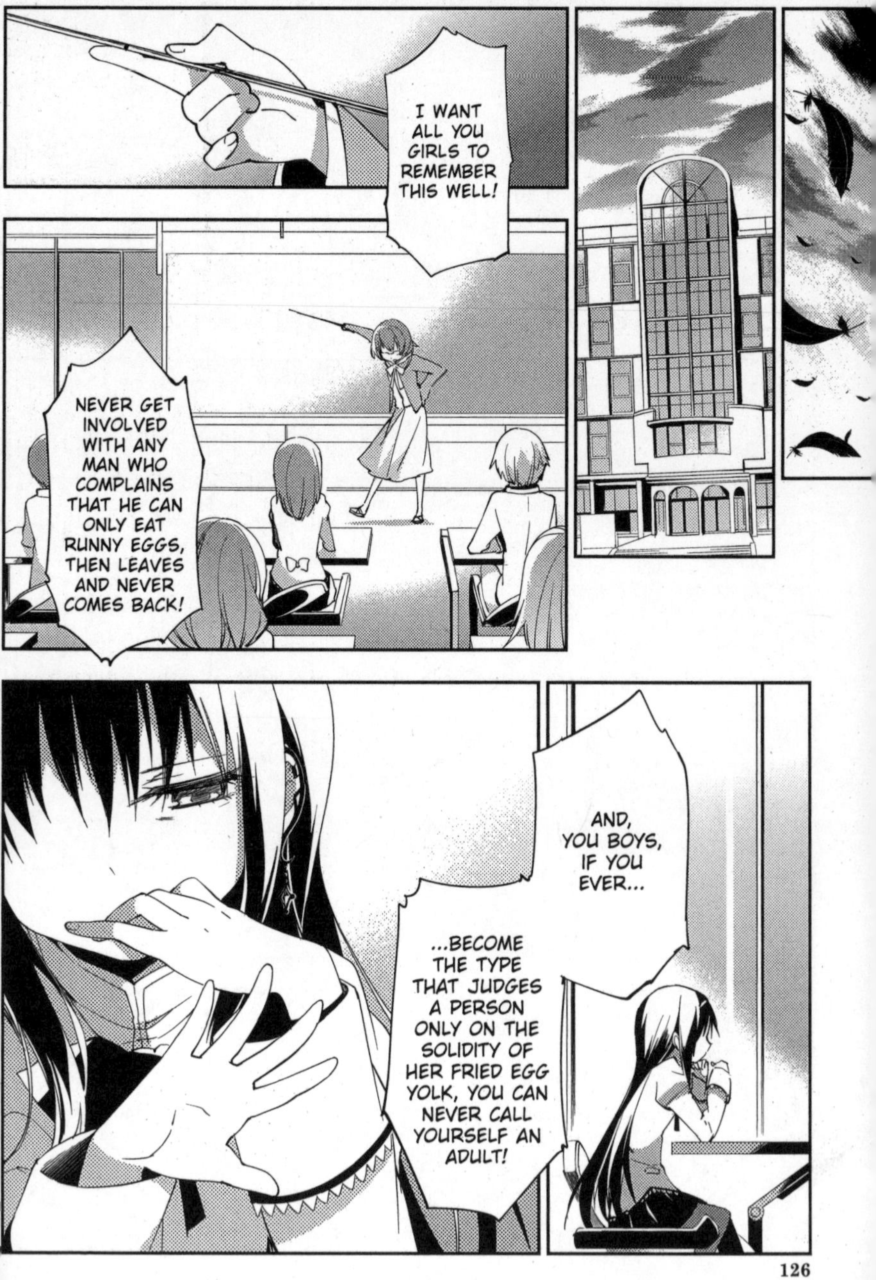
I WANT ALL YOU GIRLS TO REMEMBER THIS WELL!
NEVER GET INVOLVED WITH ANY MAN WHO COMPLAINS THAT HE CAN ONLY EAT RUNNY EGGS, THEN LEAVES AND NEVER COMES BACK!
AND, YOU BOYS, IF YOU EVER...
...BECOME THE TYPE THAT JUDGES A PERSON ONLY ON THE SOLIDITY OF HER FRIED EGG YOLK, YOU CAN NEVER CALL YOURSELF AN ADULT!

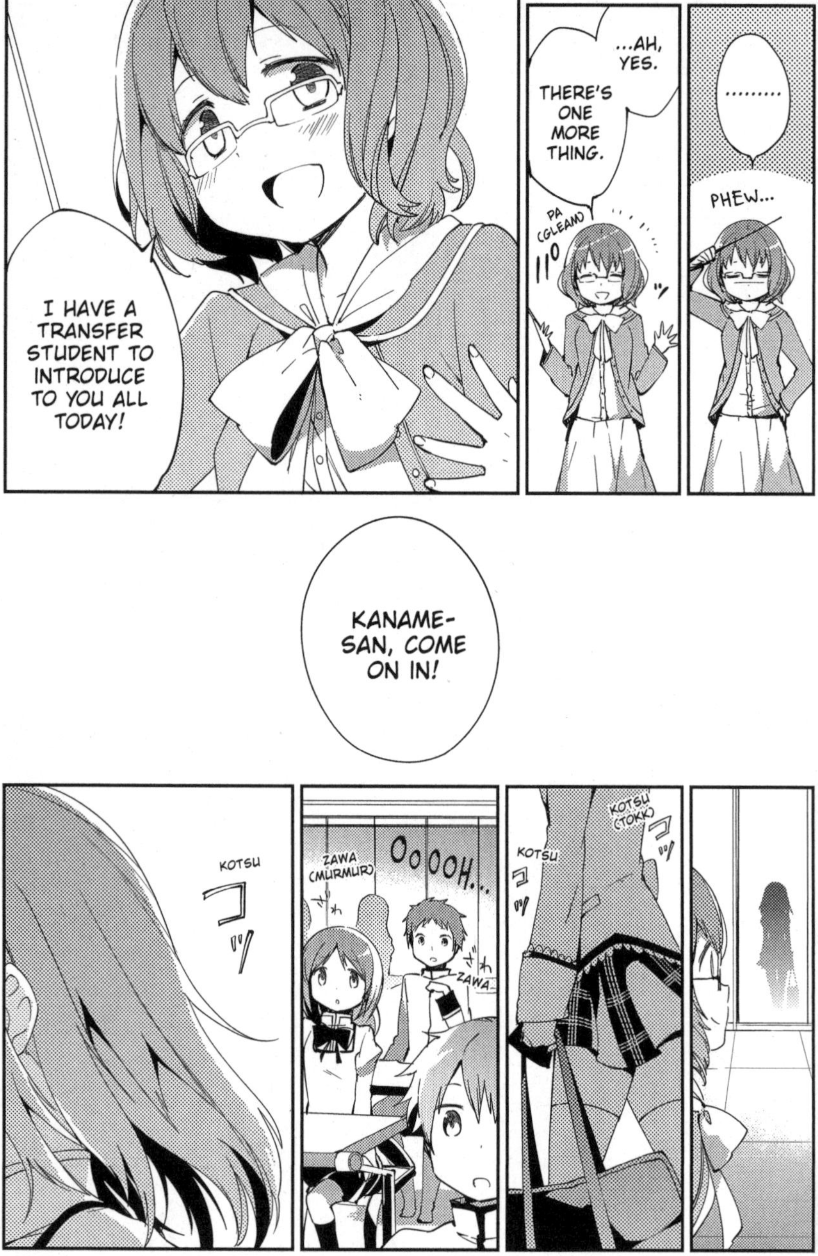
....
PHEW...
...AH, YES.
THERE'S ONE MORE THING.
PA (GLEAM)
I HAVE A TRANSFER STUDENT TO INTRODUCE TO YOU ALL TODAY!
KANAME-SAN, COME ON IN!
KOTSU (TOKK)
KOTSU
OOOOH...
ZAWA (MURMUR)
ZAWA
KOTSU

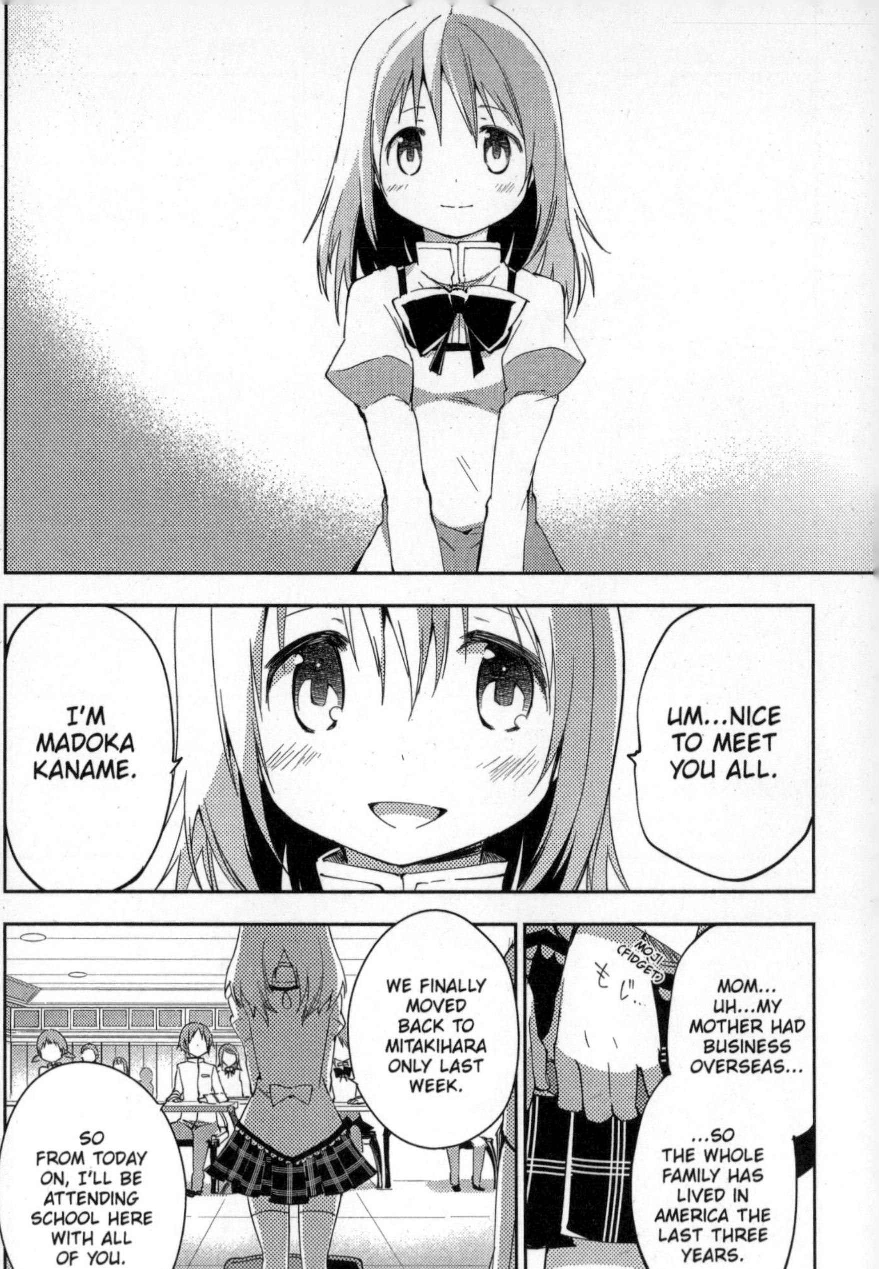
UM...NICE TO MEET YOU ALL.
I'M MADOKA KANAME.
MOJI (FIDGET)
MOM... UH...MY MOTHER HAD BUSINESS OVERSEAS...
...SO THE WHOLE FAMILY HAS LIVED IN AMERICA THE LAST THREE YEARS.
WE FINALLY MOVED BACK TO MITAKIHARA ONLY LAST WEEK.
SO FROM TODAY ON, I'LL BE ATTENDING SCHOOL HERE WITH ALL OF YOU.

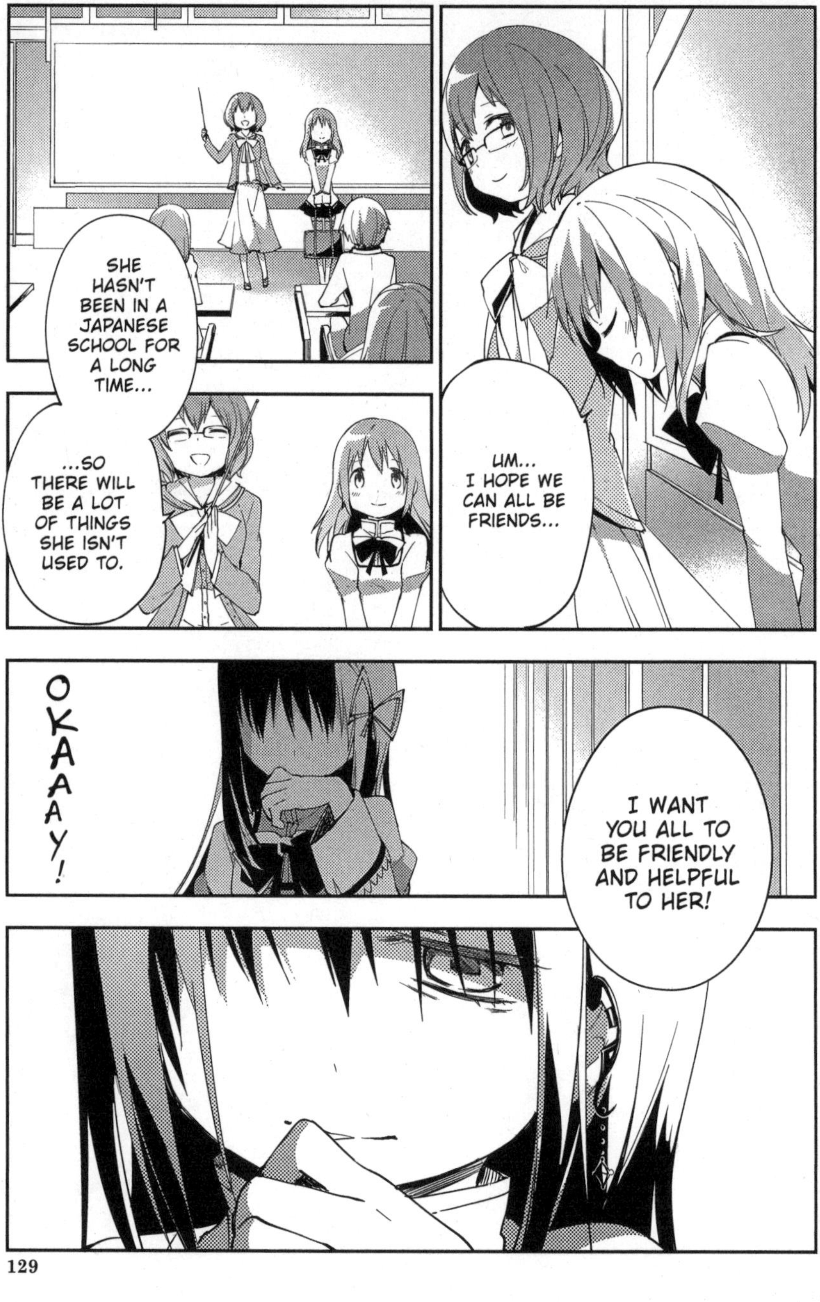
UM... I HOPE WE CAN ALL BE FRIENDS...
SHE HASN'T BEEN IN A JAPANESE SCHOOL FOR A LONG TIME...
...SO THERE WILL BE A LOT OF THINGS SHE ISN'T USED TO.
I WANT YOU ALL TO BE FRIENDLY AND HELPFUL TO HER!
OKAAAY!

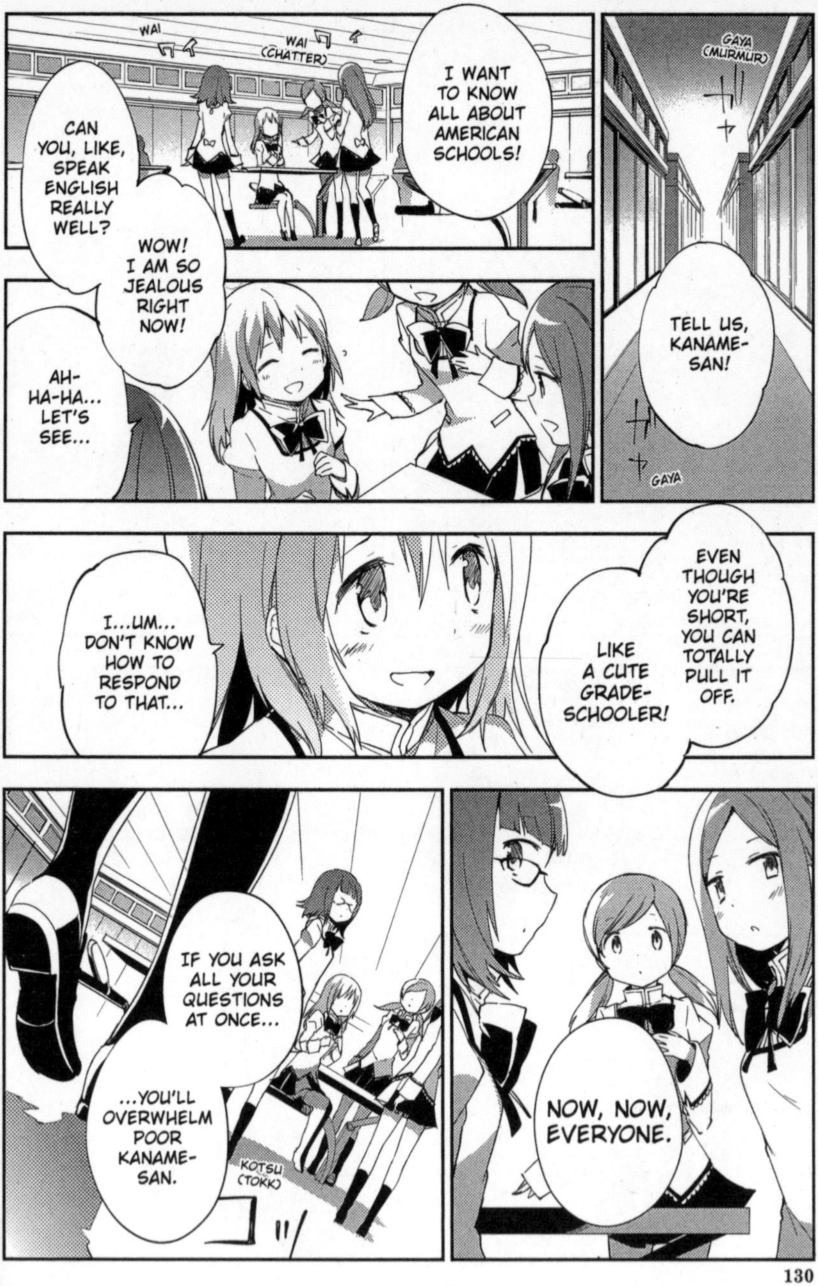
GAYA (MURMUR)
TELL US, KANAME-SAN!
GAYA
WAI
WAI (CHATTER)
I WANT TO KNOW ALL ABOUT AMERICAN SCHOOLS!
CAN YOU, LIKE, SPEAK ENGLISH REALLY WELL?
WOW! I AM SO JEALOUS RIGHT NOW!
AH-HA-HA... LET'S SEE...
EVEN THOUGH YOU'RE SHORT, YOU CAN TOTALLY PULL IT OFF.
LIKE A CUTE GRADE-SCHOOLER!
I...UM... DON'T KNOW HOW TO RESPOND TO THAT...
NOW, NOW, EVERYONE.
IF YOU ASK ALL YOUR QUESTIONS AT ONCE...
...YOU'LL OVERWHELM POOR KANAME-SAN.
KOTSU (TOKK)

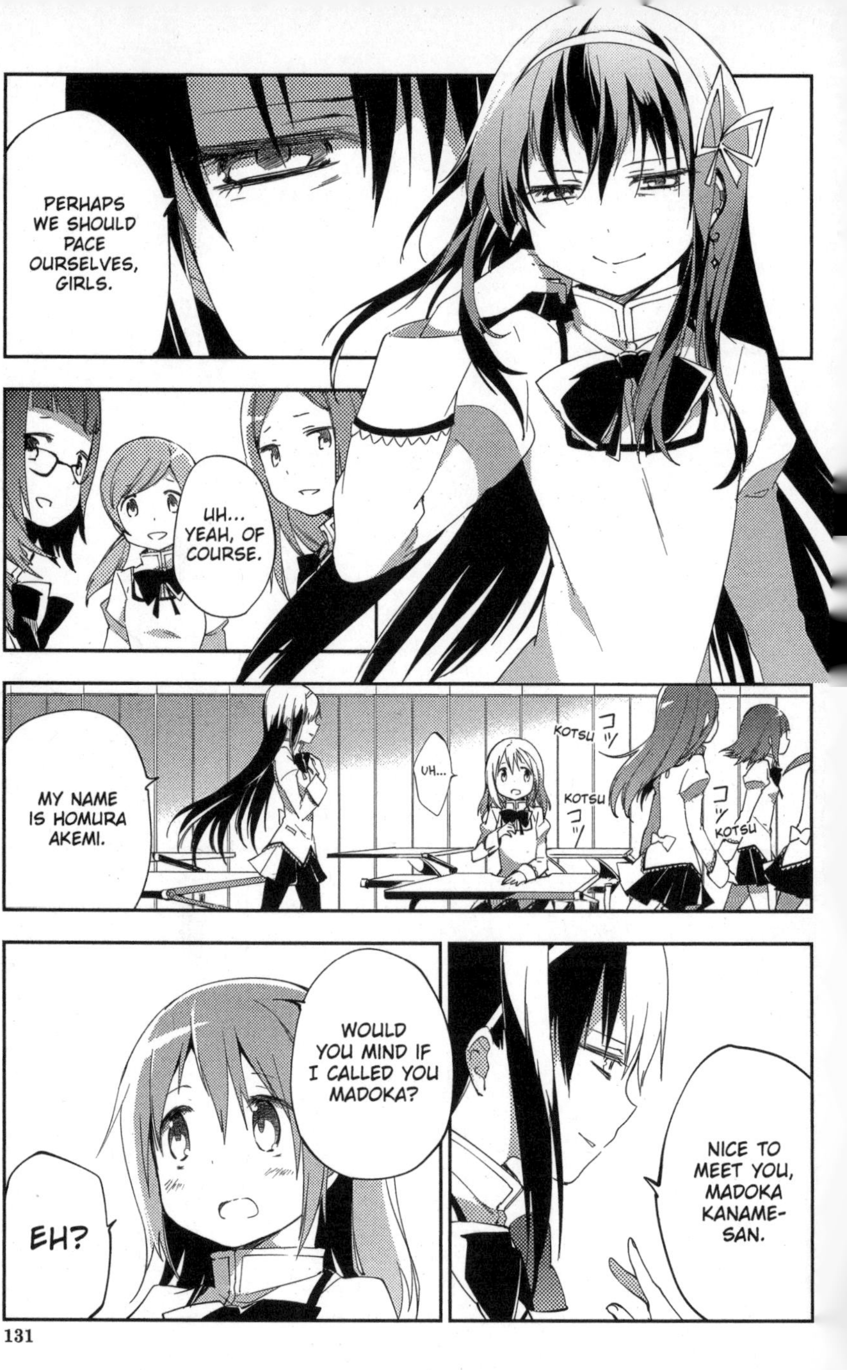
PERHAPS WE SHOULD PACE OURSELVES, GIRLS.
UH... YEAH, OF COURSE.
KOTSU
KOTSU
KOTSU
UH...
MY NAME IS HOMURA AKEMI.
NICE TO MEET YOU, MADOKA KANAME-SAN.
WOULD YOU MIND IF I CALLED YOU MADOKA?
EH?

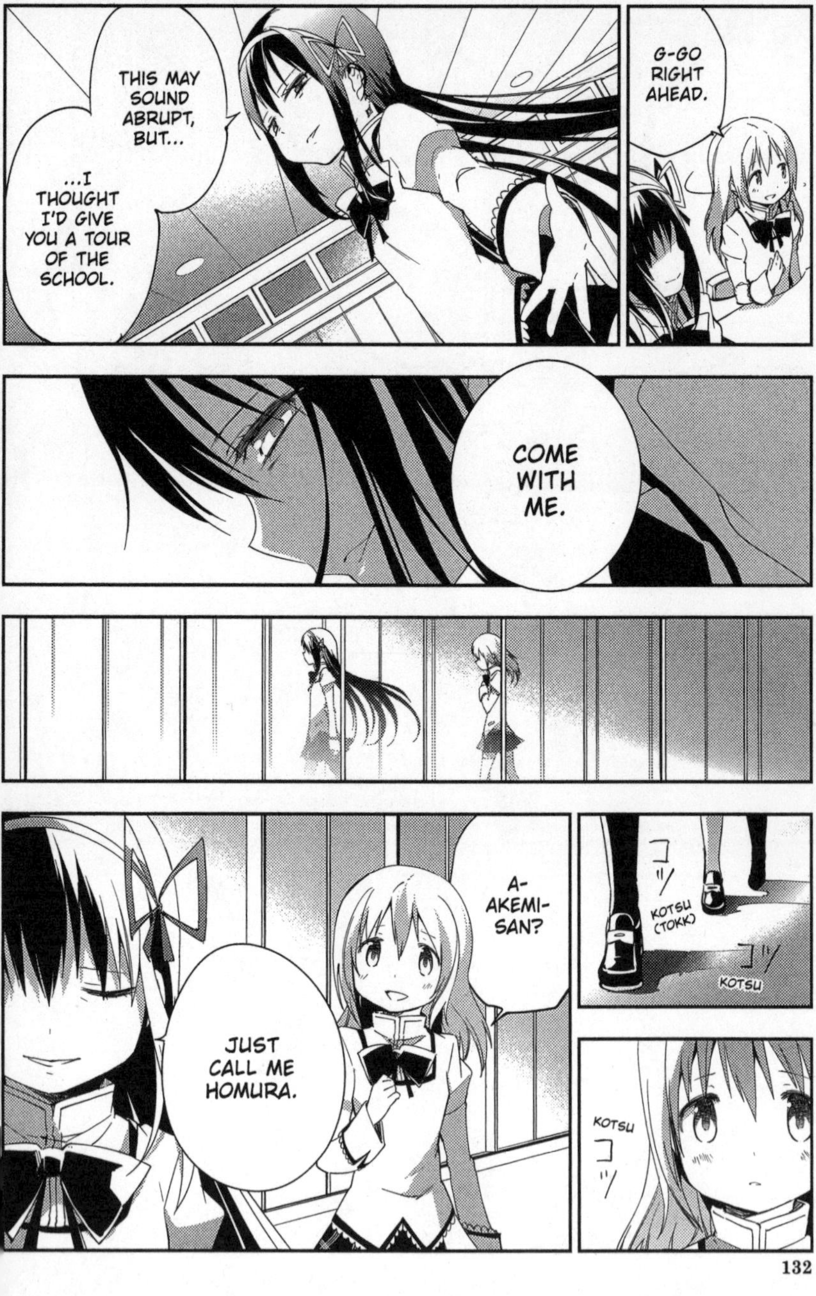
G-GO RIGHT AHEAD.
THIS MAY SOUND ABRUPT, BUT...
...I THOUGHT I'D GIVE YOU A TOUR OF THE SCHOOL.
COME WITH ME.
KOTSU (TOKK)
KOTSU
KOTSU
A-AKEMI-SAN?
JUST CALL ME HOMURA.

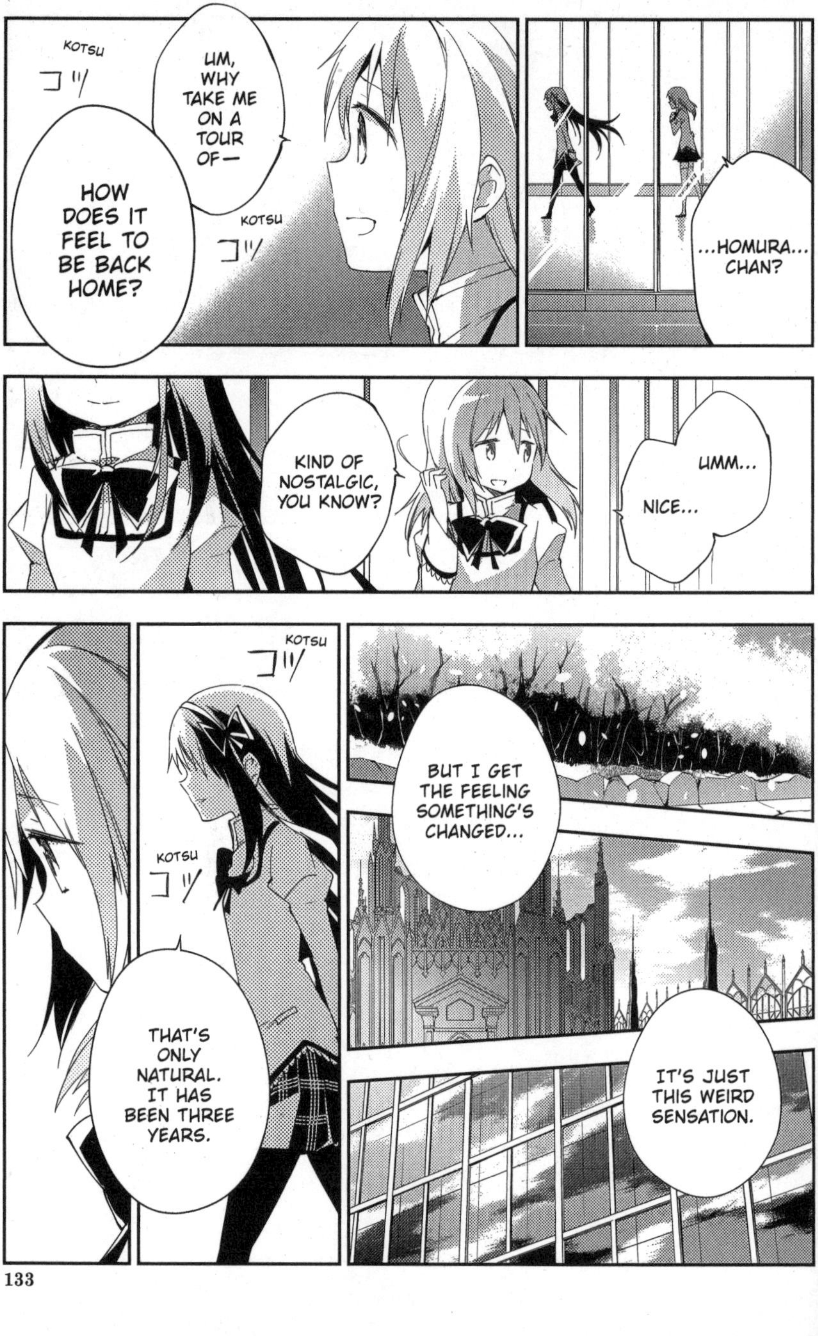
...HOMURA... CHAN?
HOW DOES IT FEEL TO BE BACK HOME?
KOTSU
コツ
UM, WHY TAKE ME ON A TOUR OF—
KOTSU
コツ
UMM... NICE...
KIND OF NOSTALGIC, YOU KNOW?
BUT I GET THE FEELING SOMETHING'S CHANGED...
IT'S JUST THIS WEIRD SENSATION.
KOTSU
コツ
KOTSU
コツ
THAT'S ONLY NATURAL. IT HAS BEEN THREE YEARS.

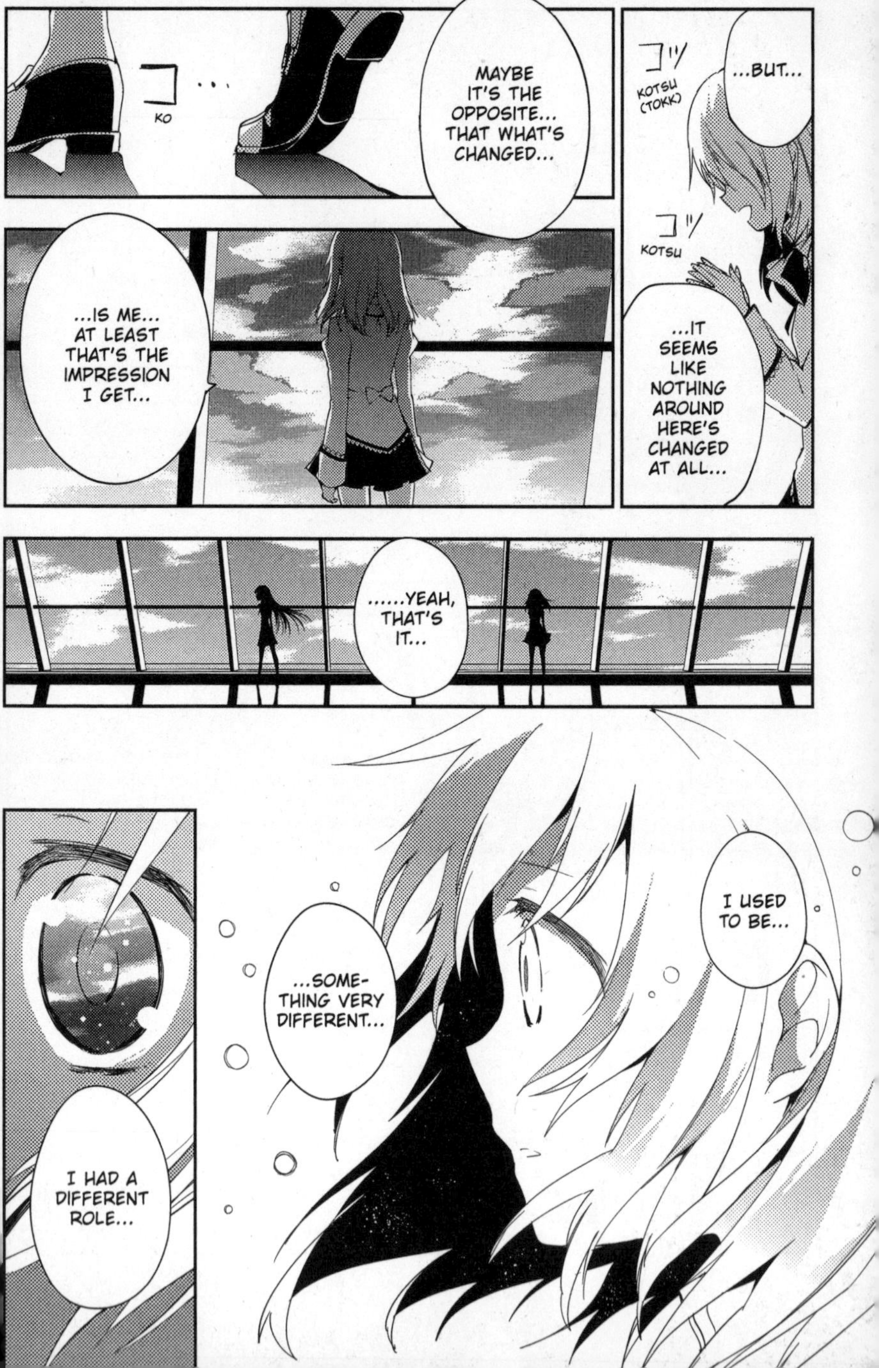
...BUT...
コツ KOTSU (TOKK)
コツ KOTSU
...IT SEEMS LIKE NOTHING AROUND HERE'S CHANGED AT ALL...
MAYBE IT'S THE OPPOSITE... THAT WHAT'S CHANGED...
コ KO ...
...IS ME... AT LEAST THAT'S THE IMPRESSION I GET...
......YEAH, THAT'S IT...
I USED TO BE...
...SOME-THING VERY DIFFERENT...
I HAD A DIFFERENT ROLE...

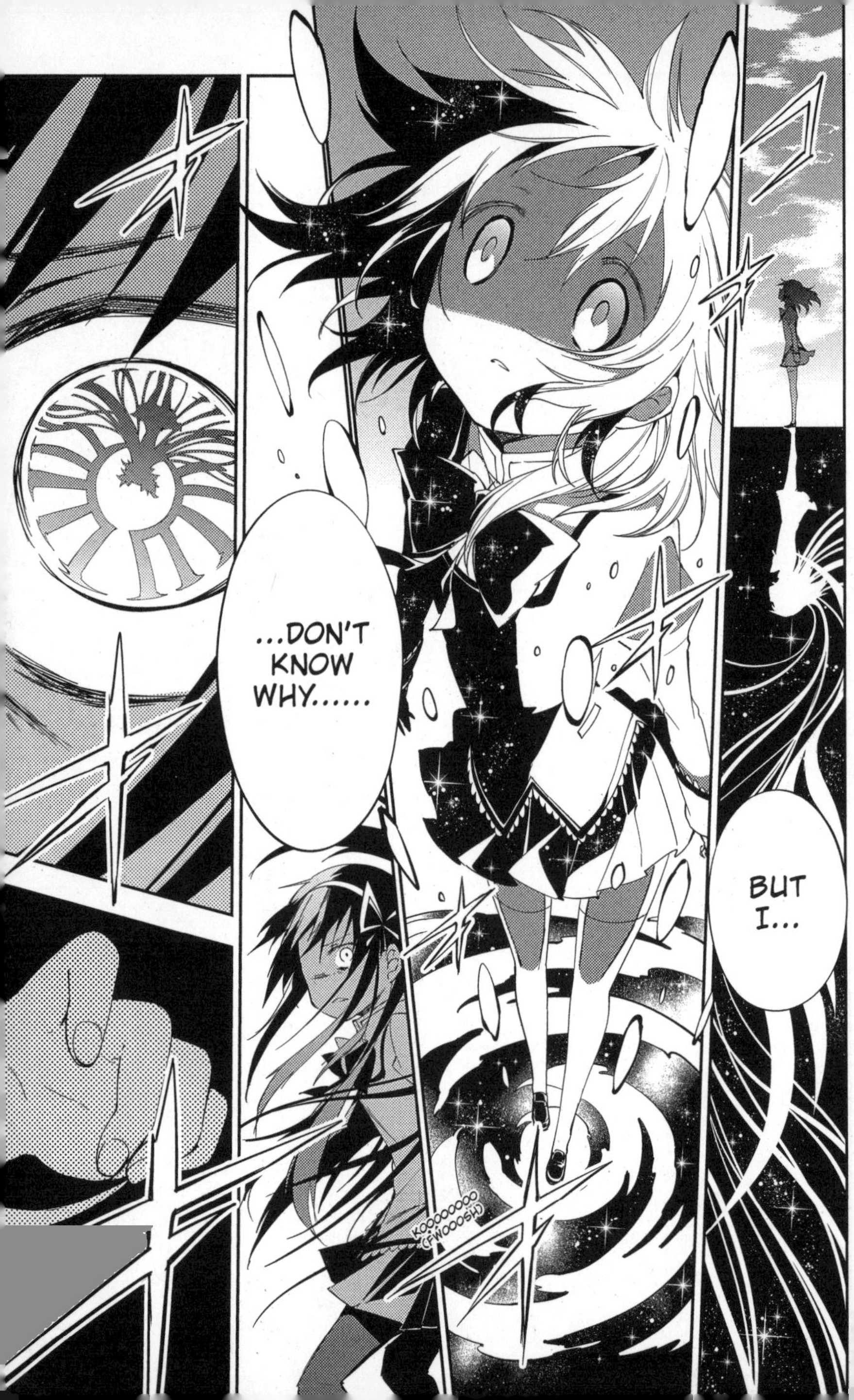
BUT I...
...DON'T KNOW WHY......
KOOOOOOOO (FWOOOSH)

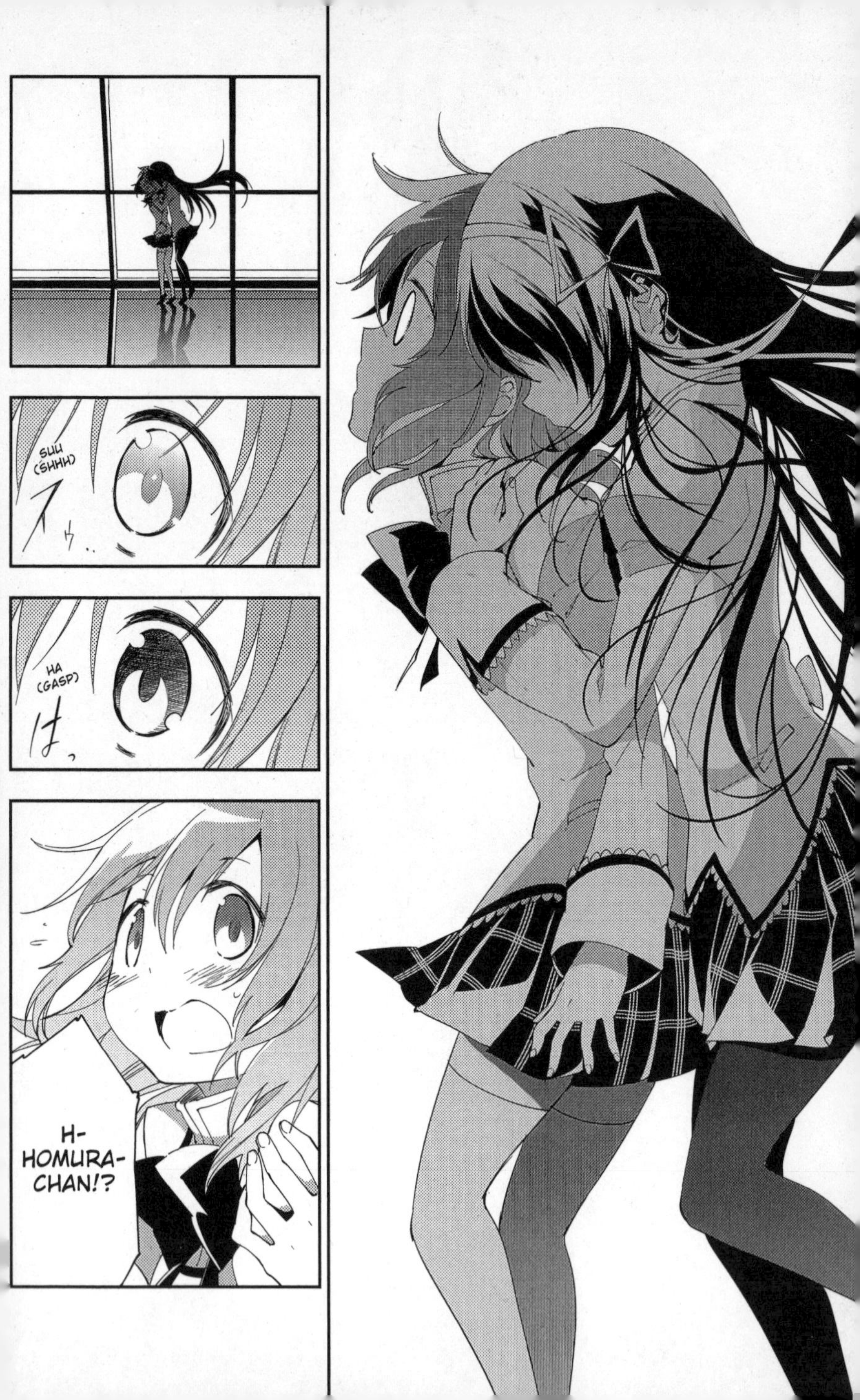
SUU (SHHH)
HA (GASP)
は
H-HOMURA-CHAN!?

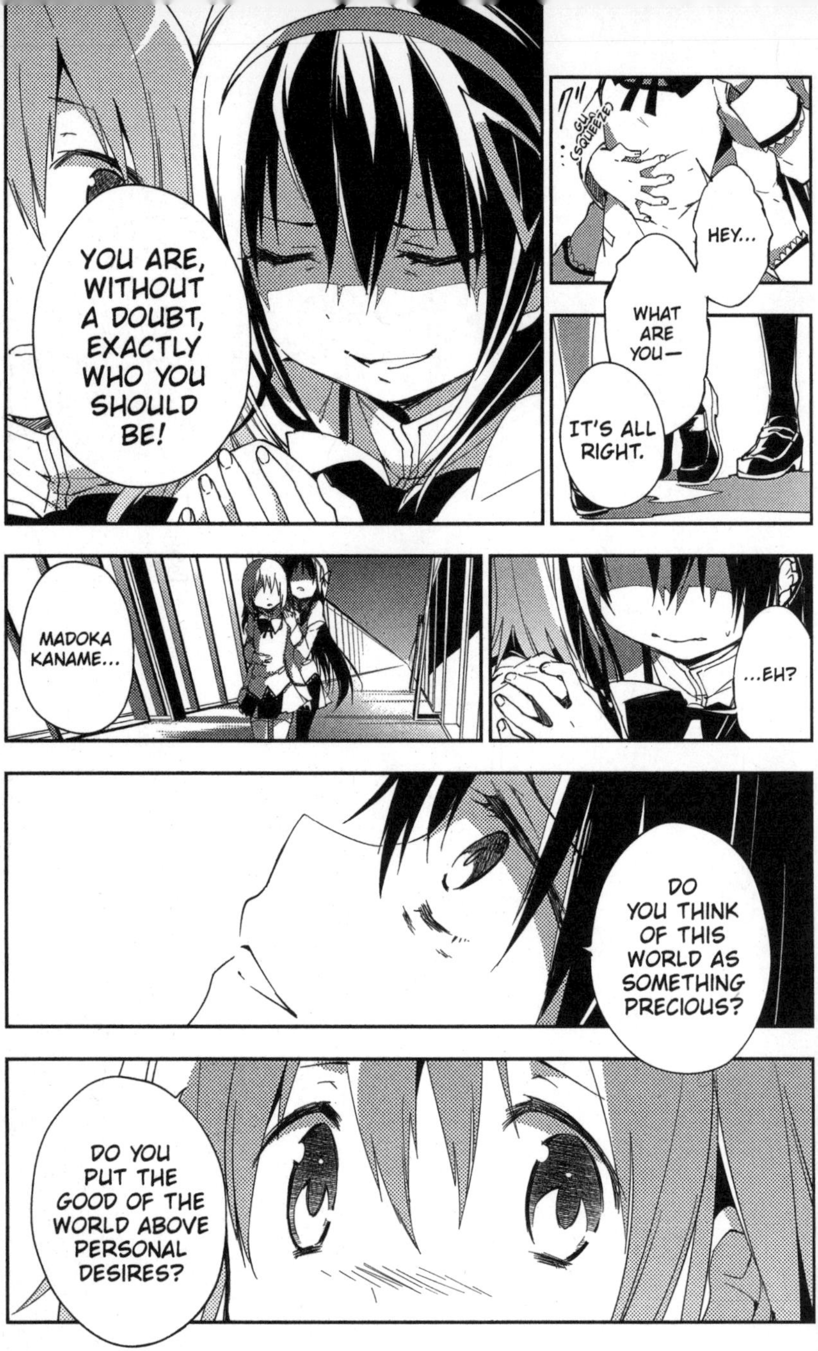
GU (SQUEEZE)
HEY...
WHAT ARE YOU—
IT'S ALL RIGHT.
YOU ARE, WITHOUT A DOUBT, EXACTLY WHO YOU SHOULD BE!
...EH?
MADOKA KANAME...
DO YOU THINK OF THIS WORLD AS SOMETHING PRECIOUS?
DO YOU PUT THE GOOD OF THE WORLD ABOVE PERSONAL DESIRES?

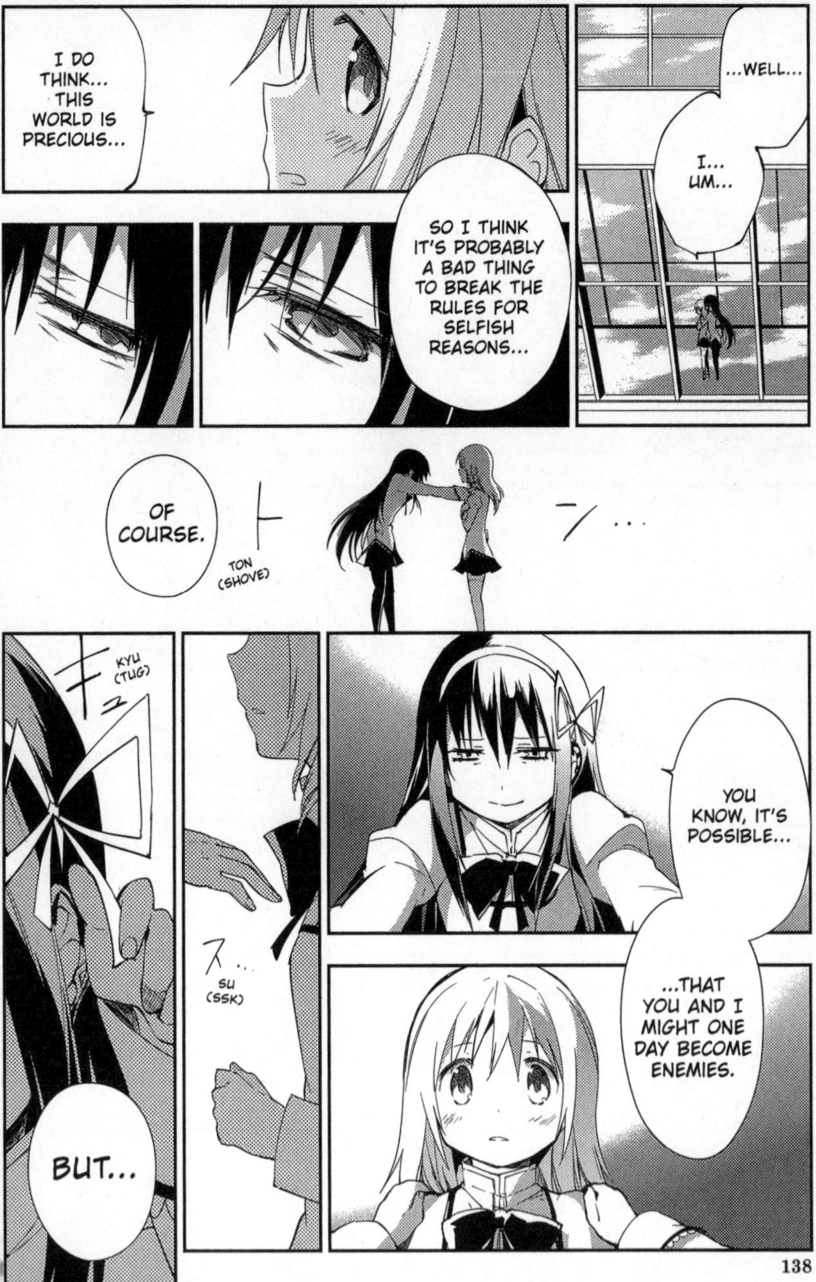
...WELL...
I... UM...
I DO THINK... THIS WORLD IS PRECIOUS...
SO I THINK IT'S PROBABLY A BAD THING TO BREAK THE RULES FOR SELFISH REASONS...
...
OF COURSE.
TON (SHOVE)
YOU KNOW, IT'S POSSIBLE...
...THAT YOU AND I MIGHT ONE DAY BECOME ENEMIES.
SU (SSK)
KYU (TUG)
BUT...

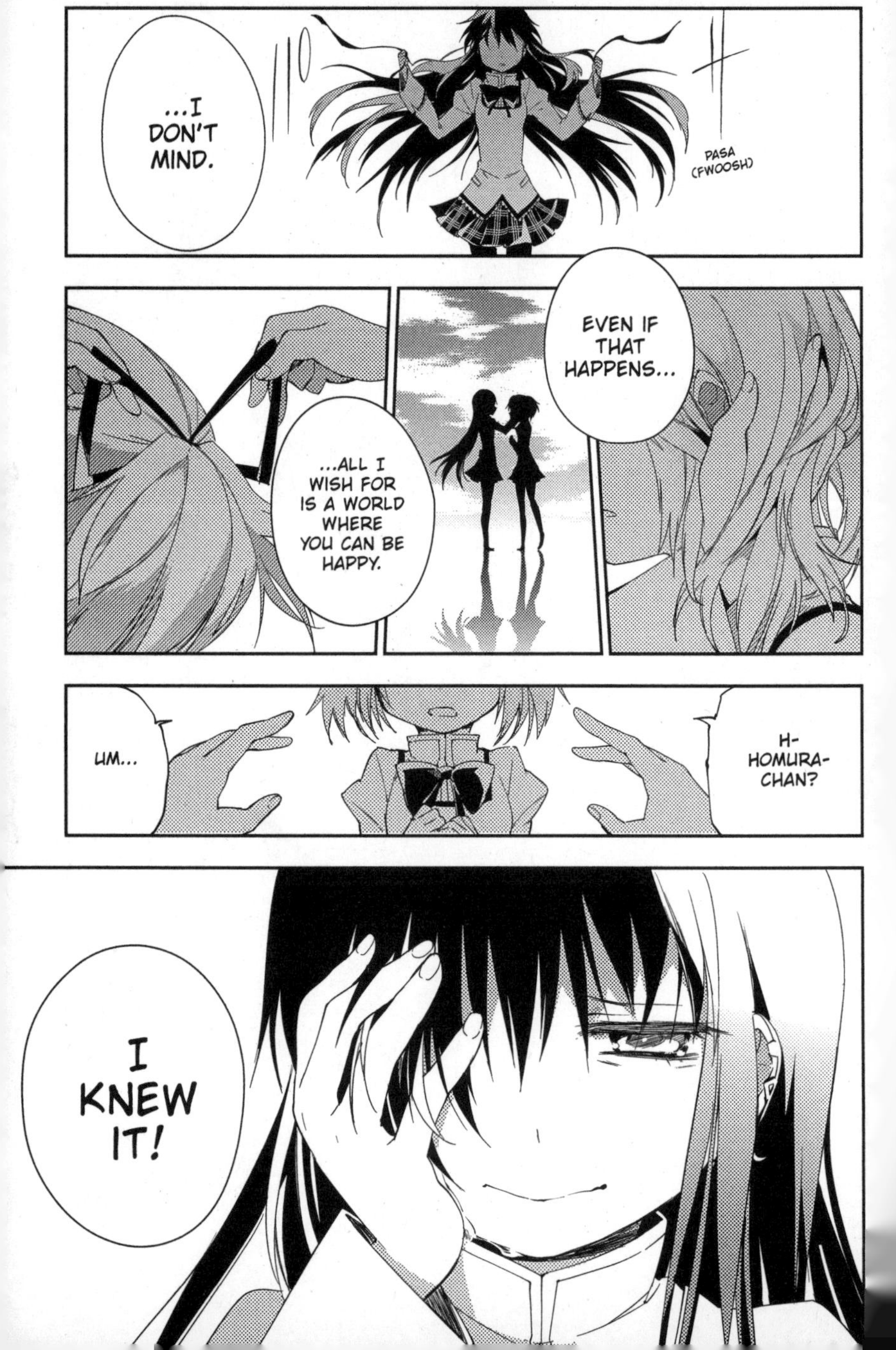
PASA (FWOOSH)
...I DON'T MIND.
EVEN IF THAT HAPPENS...
...ALL I WISH FOR IS A WORLD WHERE YOU CAN BE HAPPY.
H-HOMURA-CHAN?
UM...
I KNEW IT!

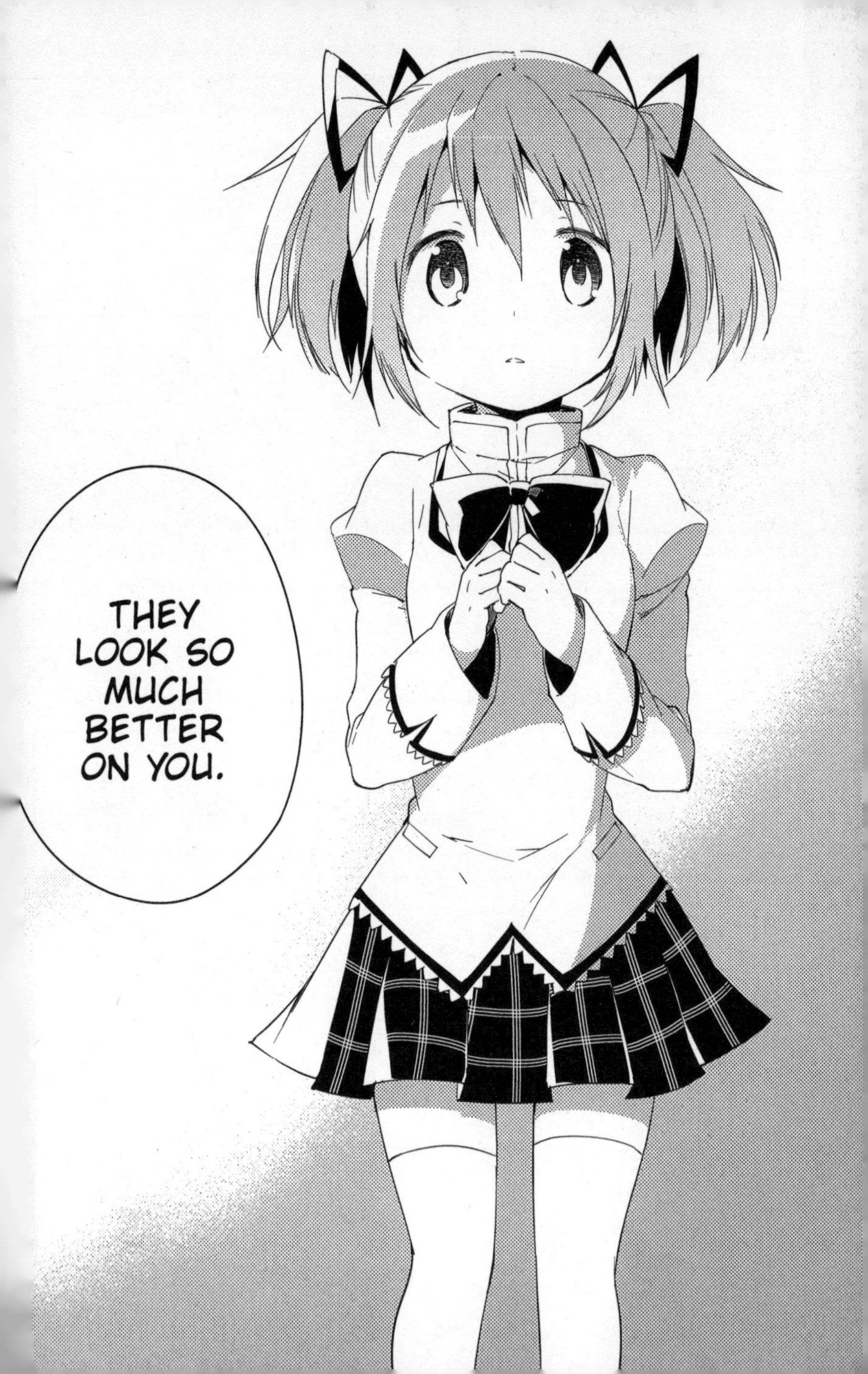
THEY LOOK SO MUCH BETTER ON YOU.

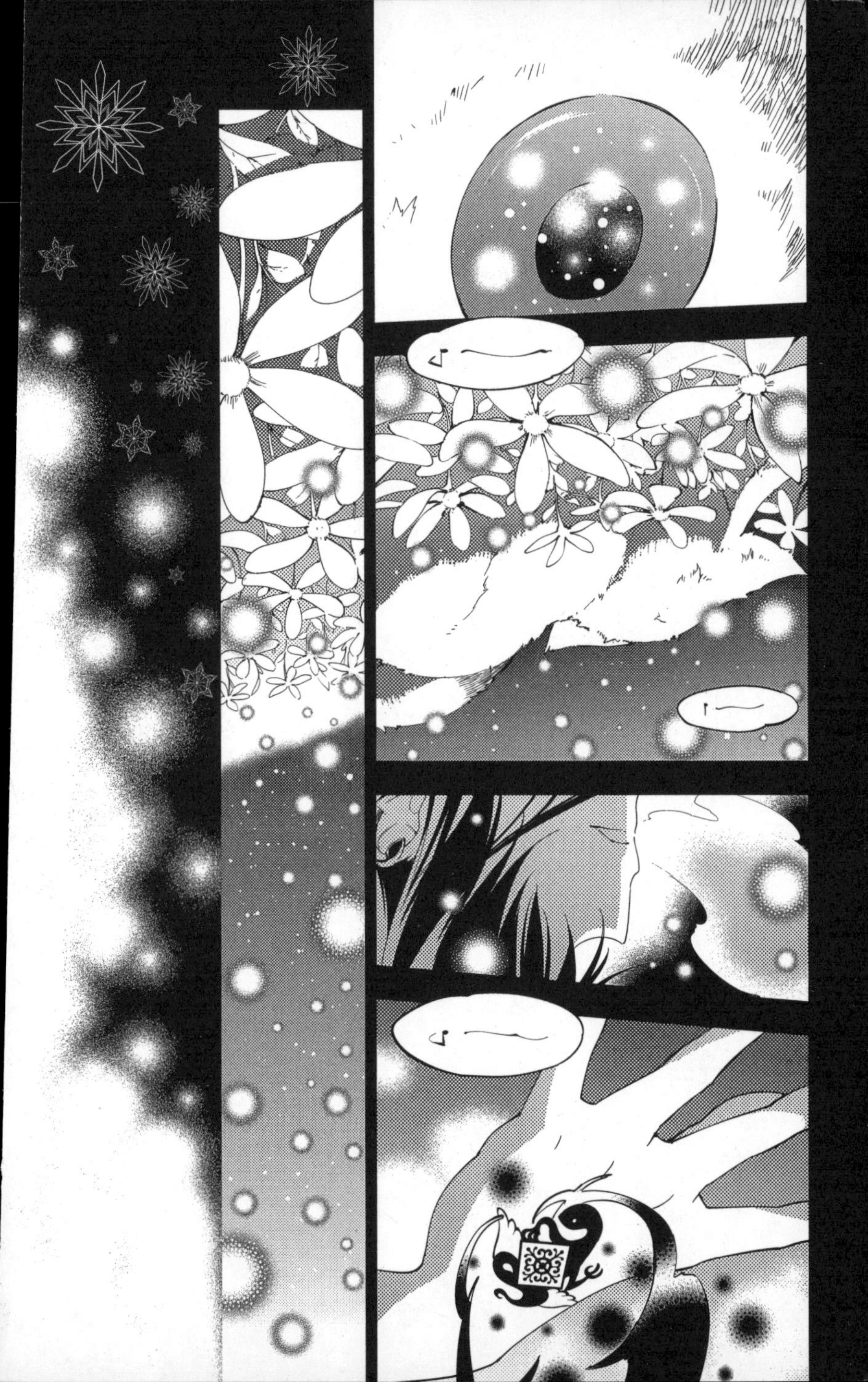

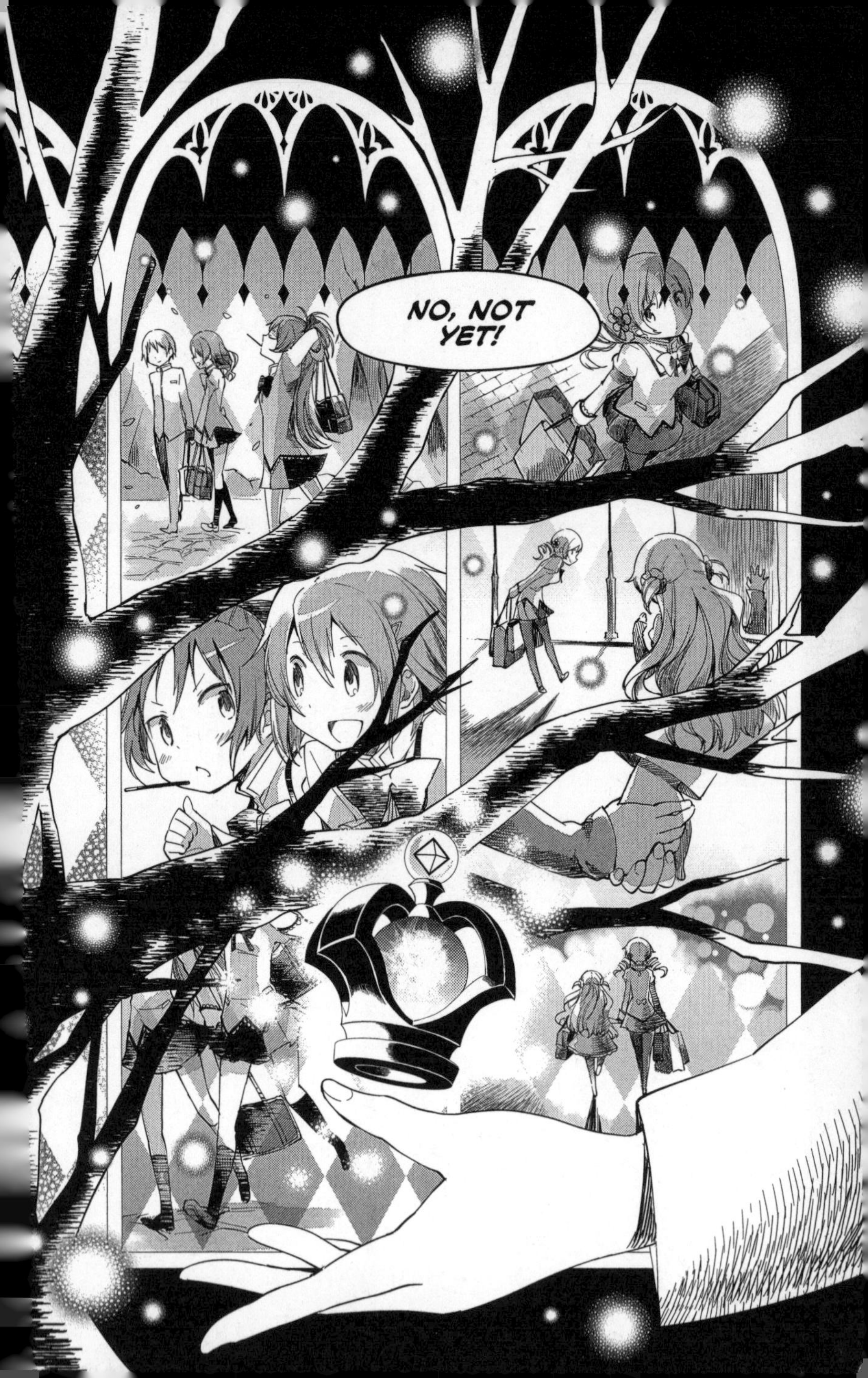
NO, NOT YET!

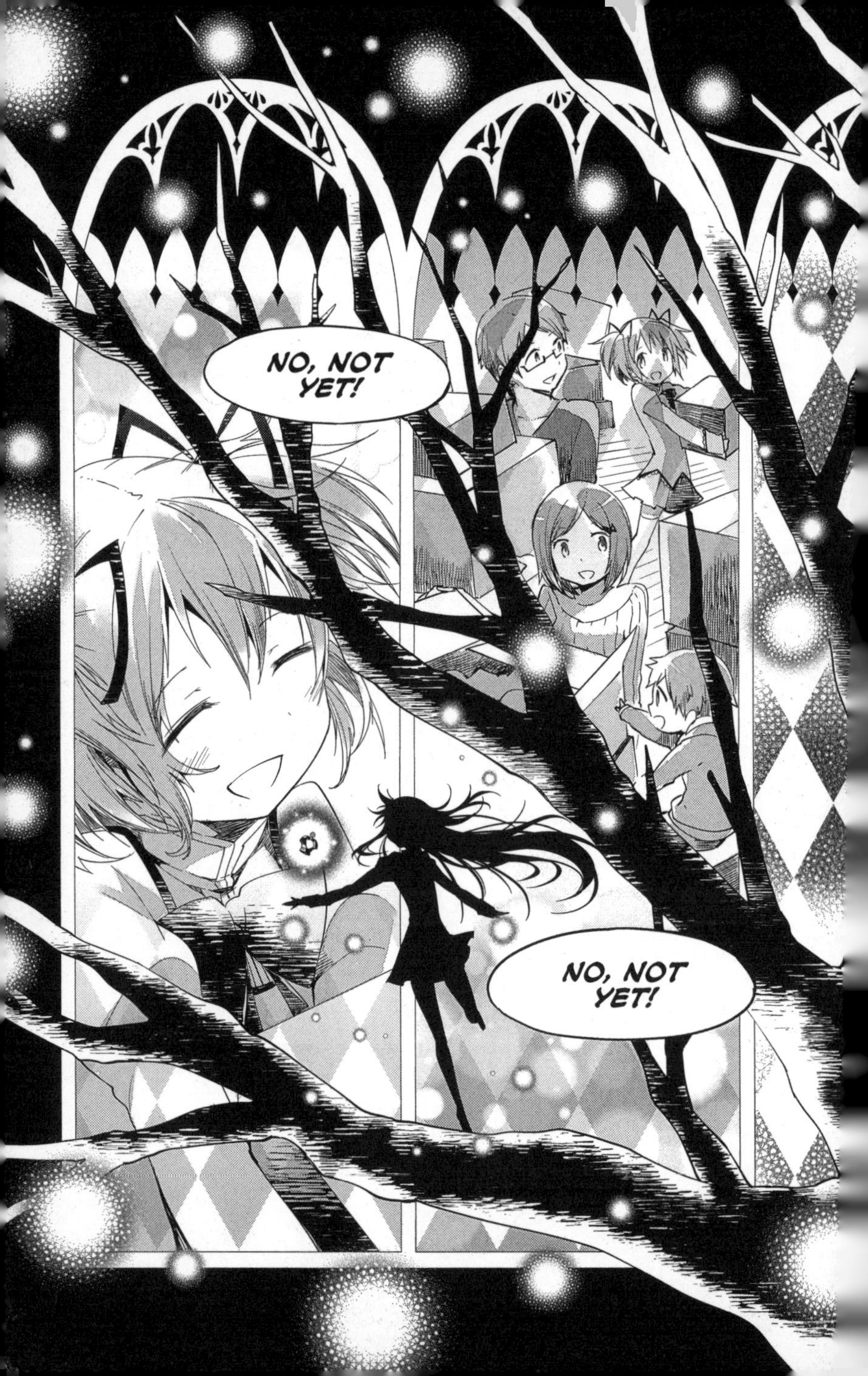
NO, NOT YET!
NO, NOT YET!

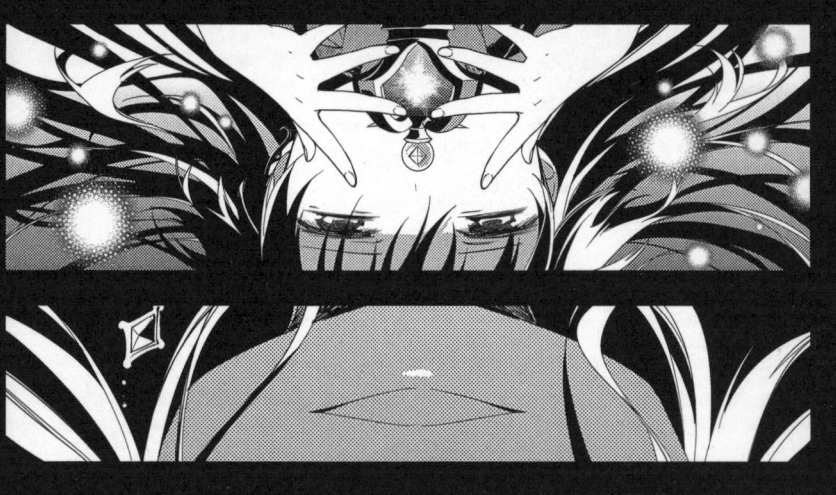

NO, NOT YET!

PUELLA MAGI MADOKA MAGICA: THE MOVIE -REBELLION-
THE END

PUELLA MAGI
MADOKA ★ MAGICA
THE MOVIE -REBELLION-

PUELLA MA[...]
MADOKA☆[...]
THE MOVIE [...]

MAGICA QUARTET
HANOKAGE

Translation: William Flanagan • Lettering: Abigail Blackman

This book is a work of fiction. Names, characters, places, and incidents are the product of the author's imagination or are used fictitiously. Any resemblance to actual events, locales, or persons, living or dead, is coincidental.

GEKIJYOUBAN MAHO SHOJO MADOKA☆MAGICA [SHINPEN] HANGYAKU NO MONOGATARI VOL. 3
© 2014 Magica Quartet / Aniplex, Madoka Movie Project Rebellion All rights reserved. First published in Japan in 2014 by HOUBUNSHA CO., LTD., Tokyo. English translation rights in United States, Canada, and United Kingdom arranged with HOUBUNSHA CO., LTD. through Tuttle-Mori Agency, Inc., Tokyo.

Translation © 2016 by Hachette Book Group, Inc.

Yen Press
Hachette Book Group
1290 Avenue of the Americas
New York, NY 10104

www.HachetteBookGroup.com
www.YenPress.com

Yen Press is an imprint of Hachette Book Group, Inc. The Yen Press name and logo are trademarks of Hachette Book Group, Inc.

The publisher is not responsible for websites (or their content) that are not owned by the publisher.

Library of Congress Control Number: 2015952612

First Yen Press Edition: February 2016

ISBN: 978-0-316-30940-0

10 9 8 7 6 5 4 3 2 1

BVG

Printed in the United States of America